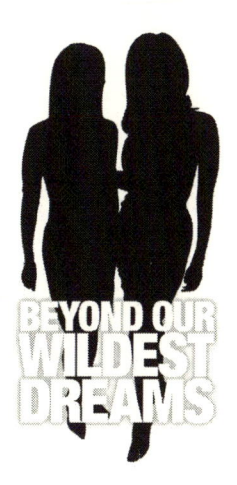

BEYOND OUR WILDEST DREAMS

Society of Singers
SINCE 1984

A portion of the profits from this book will go to the Society of Singers.

Our Dedication....

Seeing our parent's devotion to our family, taught us how to be dedicated to each other.

This book is dedicated to our loving family, our hard working parents, our sisters, our brothers, our husbands and our daughters. Thank you for all your love and support.

We thank God for blessing us with the love, talents and opportunities that have shaped our lives.

"But the seed planted in the good earth represents those who hear the Word, embrace it, and produce a harvest beyond their wildest dreams."
Mark 4:20 ~ The Message

© copyright 2011 Alberici Sisters Enterprises, LLC
No part of this book may be reproduced in any way without written permission of the authors. All rights reserved under International and Pan-American copyright conventions.

Produced and published in the United States of America.

FIRST EDITION

BISAC: Biography & Autobiography / Entertainment & Performing Arts

Billy Ingram's Dedication....

For Hank & Hope Ingram
because of their dedication.

Billy Ingram produced, art directed, typeset, researched, photo retouched, and composed this book, in addition to conducting and transcribing dozens of interviews to craft the storyline for *Beyond Our Wildest Dreams*.

All logos, initial page layouts & templates by **James Counts**.

Edited by **Dr. Bethany Sinnott**

Published by TVparty! Books

ISBN-13: 978-1463564575   ISBN-10: 1463564570
Library of Congress Control Number: 2011932600

Table of Contents

Introduction
Walking the Red Carpet at the 2009 Grammy Awards to honor Dean Martin..........7

Daddy's Girls
Meet our mom and dad..........14

All the Flowers of Tomorrow
Our mom was a popular singer in Philadelphia..........21

The strange way we grew up compared to other children..........24

Our teen years..........34

I Knew There Was Some Kind of Adventure Waiting For Me
How to win at beauty contests without really trying..........43

Auditioning for The Golddiggers in New York..........52

On Our Way
Meeting our sister Golddiggers of 1973 at NBC in Burbank..........57

How the Golddiggers got started in the 1960s..........67

Our first gig at the Vapors Club in Hot Springs, Arkansas..........70

Sun & Fun
Las Vegas debut with Steve and Eydie at Caesars Palace..........73

Here's how the book works. Text that is not indented contains the words of Maria and Linda.

> Text that is slightly indented contains the words of those persons interviewed for this book.

>> Text that is more indented and italized comes from books, newspapers, and magazines of the era or other sources.

The Wacky World of
Jonathan Winters...............................81

On the road with the legendary Italian
singer Jerry Vale...................................84

The Graduates
Taping our first Dean Martin
Comedy Hour......................................92

Maria blows it on the first taping.....100

Dean's Queens
Dean's disastrous marriage
and working with Gene Kelly
on the Comedy Hour.........................108

Our tropical getaway with the
Mexican Mafia..................................113

Vegas & Beyond
The MGM Grand opens with Dean
Martin and The Golddiggers............120

The Dean Martin Roasts with
Orson Welles, Nipsey Russell and
Don Rickles.......................................128

Puerto Rico and Tom Jones'
indecent propsal................................141

Stronger
New girls, new directions.................147

Hanging out with Sammy................154

Louis, Bob, Dean & Mike
The amazing Louis Prima's
last tour...161

Near death with Bob Hope..............169

Dating on the road...........................173

Back to Las Vegas and on
to Montreal......................................178

The Mike Douglas Show on the
beach with Robert Goulet...............183

The More Things Change
Should we stay or should we go?....187

A new series for Dean?....................191

Linda is led astray............................194

Dean's Christmas in
California 1975................................200

Vaudeville Babies
Touring the Northeast with
Donald O'Connor, Milton Berle, and
dirty old man Georgie Jessel...........207

Dean's Red Hot Scandals.................224

Red Skelton and the Beverly
Hills Supper Club............................233

A key member of our
Golddiggers family unexpectedly
dies in Lake Tahoe...........................238

Ol' Blue Eyes & Ol' Red Eyes
The last successful tour for Frank
Sinatra & Dean Martin...................243

Frank's the top.................................247

Westchester Premier Theater and the Mafia in 1977 251

Rat Pack Golddiggers......................258

Frank & Dean together again on stage and what a show it was..........262

We narrowly escape the deadliest mob hit in American history..........272

The fabulous Latin Casino..............274

The last stop on the Rat Pack tour— The Blue Max in Chicago..............280

Summer of '77..............................285
Mike Douglas and headlining with Bobby Goldsboro..........................286

Monte Carlo—summer fireworks by the Mediterranean.....................288

On the Road Again?!?
Our sister Darlene joins the act, and we're reunited with Donald O'Connor......................................299

Frank Fontaine's heart attack.........303

Dick Haymes steps in....................305

Comedians Jackie Vernon and Billy Barty..............................309

The Cotton Club Murder connection......................................312

Dean's Christmas in California 1977..............................316

Goodbyes......................................320

About the authors..........................328

Where are they now?......................330

That's me, Maria...

my sister Linda is the blonde on the left...

Over three decades of performing, wow, here we are on the Grammy Awards Red Carpet.

What are the chances? The odds certainly were against us but out of thousands of young women, two humble girls from a family of nine children were chosen to be featured singers and dancers on *The Dean Martin Comedy Hour*. Now, here we are walking the Red Carpet at the 2009 Grammy Awards ceremony with Dean Martin's family.

On this day a downpour was expected but it didn't rain on our parade as waves of anticipation carried us to this moment. Dean was being honored for his "Lifetime Achievement" in entertainment along with R&B legends The Four Tops, country icon Hank Williams, and pop singer Brenda Lee.

We felt like giggling teenagers again as we reunited with our special friends to walk the red carpet together as a group. Dean affectionately called us "my girls" and we were proud to have performed with him from 1973 through the next two decades as The Dean Martin Golddiggers. While the paparazzi snapped away, without missing a beat all of us struck a pose, just like the old days!

One of the reporters pushed forward with his microphone and pulled me and my sister aside to ask us a typical Dean question, "Ladies, ladies, tell me, did Dean Martin really drink?" We chuckled in unison and said in true Dean Martin fashion, "No, Dean didn't drink; he told us he freezes it and eats it like a Popsicle."

Once inside we were guided to our VIP seats. The ceremony warmed

Former Golddiggers at the 2009 Grammy Award ceremony in honor of Dean Martin. From left to right: Deborah Pratt, Alberici Sisters (Linda Eichberg, Maria Lauren), Susan Buckner, Marie Halton and Peggy Gohl.

our hearts and it was hard to hold back the tears when Dean was given recognition with a video montage of some special moments from television, recordings and movies. We beamed with pride for our hero, who helped shape our careers with his charm, wit and showmanship. When the time came for Dean's children to accept his Grammy, we couldn't help but recall being told the devastating news in 1987 that his son Dean Paul had been killed and the toll it took on Dean. In spite of his overwhelming sadness Dean continued to fulfill his performance commitments with us as his opening act. He told us in a tender moment that entertaining helped him to ease his pain.

As the award ceremony came to a close, it was off to the 'after party' where we listened to fantastic music and chatted with Dean's daughter Gail, who was toasting her dad with a martini. We loved the story she told about her grandson recently buying a skateboard with Dean's picture on it, "With two other guys...." That would be the Rat Pack.

As we celebrated that evening it all came flooding back—the stars, the memories....

Touring with Frank Sinatra and

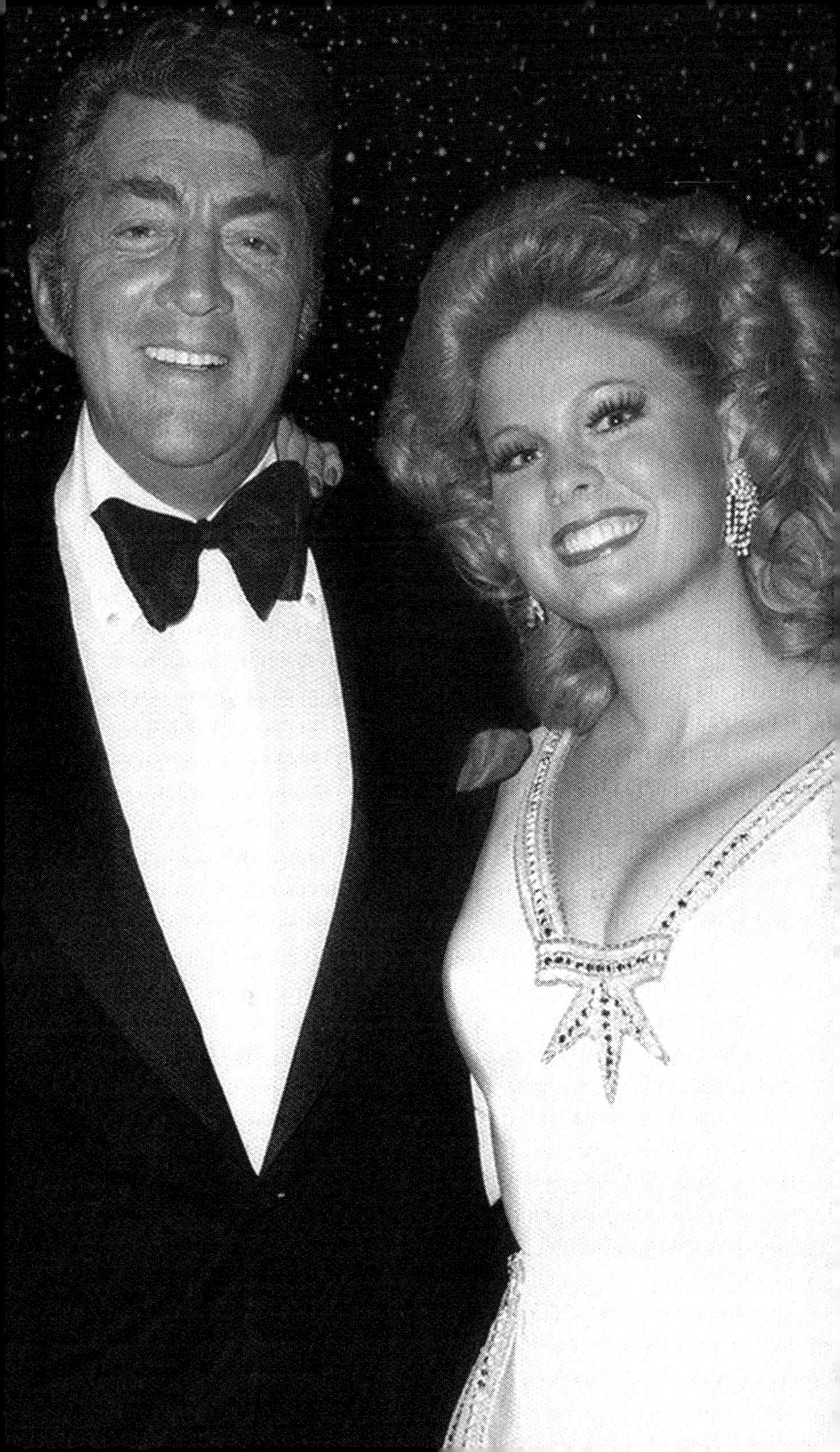

The Golddiggers of 1973 - Clockwise from the bottom: Patti (Pivarnik) Gribow, Linda (Alberici) Eichberg, Robin (Hoctor) Horneff, Maria (Alberici) Lauren, Colleen Kincaid, Deborah Pratt, Susan Buckner, Lee Nolting

Dean Martin on the same bill, hanging out in the dressing rooms and at home with Sammy Davis Jr.; taping the Dean Martin TV show; opening the MGM Grand in Las Vegas with Dean and then appearing at Bally's for so many years until Dean's final performances. What an experience. What fun!

Spending all of that time in Las Vegas with Dean opened our eyes to who the legendary entertainer really was on a personal level; the man behind the laughter. And the sorrow.

As my sister and I searched for our friends through the crowd we were stopped by another news reporter, "How did you like performing with Dean Martin?" He became enthralled with our stories of singing, dancing and palling around with Dean Martin and the Rat Pack. Then he posed the question, "Are you ladies still performing?" We enthusiastically proclaimed, "We never stopped!" We told him that we were still going strong performing reunion shows with some of the former Golddiggers in our show that was aptly called *Showstoppers*. After all, the superstars that we performed with were all showstoppers! As we told him about our experiences, the reporter's eyes were glistening with excitement. It became obvious to us that there was still a strong fascination for this past era of entertainment by how quickly he fired question after question at us.

The reporter realized he had made his catch for the evening and he reeled us in when he remarked, "You sisters should write a book." We laughed it off at first but then, after being told the same thing by *TVparty!*'s Billy Ingram, we thought, "Why not?"

Throughout our careers we starred in everything from television extravaganzas in Hollywood to a college tour with Bob Hope—even a command performance for the Royal Family of Monaco, where we danced with the Prince. We lived out our own Cinderella story and the life we enjoyed was truly beyond our wildest dreams.

Well, here it is, a story of sisterhood and that glamorous time in show business that will no longer be. We were blessed to perform and learn our craft from the best in the trade. We discovered first hand Sinatra's impeccable vocal timing, Gene Kelly's attention to precision, comedy timing from jokesters Milton Berle and Dom DeLuise, down-to-earth goodness from country stars like Lynn Anderson and Crystal Gayle and the cool charisma that was Dean's alone. It's a privilege to tell these wonderful stories with some of our colleagues and our "Golddiggers sisters."

Over the years, there have been about a hundred young women who have worn the title "The Golddiggers." Each of us in our own unique way contributed to the longevity of the legacy. Many of us grew together as entertainers, changing with the times throughout the evolution of music and entertainment.

As a group, we grew from wide-eyed girls to womanhood, from go-go boots to evening gowns. We changed our look and our sound but not our hearts. These wonderful ladies with whom we traveled for so many years are now our lifelong friends. Oh, the adventures we had together! Our life has been a whirlwind of surprises with many challenges, ups and downs, but my sister and I still kept plugging along and held on to each other and our family values. Yes, there was danger as well but our faith carried us through it all. We came from a resilient family and it all started with our parents, their struggles, an unusual upbringing, and our dad who almost didn't survive long enough to bring us into the world.

Daddy's Girls

Al Alberici (our Dad): You have to be motivated to learn things in this world. And I sure was motivated.

I guess God put me in the position I was in, to motivate me to learn things so I could be able to help my family. He knew in the future I would have this big, large family. He knew it before I did.

I was brought up in a typical Italian family in South Philadelphia and, like everybody else, I only would eat what I liked which was mostly pasta. The food was put on the table and you ate whatever you liked. Because of that, unfortunately, I used to eat only the foods that tasted good, not what was good for me.

I guess I was thirteen or fourteen years old. I'd been sick, in and out of hospitals for a long time, and the doctors were going to operate on me. They were going to cut my intestines out, take it out, open it up, make it smaller, and put it back. It was a very dangerous operation.

They had Chinese doctors, Japanese doctors, all kinds of doctors... these doctors were going to operate on me the next day. They were talking and they were looking at my x-rays. I was layin' in bed and they were feeling my intestines and stomach and all and I thought to myself, "When you doctors leave here, I'm scrammin'!" They all left, I got up out of bed and I left that hospital. I took off. I went home and hid in my brother's car—then my sister saw me and they took me back to the hospital.

I felt I was being used as a guinea pig. One doctor, a very wise doctor, said, "No, I don't think we should do this operation. I believe that you should start eating roughage, fruits and vegetables." When I came out of the hospital I must have weighed a hundred pounds, I was very, very thin. In the next six months I got myself up to a hundred ninety pounds. I sent away for the Charles Atlas course, with exercises, and food information. That was the beginning. From eighteen to about the age of twenty-two I was a perfect specimen, very strong, healthy. I started to learn how to take care of myself.

Lillian Biro Alberici (our Mom): We had all of the Hungarian traditions in our home. We grew up in a Hungarian church, my mother was a professional dressmaker and she would make the Hungarian costumes.

I was always singing. My whole life I loved music. I was kind of bashful, but I loved it so much that I just got out there and sang. When I was 16 my brother's friends had a band and I went and sang a little bit with them at the YMCA. They liked me so I started singing with them on Friday nights. Then one person or another would tell me about a band that needed a singer or somebody would get in touch with me so I eventually started singing with larger bands. I worked three nights a week until I was 18.

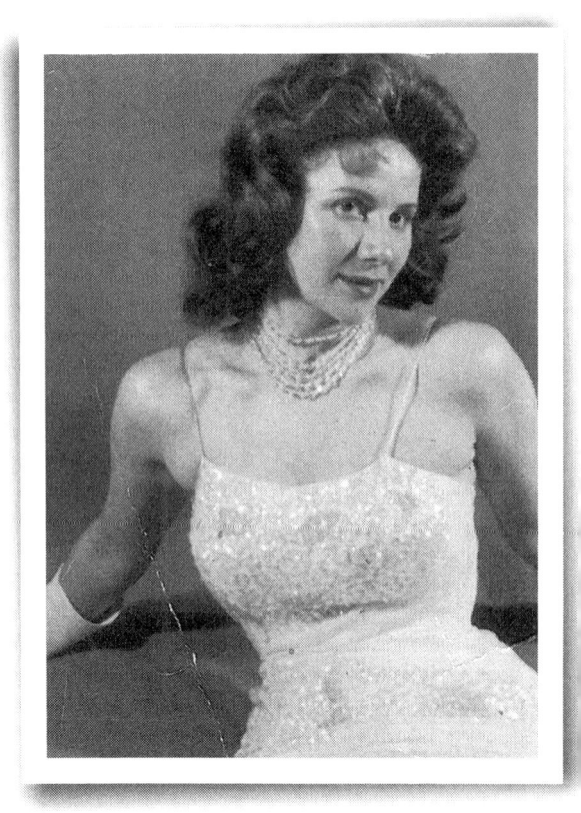

When my husband and I met, I was singing at the Brookline on the Boulevard club on Roosevelt. I sang the 'Boogie Blues' which was a standard arrangement, exactly like Anita O'Day's so I knew it word for word. I sang it and everyone's clapping and clapping and clapping and yelling, "One more time! One more time!" That had never happened to me before. So I had to repeat it one more time so they could jitterbug again.

When my husband and I were dating he was into bodybuilding. He was sickly when he was young so we'd go to health lectures and they'd say, "just eat whole wheat flour, no white flour." So we did that. Then we'd go to other lectures and they'd add on, "no sugar, honey's good" and different things like that so, little by little, we changed to being completely vegetarian.

We eloped. I was raised Presbyterian but Al's mother wouldn't consider us married unless I converted to be a Catholic. We remarried and had our own little celebration after that. We lived with Al's family; because I'm Hungarian, his Italian mother, who only knew a few words in broken English, used to call me a Gypsy—"Gy-pa-see!" The few Hungarians my mother-in-law had seen in Italy were all gypsies.

When I was having my first daughter, Maria Elena, my sister-in-law's brother was a doctor and he suggested, to save money, that we go to his hospital that was completely staffed by nuns. They all spoke Italian and I was the only patient in the place because it was a very small hospital. So here, for the first time having my baby, I'm walking up the steps to the room, no wheelchair, no elevator and nobody spoke English.

They heard Maria Elena screaming when she first came out and the nuns told my husband, "She's going to be a singer!" because she had wonderful vocal chords.

Lillian Alberici: Linda was born on Thanksgiving Day. I remember hearing the Philadelphia Mummers parade outside the hospital, She was so beautiful, I just wanted to make a porcelain statue of her. She had gorgeous blonde hair and lovely green eyes. I would kid her that she interrupted my Thanksgiving Day dinner.

Maria: Probably my first memory of Linda was as a baby, her skin was so fair and the light eyes—she was like a doll. Everyone would "ooh and aah" when they saw her.

We were like night and day. I was dark next to her. I felt a little odd and out of place. When I looked at pictures in magazines, I couldn't find any child that looked like me, except for the poor child with a sad face holding on to an empty plate. The caption usually read, "Feed The Children." Sometimes I imagined I was one of those children and my parents had

Maria Elena was named after the hit Tommy Dorsey song.

secretly adopted me.

My thoughts of feeling not too pretty, magically disappeared when my parents poured their love and attention on me, I loved when my father gave me 'fun rides'. He would lift me over his head to fly like Superman. Before Linda started crawling, my father would hold her feet in one of his hands where she would balance and stand in his hand. All of my aunts, everyone, would gasp. His Mom would cry out, "You craze!" meaning, "You're crazy!" My cousins and I loved it. It was like being at a circus show. I didn't worry because my dad seemed so confident and smiling and I could see his other hand ready to catch Linda if she should wobble but that never happened. Dad loved showing everyone how well Linda could keep her balance. My father was very demonstrative when it came to his children being healthy and fit.

Lillian Alberici: Making vegetable juice, that was my job. I had this huge hydraulic press to make vegetable juice for all the children. Other mothers had different things in their baby bottles, I had goat's milk and carrot juice in mine plus I nursed them all until they were at least two years old or until I'd be pregnant with the next one.

Al Alberici: Both of our families were European immigrants and had difficulty understanding what we were becoming involved in. However, my family did see me become very healthy after being sick for so many years. My mother-in-law, on the other hand, argued if our children didn't eat meat that their growth would probably be stunted. Changes in nutrition and lifestyle were just in their infancy; I had to really call on my courage to put those lifestyle changes into practice with my family.
I wouldn't let my kids be vaccinated. Why add an unnecessary burden to the body? Instead concentrate on lifestyle choices that promote optimum health.
In the beginning I think people had doubts about whether I really cared about the kids. But I had learned to question authority and made the study of nutrition, health and fitness a lifelong endeavor. My children grew up without any major sickness and no need for doctors and drugs, thank God. I have always had their best interest at heart, they are my legacy.

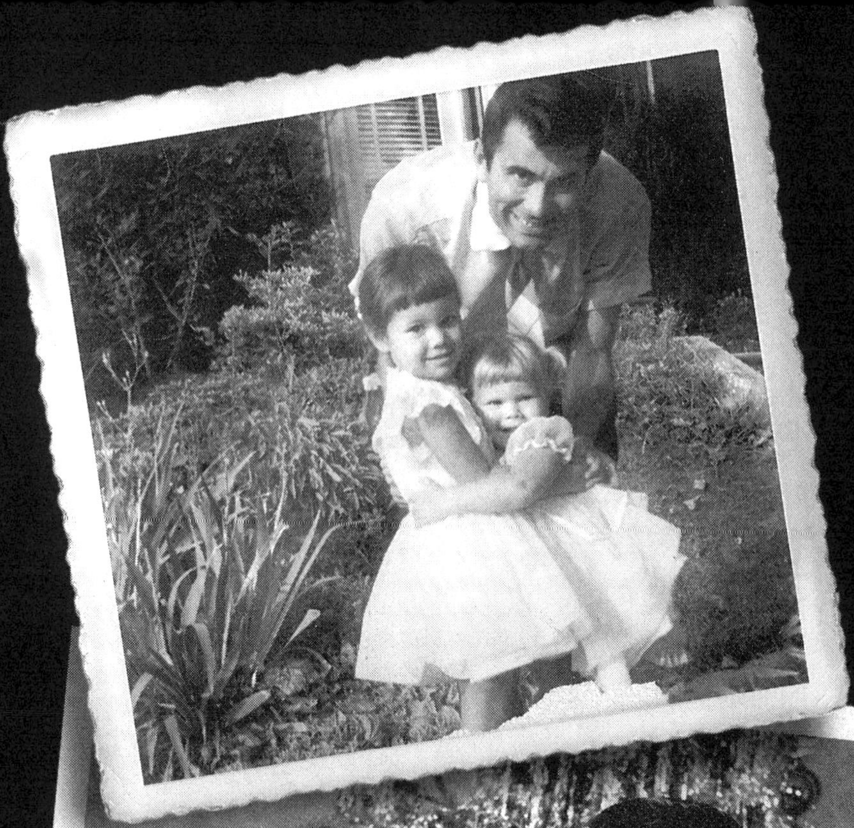
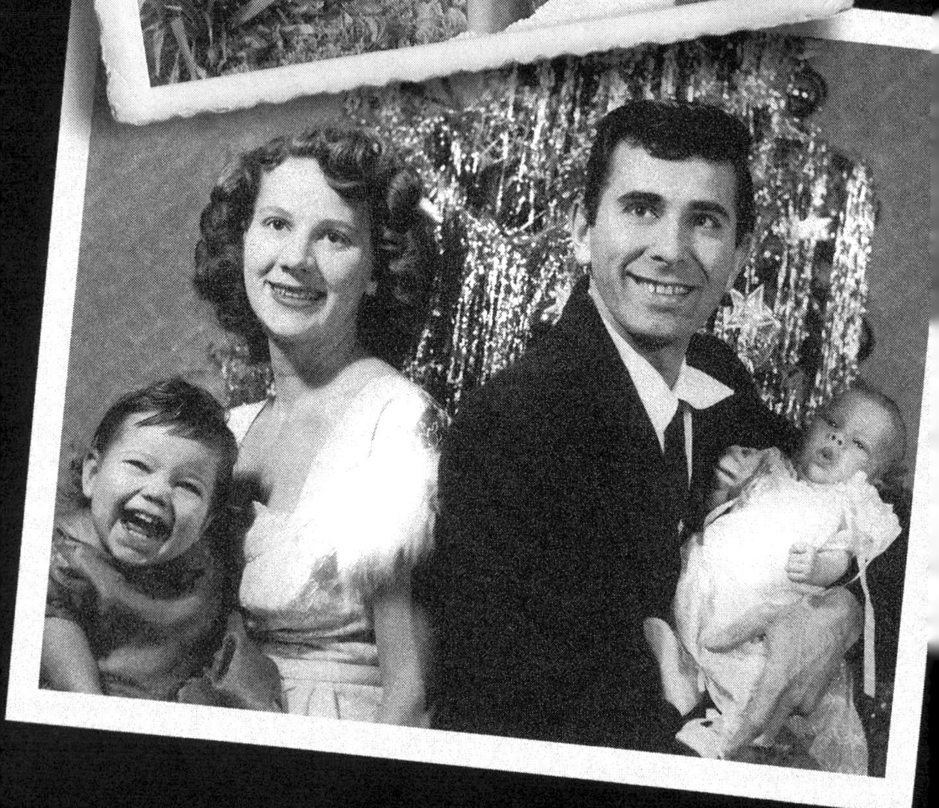

All the flowers of tomorrow are in the seeds of yesterday.

Linda: Every two years our family grew and that was hard for Mom. She would hide her pregnancies because she always got an ear full from her mother. Somehow the size of our family upset my grandmother. I don't know if it wasn't socially acceptable to her or due to the fact that she knew the sacrifices my mother would have to make. Whatever her reasons were, our grandmother loved all of us as much as any grandmother could. As our family continued to grow, it took Mom further away from her dreams.

> **Ed Gebhart, "My Kind of Town":** *You may remember Mrs. Albert (nee Biro) Alberici. She appeared at scores of private banquets over a number of years as Lee Richie, an excellent vocalist who was very big at the Downingtown Motor Lodge and appeared so frequently at the Alpine Inn in Springfield that Mike Puppio was tempted to name the room after her. Mrs. Alberici still has the good pipes and has the type of beauty that is ageless. She could throw on a gown, step on a stage and you'd swear she'd never been away from showbiz. At present, however, showbiz is a little out of the question.*
> *She is far too busy running her household in Newtown Square. As households go, it is a sweetheart. It contains nine of the healthiest, most talented kids you are likely to see this side of the Olympics.*

Lillian Alberici: We settled in the Philadelphia suburb of Newtown Square. I sang in clubs a bit but then it got to be too much, I had to raise my children so I didn't start singing again until I had my fourth child. I gradually started performing on weekends, my husband would drive me or we'd take the kids in the car or have somebody watch them.
I got the opportunity in 1960 to play the Latin Casino the night it opened in Cherry Hill, a very big, elegant nightclub. This little combo and I would sing from the balcony between the big acts. All the great stars played there. When Sammy Davis Jr. performed, his show would always go overtime and I would worry about getting home late.

Maria: Who inspired us to be entertainers? Our mom was our first inspiration. I loved hearing about the stars and their shows from my mom.

I especially remember my mom going on and on about Sammy Davis Jr. and how he sang, danced and played musical instruments. My mom seemed amazed at how talented he was and how hard he worked during his performances. I knew my mom was not easily impressed by entertainers, so I made a mental note. I wanted to be an entertainer and hearing about Sammy let me know at a young age that I had to do more than just sing to gain the respect of an audience, I had to be able to wow them too.

My mom knew how to do that. When she put on a sequined gown she looked like a star. She'd be around the house and just be Mom doing the housework and then she would put on what we called her 'equipment.' She had a waist cincher, it made your waistline about four inches smaller, like Mae West. She had beautiful gowns, and these hairpieces that she sometimes put on, it was definitely a startling metamorphosis.

Linda: It never took Mom very long to get ready for her jobs. She would go into her bedroom and, before you knew it, all of a sudden, we would see this singer come out. She was transformed like Cinderella.

Lots of times the younger ones would get upset when they saw her ready to go, so she would leave her gown on underneath her housecoat and then, "Shazam!" she'd take it off right before she ran out the door.

She had some of the most elegant gowns around. An exclusive store in Philadelphia was going out of business and my father bought ten dresses, all beaded and sequined. She would buy

Chuck Anderson, Latin Casino guitarist 1969-1973: The Latin Casino was right up there with any place in Vegas or the Copacabana in New York. It was one of the major showplaces in the United States. They started off in Philadelphia on Walnut Street and then moved to the lucrative Cherry Hill, New Jersey location, and it was there for many, many years. it was like the East Coast version of Las Vegas. Inside it was large; it seated 3,000 people with long tables that were set up perpendicular to the stage so they fanned out. Up on the second level they had the 'gangster tables,' where you sat if you were with somebody you wouldn't want to be seen in public with.

People came from all over the Tri-State area to the Latin Casino. Everybody felt that they were in the coolest place on earth and actually they were. Of course, they had the best entertainers anywhere. There was no argument about the level of talent, everybody that played there was a headliner. Sammy Davis Jr., Peggy Lee, Frank Sinatra, Trini Lopez, Perry Como—you had to be at the top of your game to play the Latin.

"It is not enough to be Hungarian; you must have talent as well." - Alexander Korda

dresses off the rack and put bottoms on them, turn them into fishtail gowns. Our idea of glamour came from our mother, she had glamour down.

Lillian Alberici: I wrote my own version of 'Let Me Entertain You' to open my shows. Sometimes, I even did my own audience participation thing. I had a bag of instruments, tambourines, bongos, triangles, and different things like that. I'd say, "I always dreamed of singing with a big band but somehow my wish never came true. You've been such a wonderful audience, wouldn't you like to see my dream come true? Now, who would like to be in my band?" So, all in fun, people came up to play my toy instruments and dance on stage as part of 'My band'. It was a funny bit and the audience enjoyed it.
Later on the kids would come with me when I was singing at some place if it was easy for them to be there. They would tag along and the owner or somebody like that would see them and ask them to sing a little bit in my act.

Maria: I enjoyed watching my mom perform. She had personality, a cute sophisticated and sexy way of flirting with the audience as she sang. Sometimes my dad would get jealous and my parents would argue. Deep down I think he knew it was just entertainment but he could be insecure. Back home, my mom taught us songs when we would help her clean the house. There was always plenty of cleaning to do so she would try to make it fun.
When one of the younger ones would hold on to her leg while she was trying to do some work, Mom would get out the pots and pans and a wooden stick. She would let them "play the drums" for a while until she got her work done or got a headache—whichever came first!

Linda: We would watch movies on TV with our mom as we helped her fold the laundry. Marilyn Monroe and Jane Russell in *Gentlemen*

"If you keep on believing, the dream that you wish will come true." - Cinderella

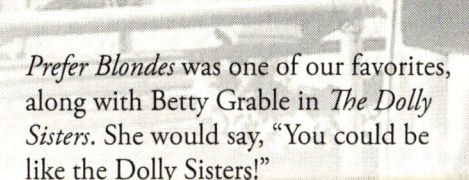

Prefer Blondes was one of our favorites, along with Betty Grable in *The Dolly Sisters*. She would say, "You could be like the Dolly Sisters!"
We used to visualize ourselves doing those campy, old-fashioned numbers. We loved the Maguire Sisters, the Lennon Sisters, the King Sisters, all the sister groups. Sometimes our parents would let us stay up late and watch the June Taylor Dancers, who were the opening act on *The Jackie Gleason Show*. They used to lie on the floor and make interesting kaleidoscope-like designs using their moving arms and legs. I was fascinated by the many floral-like patterns they would create every week.

Maria: We started to put on shows for our family and friends. My song was usually 'Somewhere over the Rainbow' and Linda would sing the Doris Day song, 'Que Sera Sera.' She had a soft way of singing it that was lovely, just like Doris Day. After our solos we came together and sang 'The Trolley Song,' complete with hand motions.
We were drawn to musicals because of our parents and, once in a while, even our dad got lured into watching them with us. This was an unusual treat because most of the time he would turn off the TV set, proclaiming that it was "A waste of time!" My parents always seemed to be in survival mode with so much work to do that even Mom would sometimes complain, "What I need are less singers around the house and more dishwashers," but all I could think of were those Dorothy Lamour movies with Bob Hope and her swimming at the beach surrounded by palm trees. I thought, "I'm going there."

Linda: Maria and I, along with the rest of our siblings, went to Catholic school through the eighth grade. Everyone had to wear uniforms and the nuns told us we had to buy them from a special uniform store. In order to save money, we bought our uniforms from a different discount store or our mother made them for us. The fabric was slightly different and the dye lot was a little off so we were treated like freaks. The nuns had no mercy. They really rubbed it in that we didn't have the exact uniforms as everybody else.

The Catholic school also required us to use special pens and school supplies that we could only buy from them. They were more expensive than what you could buy elsewhere. Sometimes I got caught using regular store brands. It was so humiliating. All through school I was ridiculed because of these things and also because my father, having so many kids and working so hard, was usually late getting us to school. One nun I had as a teacher would say, "You'll be late for your own funeral."

Pretty much everything Maria and I did was a little out of the ordinary so naturally that caused problems for us at school. We were supposed to sell candy to raise money for the school but my father would not allow us to. It was junk food! We were made fun of a lot.

I would dread lunchtime because I had whole wheat bread sandwiches and this was the Wonder Bread era. The other kids used to say, "Eeew, what are you eating?" They just reveled in embarrassing me.

Maria: We were vegetarians living in meat and potato land. It took a lot of courage to eat lunch in the school cafeteria. I was the only one eating a sandwich made of brown colored bread with lots of green things like lettuce and sprouts hanging out the sides. I saw everyone staring at my lunch. I looked around at the other lunches made of bleached white bread, neatly enclosing processed cheese and bologna. It's no wonder we didn't mind walking a mile or more home for a hot lunch.

We loved to eat, we just ate healthy. We had fantastic recipes, everything that today you find in health food books we were brought up on. Making cakes out of natural things. We even made candy out of ground up nuts, honey, maybe a little non-fat dried milk, and carob powder instead of chocolate. It was delicious but didn't look so good to the eye, however. The kitchen was a place for creating concoctions and discovering who could make the food taste the best. One person would flavor it up one way and say, "Taste this." That was a big thing, "Taste this, look how I did it."

Linda: For dinner Mom used to make nice stews and lentil soups. She prepared rice with celery and parsley, we liked that. We had pizzas made with a high protein soy flour, and always a big gigantic salad with lots of vegetables.

Collard greens, kale, mustard greens, black eye peas and lima beans were often part of the menu. We were eating veggie burgers made with ground up sunflower seeds before anyone had ever heard of such a thing. My mom molded a turkey once out of nut loaf for Thanksgiving. She made it with nuts, tofu, wheat germ and spices.

As our family got larger, our father would buy fresh produce in bulk at wholesale prices. There was always lots of fresh fruit and raw nuts to eat. Dad had us take lots of vitamins too. We didn't like that part too much.

Maria: My father kept a very tight rein on us. We wanted to do so many things but he wouldn't let us. He didn't want us out where we could be eating junk food. In our house there was no white flour, no white sugar, meat was raw nuts, and we went to a farm to get the raw goat's milk.

Linda: If we ate cake at a birthday party that would be the equivalent in anyone else's family to smoking pot. "You did what?!?" Dad was a little bit too much....

Photo: Linda, John and Maria Alberici.

When we came home from parties my dad used to pull us aside and say, "Look in my eyes. Did you eat junk?" I felt as if he were God and there was no way we could lie because he would know anyway.

Maria: I remember at a neighbor's birthday party there was ice cream. Dad said, "Okay, you can have a little taste of it just to be polite." This ice cream—I thought I'd died and gone to heaven. I'd never tasted anything like that in my life. My mom used to make ice cream with natural ingredients like avocados, natural vanilla or carob, frozen goat's milk, honey and whip it up in a blender. She was very inventive and we were an imaginative bunch. If we were told, "Look, I made ice cream, yummy...." we would anticipate a delicious dessert. Since we had nothing to compare it to, it would taste good to us.

One day my brother and a couple sisters gathered some small change together and said, "Do you want to be in our club?" I was thinking, 'What club?' "Come with us," my brother said, with a devilish twinkle in his eyes. I followed them to the corner candy store. "We can't go in there!" It was forbidden. I followed them in and we gazed for a while at the variety of candy that was displayed. Which one would we share? Just then, I heard one of my sisters say, "Look, that one has almonds in it. It must be healthy!" We always ate almonds, even almond butter at home. Yes, I had convinced myself, so we bought and ate the chocolate bar with the almonds. We were sworn to secrecy!

The Most Wonderful Time of the Year

Linda: Christmas was magical, it was the big holiday. My parents scrimped and saved and we did without all year until Christmas came. Christmas was the end all in our family.

My parents did everything on Christmas Eve without us knowing it. It was amazing. They probably stayed up until 4:00 in the morning and then we would wake up at 6:00 and would want to go downstairs but they wouldn't let us because Dad wanted to have the movie camera going. So we had to wait at the top of the steps, and wait and wait and wait—it was like torture. It was probably only thirty minutes but to me it felt like three hours.

>**Lillian Alberici:** We always tried to get them nice gifts, of course at bargain prices. We'd wait until the last minute. Some of the stores were open until twelve midnight, we'd wait until 11:00 and get the bargains.

Maria: So there's movie footage of us running down the stairs and seeing the presents. To us, the tree was decorated like it could be in a *Home Journal*.
My family, and my father's brothers and sister's families, had quite a tradition with Christmas tree contests. My dad would spend a great deal of time tying on extra branches if there was a bare spot on the tree.
My parents took a lot of

pride in their tree, even though they only had a few hours on Christmas Eve to get it together.

Linda: They always wanted us to experience the fairy tale side of Christmas and the big surprise of seeing all the decorations, gifts and everything magically appear when we woke up on Christmas morning. Our parents' reward was our squeals of delight as we ran down the stairs and immediately tore into the presents, thrilled to see what we unwrapped. One thing about my parents, they could go in spurts. They could go all out when they had to, like doing Christmas in one night. It was crazy. There was one Christmas, I was about twelve or thirteen, when we almost didn't have a tree. My father went out a little too late on Christmas Eve to buy one. My brother and I went with him but all the Christmas tree lots had closed early because of a severe blizzard. The last lot we went to had dozens of leftover trees just standing there frozen in the snow.
Dad said, "What a shame, they are going to have to burn them all. If we take one we will be doing them a favor." My father had just a tiny bit of what I call 'South Philly scruples' but even I couldn't imagine my little brothers and sisters waking up to Christmas without a tree. So I volunteered to climb the fence and get the tree.
The blizzard was so bad that we didn't make it home for hours. My dad and I spent quite a bit of time helping drivers who were stuck in the snow on Baltimore Pike. I never saw snow so thick and so high on a main road. There were many people in need of help. It was pandemonium! My brother John, who was a year and a half younger than me, helped dig out cars too but also spent a lot of the time in the car sitting on his hands. It was absolutely freezing!

Maria: Back at the house we were waiting for them to arrive home and it was getting late. With the weather being so awful, my mom and I were worried and hoping that they hadn't gotten into an accident. When they finally made it home with the tree, we were so happy! Dad bragged about Linda's heroism and made it clear that she wasn't stealing. As I adorned the tree with decorations, I thought how lucky we were to have this special tree in our home to share the Holidays with us—and how lucky the tree was too!
Singing Christmas carols was a big thing in our family. our dad was inspired to create a Christmas song for us and every year at Christmastime, the whole family would sing it like an anthem. Dad would lead us and teach us the catchy melody and lyrics. Then, Mom would start in with a harmony and Linda would add another harmony. Some of the younger kids would keep the beat and Dad would swell the high note at the end. We all joined in with gusto and I would go for the

highest note! Come to think of it, we all went for the highest note. It was a riot!

We would sing the song in the car on the way to visit our relatives during the Holidays and it made the time go by, without all of us kids asking, "Are we there yet?"

During the year, there were lots of hand-me-downs but not at Christmas! No matter what struggles the year had brought us, we all pitched in to help one another. Yes, we quarreled.... we were a vocal bunch but we sure could sing! In that moment of sheer exaltation, we shared a special bond. We were united in song and all was right with the world.

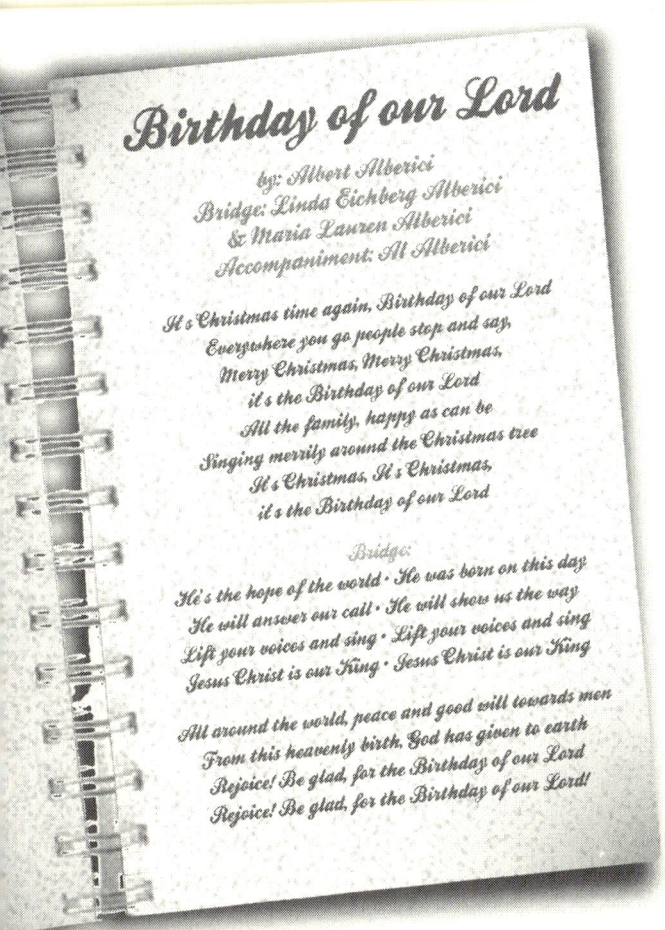

Birthday of our Lord

by: Albert Alberici
Bridge: Linda Eichberg Alberici
& Maria Lauren Alberici
Accompaniment: Al Alberici

It's Christmas time again, Birthday of our Lord
Everywhere you go people stop and say,
Merry Christmas, Merry Christmas,
it's the Birthday of our Lord
All the family, happy as can be
Singing merrily around the Christmas tree
It's Christmas, It's Christmas,
it's the Birthday of our Lord

Bridge:
He's the hope of the world • He was born on this day
He will answer our call • He will show us the way
Lift your voices and sing • Lift your voices and sing
Jesus Christ is our King • Jesus Christ is our King

All around the world, peace and good will towards men
From this heavenly birth, God has given to earth
Rejoice! Be glad, for the Birthday of our Lord
Rejoice! Be glad, for the Birthday of our Lord!

Linda: We watched the local TV children's shows growing up—*Pixanne, Gene London, Sally Starr;* we loved Sally Starr. One of our favorite shows was *The Three Stooges*. They reminded me of how our brothers and sisters used to goof around. My mom liked to watch *The Shari Lewis Show*. We would watch together, as we helped Mom with chores, usually folding cloth diapers.

Maria: When I was very young, I remember a TV show called *Romper Room*. My favorite part of the show was the closing segment, when the host, a sweet young lady with a soft voice, would hold up a Magic Mirror. The hand mirror would transform so that you could see her face through the mirror. She would say, "I see John and Jane and Billy...." and I would straighten up my posture, smile and sometimes wave to the TV. I wanted the Magic Mirror to see me and have the nice lady say my name, Maria Elena. There wasn't a chance that was ever going to happen and my mom knew it. After the show ended I must have looked so disappointed—again. Mom told me, "Maybe she'll say Mary, that means Maria in English," but that wasn't the name that my parents and relatives called me. If it was a Magic Mirror, it should know my real name. Shouldn't it? My mom never wanted to disappoint her children so one day she surprised us. She must have taken the glass out of a hand mirror she had, because she had her own version of the Magic Mirror. She looked through it and said, "I see Maria Elena and Linda...." she would tell us how good we were or how we could be better. Who needed *Romper Room* anymore?

Whenever we could, we would exercise with *The Jack Lalanne Show*. He reminded me of my father, especially when he would joke around and start singing while he was exercising. Jack Lalanne was entertaining and made exercise fun, my mom liked that. My dad loved that he was motivating. If Dad was home, he would passionately encourage us to exercise during the show and even through the commercials.

When I got older, once in a while, my parents would let me stay up and watch *The Bob Hope Specials, The Frank Sinatra Show* and *The Dean Martin Show*. They were a little past my bedtime but when I heard the applause, laughter and songs coming from the TV set into my bedroom I couldn't stand it! I would sneak out of bed and tell my parents that I couldn't sleep and ask them if I could watch. Because I was the oldest and

Photo: New York's Romper Room lady Miss Mary Ann in the 1970s.

wanted to be in show business, they would make an exception. They were fantastic variety shows that would give me sweet dreams and, the next day, I would re-choreograph everything I saw in the mirror. Judy Garland had a show too. I remember when Liza Minnelli went on her program as a young girl and that made an impression on me.

Linda: There was a local TV series called *Al Albert's Showcase,* it was a big East Coast talent show. People knew the host as the lead singer with the original Four Aces.

Dad had this idea for all his daughters to sing together on the show. It was incredibly exciting to think about. Maria eagerly took control and taught us something from the *Sound Of Music*. When we had our audition to get on the show, the producers were grinning from ear to ear. They loved us; we were going to be on TV!

Maria was about thirteen and I was eleven; we both had braces on our teeth and we were not feeling too pretty. On the day the show aired we all kept scooting closer to the television set until we heard our father yell out, "Get back from the TV, the radiation's bad for you."

First Maria appeared on the TV set and sang an expressive and emotional solo, 'Somewhere Over The Rainbow.' She never stopped smiling, braces and all. I, on the other hand, was not anxious to show my 'tinsel teeth.' After Maria's song, Al Alberts interviewed her and she told him, "I have another sister." Then I came out and said, "Well, I have another sister" and the rest of my sisters came out one by one saying, "But I have another sister," until all six of us arrived on stage, all the way down to about three years old. We sang 'Do Re Mi,' complete with arm movements. It was a cute bit.

After my mother had her seventh child, she sometimes had help around the house. One housekeeper would rush out at a certain time on Thursday nights, "I have to leave, I have to go home and watch my Dean Martin. I'm leaving right now. I have to watch Dean Martin." I thought, "Who is this Dean Martin, why is he so important?"

Al Alberici: My impression of Dean Martin is that he was one of the fortunate ones who made it.

"Two Different Faces But In Tight Places We Think And We Act As One"

Maria: When we were around eleven or twelve years old, we started tagging along on Mom's singing jobs and we would sing a song in her act. That's how we got our experience. Then, we started singing on our own, doing little jobs here and there and performing in musicals.

Linda: We had to get the leading role or our parents wouldn't let us do it because they wanted us to be at home helping them. They believed as long as you had the lead that's a lot of hard work and it looks good on your resumé.

Maria: I think because my parents had to put most of their energy into taking care of a big family, they were living vicariously through us. And we did learn a lot from our parents because they were very talented. I learned showmanship from my mom. Now my father, however, he wasn't the type to sing in public because he would get nervous, he wanted perfection, but around our house his singing was magnificent. We would sing together to the famous musicals like *Oklahoma* and *Carousel*, most of the duets made famous by Shirley Jones and Gordon MacRae.

>**Lillian Alberici:** My husband loved to sing also, as a matter of fact he took lessons from Mario Lanza's teacher Enrico Rosati in New York, but he was busy making a living. When it came to singing in public he was kind of shy.

Linda: Dad gave us voice lessons a couple of times a week and always made sure we had the best piano and dance teachers although Maria wishes she could have started dancing a little earlier.

Maria: I can remember passing by the neighborhood dancing school when I was about twelve years old. I would look in the window and wish that I could take dancing lessons. My parents finally noticed my passion and the owner gave us a family discount. My wish for dance lessons came true!

We were able to start performing at a very young age. Slap some makeup on us and we looked all grown up. We were working as young teenagers, thirteen, fourteen, just doing our thing.

At home, we would be busy doing school work or helping around the house and then it was rush-rush-get ready. Either our dad would drive us to our singing jobs or our uncle would take us with our mom.

Philadelphia had some soulful musicians that knew how to express old-time blues songs. One of my favorites was the Louis Armstrong song—"If I ever had a cent, I'd be rich as Rockefeller, gold dust at my feet, on the Sunny Side of the Street."

After our singing job, we would go straight back home to sleep because we knew that we would have to wake up early the next morning.

We had seen our mom doing it. She'd work around the house then all of a sudden she was dressed up and off to a job. The next morning she wouldn't be able to sleep late, she'd be in the kitchen making breakfast so that's how we were. We didn't know any better. My parents would wake us up early in the morning, they wouldn't let us sleep. They'd open the windows to let the sun shine in and sing a song, "It's a good day...."

Al Alberici: My main philosophy is to have a closely-knit family. Children should realize a house divided falls and a house united stands. Where there is unity there is strength.

Linda: I think our father was balanced between spirituality and church doctrine. In those days the Catholic Church was very legalistic, all about rules and regulations. My father was looking for something more spiritual, more about the personal relationship with God and Jesus. Sometimes we couldn't go to church on Sunday and that was okay. We prayed together at home. This wasn't all right with the nuns and the priests—being raised Catholic, it might be a sin but it was okay within our family. We honored God in our hearts in a different way. My father knew the truth about God's grace and having a family of eleven required a heaping portion of that grace.

On Sundays we usually went to visit grandparents, my dad taught us to respect our elders. Whenever we were together in the car for long trips we prayed as a family. My father could pray out loud for forty-five minutes straight, from the beginning of the trip all the way to the end. He was either really long-winded or inspired by the Holy Spirit. I haven't decided which.

My father followed his heart and learned about alternative healing and fitness methods, including yoga. I remember as a young girl, being intrigued by the postures and the science of breath. Dad talked often

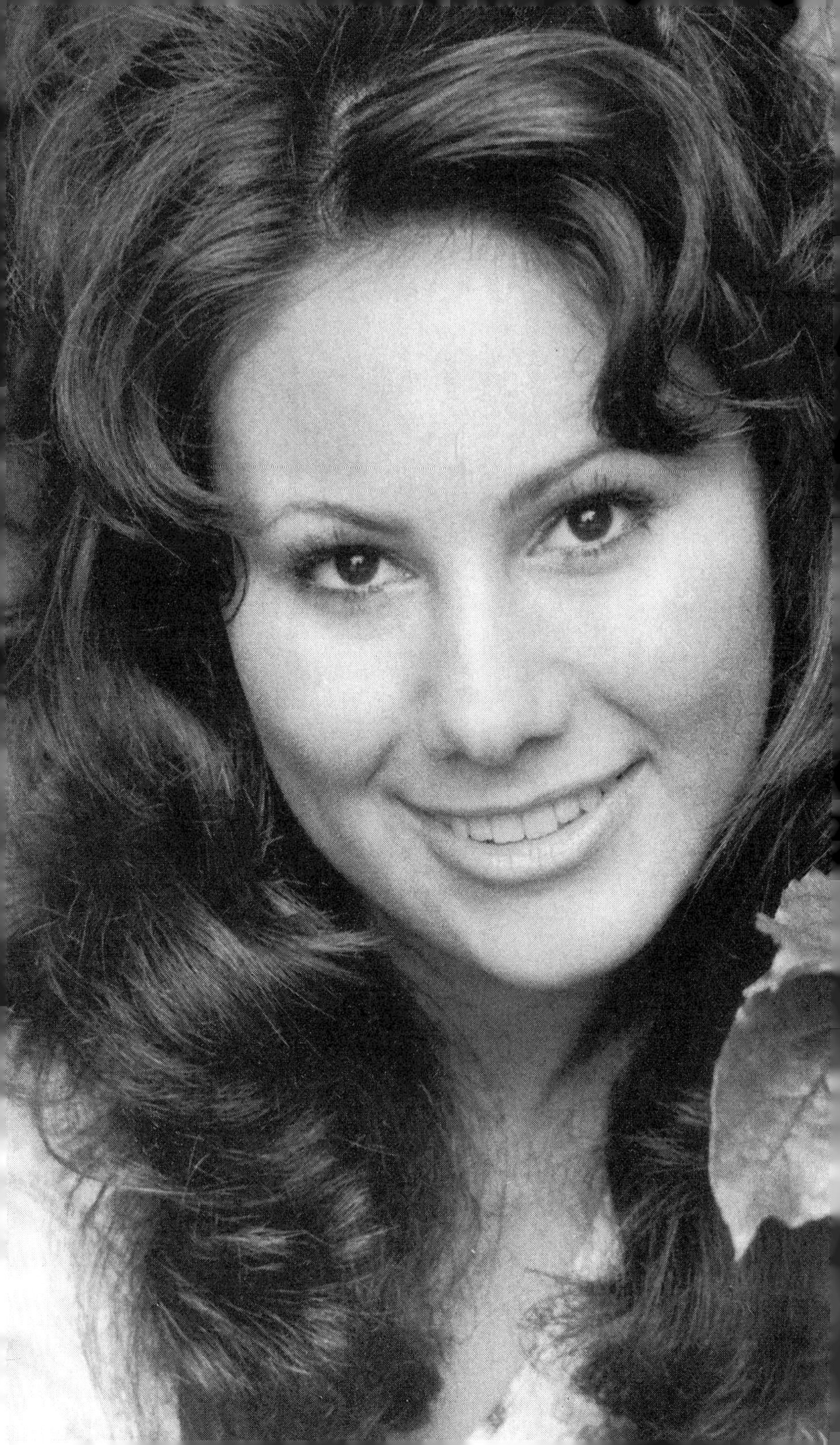

about Prana and fresh air. He always slept with the window open even in winter. He would come into our rooms at night and open *our* windows too. In the winter, if I was awake, I would close them as soon as he left.

Maria: I escaped the cold of winter by reading the inspired writings of Paul Bragg. He lived in California and wrote about the benefits of natural foods and simple living practices, like jogging with his daughter. He philosophized on the connection between the body, mind and spirit and how it relates to wellness. These beliefs and Dad's motivation laid down a strong foundation for me.

Dad was passionate about business too. My parents saved their money, worked hard and we also helped them with their businesses. We moved from Philadelphia at a young age to Yeadon, then we moved out to Newtown Square. Each move took us further away from the city and more into the country. Eventually, we had many acres surrounding our home. Our back yard was like a park.

My father's main business was selling tombstones to mark grave sites. After a while in the monument business, my father and his brothers bought three catering halls to hold wedding parties. People would joke that my father married them and buried them.

Linda: My dad always gave God the credit for his 'luck' in business. He was successful in buying and selling small apartment buildings. I enjoyed going with him to work on the apartments because it was a diversion from the usual house work. I learned about painting, carpentry and plumbing. I liked knowing how to fix things. My dad used to call his children who helped him "my partners."

Maria: When we were growing up, we were taught to be seen and not heard but I found out that I could be heard when I sang. It was a way to express myself and it pleased my parents, especially my dad.

Linda, though, was pretty vocal about her opinions. I was more introverted, except when it came to singing and dancing. That gave me my self-worth which was a good thing because, when Linda started puberty before I did, I felt a little left out with my thin physique. I worried that maybe my growth was stunted because I was so thin.

Linda: I went through puberty at a very young age. Even though I was younger than Maria, my best friend and I had breasts and she didn't; she had to go through that psychological trauma. Nature has a way of evening the playing field, she started exercising and developed curves. She became Miss Body Beautiful a few years later.

"Three E's: energy, enthusiasm, empathy" - Al Alberici

Maria: What brought about my transformation? I guess adversity makes you want to be strong. All through grade school, I felt like Linda was my protector. We were often made fun of because our family was so different. The other kids would call us "Alber-creatures!"
I would try to ignore them or make a retort like, "Sticks and stones may break my bones, but names will never harm me." That was a little saying my mom taught me but it wasn't true, words do hurt. I would run away when it got to be too much to handle.
But not Linda, she would be ready to sock 'em one. She was tough. Once in the neighborhood she twisted a boy's arm behind his back and he never bothered us again. I felt physically and mentally fragile. I started lifting weights. I set my mind to succeed in my life and make something out of myself but ultimately what saved me was my personal relationship with God. This was precious to me. No matter what, I could walk and talk with the Lord and that made me feel nurtured, protected and guided.

Linda: Throughout my pre-teen and early teen years I remember my father showing off my strength and athleticism. I went through a husky period then. My dad would take me into the sporting goods department of stores and show people how much weight I could lift. I was glad I could make him proud of me in some way but I secretly wished that he would be proud of my singing like he was of Maria's.
I was the second child so I found my niche as the extra son my father didn't have. I got very involved in sports, I used to get my self-esteem by how great I played softball. I was the great softball player and the athlete in the family.
I remember the last time I challenged a boy to a duel. It was my senior year of high school. There was a boy who used to tease me a lot so I bet him I could beat him in arm wrestling. I won but it wasn't easy, I knew my arm wrestling days were numbered. By that time I had discovered the many benefits of charm and lady-like behavior so I was ready to give up the tomboy act.

Maria: What were my favorite teen experiences? When I was sixteen years old, St. Joseph's University announced they were putting on *West Side Story*. I immediately began to prepare for the part of Maria, at home with my father as my vocal coach. It was the perfect part for me, it required dramatic acting, singing and dancing. Well, I got the part and a summer full of classes in diction and choreography. I soaked it up like a sponge. It was a wonderful experience and, on closing night, I received dozens and dozens of flowers on stage.

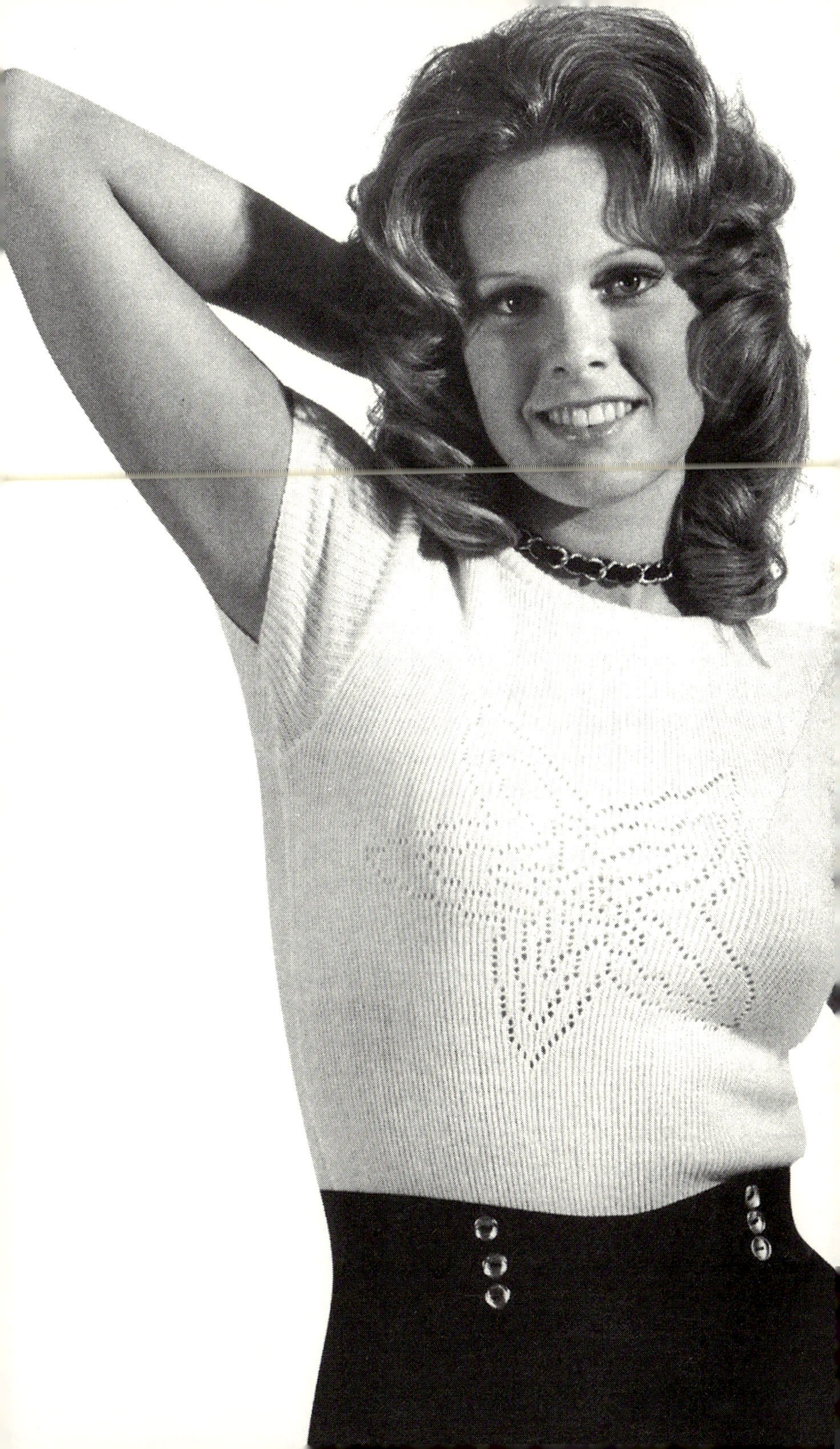

I struggled to hold back the tears because it was the first time that I felt like a star. I was on my way!

A local TV series that I loved to watch with my brothers and sisters heard about my performance in *West Side Story* and gave me the opportunity to play Snow White. I would appear on the Gene London TV show during the segment called "the land of make-believe," a musical and dramatic adaptation of famous fairy tales. I really related to the character of Snow White because, back then, she was the only brunette Disney character. Luckily we taped in the cold of winter when my skin color was more fair, like Snow White's. In the summer sun, I tan easily!

Linda: We went to Catholic school until my last two years of high school when we went to Marple Newtown High where they had a drama department. I was there for two years but even though Maria was only there for one year she made a big splash in the drama department.

> **Jan Kubicki, Drama teacher, Marple Newtown High School:**
> Maria Elena came in her senior year. I was teaching drama and I couldn't believe what I was seeing because she was so eccentric and theatrical. Very flighty and dramatic, there were no small gestures—everything was large. Linda, on the other hand, was more subdued and very practical.
> All the boys at school were enthralled with Maria but they were afraid of her father. It was a shame in a way, she couldn't have a normal life because the father was always intruding. Everything she did he was there.
> He was an extreme case and word got out. She never had a date, never went out with the kids to the football games, she always went straight home after school or rehearsal. She was liked by everyone, she was part of the group and everyone admired her talent and liked her personally but she didn't have a lot of friends. We were doing one of those New York avant garde plays at the time and Maria was quite sensational in it. When she moved your eyes were riveted to her. We entered the show in drama competitions around the state of Pennsylvania. For some reason between the regionals and the state finals her father decided that Maria wasn't going to be allowed to go with the rest of the kids and stay overnight in a motel to perform the next day. He was adamant. So we started rehearsing with another girl in the part and unfortunately the girl wasn't suited for it. Everyone was kind of dispirited about it. Then at the last minute, to everyone's relief, he let her go.

"Musical comedies aren't written, they are rewritten."—Stephen Sondheim

Maria: Linda also performed in the play so my father let us go to the state competition but only after much persuasion. Dad made it clear that we would be responsible for each other. I relished this newfound freedom because it was my first time sleeping away from home. I was going to make the most of it and have some fun! Some of the kids in the play would sneak away and smoke those "funny" cigarettes. Afterward, when they were stoned, I would have deep conversations with them. I guess, I was naturally high and didn't need to smoke anything. For instance, the kids dared me to go into our drama teachers room and lie on his bed. What would he do? Peer pressure! Without thinking, I took the dare.
Afterwards, one of the female teachers and chaperones gave me a talking to, and I never did anything like that again. You see, back then, I related life to the early musical comedies that I watched growing up. The world was my stage and the audience was watching.

> **Jan Kubicki, Drama teacher Marple Newtown High School:**
> It was a joke, her idea of a joke, the innocent, chaste Maria Elena was offering herself up like a piece of luggage in a motel room. It was funny and everyone laughed but I wonder what she would have done if I had jumped on top of her, you know? She probably would have screamed so loud her father would have heard her back in Philadelphia.
> We won the competition and before we left Penn State that day the head of the theater department offered Maria a full scholarship because they were so impressed with her.

Maria: Linda and I learned how to be leading ladies in musical comedies. Jan Kubicki also directed me in the musical *The Fantasticks*. It was easy to relate to my character Luisa, especially when she said, "Please, God, please don't make me be normal." I could very much relate to that, it pretty much became my motto in life. It's like, I wasn't raised normal, I am not normal so please don't make me normal, that would be taking my soul and making it something it wasn't.
The next year Linda had the lead in *South Pacific* in high school. I thought she was brave when she cut her long hair very short to emulate Mary Martin and Mitzi Gaynor. The leading ladies who starred in the Broadway and movie productions had short hair. In the song, 'I'm Gonna Wash That Man Right Outa My Hair,' Linda actually did wash her hair on stage.
When the family saw her short hair for the first time, we were shocked! My father liked all the girls in our family to wear their hair long. That

year, at graduation, Linda won the "Most Talented Girl" award just like I did the year before and that was sweet.

Linda: It was in high school that I finally got accolades about my singing and acting talent from my teachers and classmates. That encouraged me to eventually pursue vocal music as my major in college.
Maria and I used to do a lot of college summer theater. Besides performing at St. Joseph's College, we both played in *Age of Aquarius* at Villanova, and then we moved on to professional dinner theater. We starred in *A Funny Thing Happened on the Way to the Forum* at the Brandywine Dinner Theater. There were two leads and we got them both. Without music and theater, my life would have been so boring. I would have been home folding laundry and cleaning. I was grateful for the diversion and I loved it. Maria was different; she knew it was her fate.

I knew there was some kind of adventure waiting for me...

Linda: Maria and I developed a sister act. Our parents encouraged us to sing together, they said, "two are better than one." We actually had a professional writer, Russ Faith, develop some special show material for us because we were doing more and more in our mom's act. He wrote tunes for some of the singing stars that came out of Philadelphia like Frankie Avalon, and he mentored Andrea McArdle, the star of the Broadway musical *Annie*.

It wasn't long before Maria and I were doing gigs on our own. There were nice supper clubs around town with swinging bands where we performed. Dance clubs were popping up all around Philadelphia and the recording industry was growing. It was like a little New York. During all of this, we began recording for a producer at the hit-making Sigma Sound Studio.

Maria: That's how we continued to grow as entertainers. Plus we sang at our father's catering halls, where we would check coats and hats at the wedding receptions and then run up and sing with the band.

We also worked conventions, small nightclubs and country clubs like the Downingtown Inn. A lot of the hotels had lovely dinner showrooms at that time. Most of the places where we performed were managed by people our mom had worked with before, so they took care of us like we were their own daughters. Alcohol was served at these places but we were too young to drink and wouldn't dare.

Linda: We had a steady gig at the West End Boat Club, by the Delaware River, singing standards with the band and we also performed with Al Raymond. He had one of the most well-known big bands in the Philadelphia area at the time.

Maria: Our mom used to sing with him years earlier. Singing with the big bands was very good training for timing, phrasing, and it helps you become more versatile. That's how Frank Sinatra and a lot of those famous singers got their start and my father was very wise to that. For being so cloistered Dad let us do these jobs because he knew this was a way for us to get our training.

When I was younger, I loved going through my mom's scrapbook. Inside were newspaper clippings of her winning the Miss Lawndale beauty contest. In one picture, she was surrounded by lovely flowers and she seemed to glow. I wondered if I would ever have the chance to blossom into this kind of beauty.

Next step to fame, beauty contests? I knew I needed to get out of the house and into the world—somehow. So, one day, a very popular radio station publicized a Miss Hot Pants contest. Maybe this would be a way to meet people and if I won, gain some recognition. Wow—I won! It was all over the radio and newspapers. Things were beginning to happen. I knew I wanted to be in show business and reasoned that pageants could be a stepping stone. A girl in those days, how did you get yourself out there? So on a whim I entered the Miss Pennsylvania World contest in 1971.

> **The Evening Bulletin, June 21, 1971:** *Maria Elena Alberici, 19, of Newtown Square was named Miss Photogenic Friday night by newsmen at the introduction show of the Miss Pennsylvania Pageant at the Franklin Mall. Evening gown and swimsuit competition were held Friday night. The finals and crowning of the new Miss Pennsylvania will be tonight.*

Maria: The gown I was planning to wear in the pageant was all wrinkled, I tried to iron it but there was no ironing board. It was hopeless.

"If you can't run, walk, if you can't walk, crawl, if you can't crawl, wiggle like a snake."—Dad

I brought a backup gown that my grandmother made and I wore that instead. It probably was a good idea because the dress I was going to wear was a lot more demure. The one that I ended up wearing was a little more sexy and sophisticated. It was made of white shimmering material that hugged my body. My bikini bathing suit was fire engine red.

> **News of Delaware County:** *On June 21, Maria Elena Alberici accomplished a life-long dream winning the "Miss Pennsylvania World" contest. She will represent the Keystone state in the Miss World contest to be held in Hampton, Va on September 27 with Bob Hope as the master of ceremonies.*

Maria: When I represented the pageant for Miss Pennsylvania World I made public appearances. I discovered pageants were a business and the winner is the product. I would get paid and so did the heads of the contest.
Basically, they were my agent for a year and would negotiate each contract with the potential buyer—"Come meet Miss Pennsylvania at some special event." Going to the Miss World nationals was my first time away from home for more than one night, I had to be in Hampton, Virginia for three days to do all the activities and publicity. I didn't have my parents or Linda with me but I had a chaperone, my parents traveled to see me later at the actual pageant. It was practically my first time eating in restaurants. I was very nervous about it. Which fork do I use? Would the peas

roll off my fork? There were photographers taking pictures and newspaper people trying to talk with us while we ate. Suddenly, I wasn't so hungry!

Linda: Our family was too big and we ate too healthy to go out to eat. My father was very particular when it came to ingredients. On one rare occasion when we did eat out he asked the waiter, "Would you bring me the salad dressing you're using; is it hydrogenated?" He would have to read the ingredients. Hydrogenated oil is very bad for you so he would want to know. My father knew all about margarine, hydrogenated oil and trans fats back then, this was in the 1960s and 1970s. He called artificial fats "poison." He said, "It will harden your arteries." People used to laugh and say, "You're crazy." My poor father got ridiculed so much because of his belief in health foods.

> **Ralph Pepino, fitness trainer and family friend:** Maria went on to the Miss World USA contest in September of 1971 which was held at Hampton Beach, Bob Hope was the emcee. She represented Pennsylvania and we all went down there for the weekend. What happened down there was—if your daughter won, you had to release her to the organization and they would take her around the world. Al never signed that release. I'll never forget it. And they could not give Maria Elena the title because Al, all night, he was fighting with the head of the contest. Eight hours!

Maria: They started giving me a hard time after that. They took me into the back room and checked to see if I was wearing any padding. I didn't see them do that with any of the other girls. I had snaps and hooks in the back of the dress and when they were finished examining me I asked them to re-fasten my dress. They didn't do it and when I came backstage between numbers my mom said, "They didn't snap and hook your gown, here let me do it before you go out again." Little things like that.
They brought in a new judge at the last minute which was kind of weird. "Meet your new judge, our hairdresser." She was really tight with the pageant officials. I think they decided they didn't want to deal with parents.

> **Ralph Pepino, fitness trainer and family friend:** Finally, the head judge said, "Al, you didn't sign the paper. We could not give Maria Elena the title. Yes, she deserved it." I felt bad but Al wouldn't release his daughter. No one could beat her that day, she was it.

Linda: Nothing got past my father. When he talked to people he would

"I once spent a year in Philadelphia, I think it was on a Sunday."—W. C. Fields

think like a detective. He would be very disarming, very charming, so they didn't know they were being interrogated. He would get people off their guard and they would inadvertently give all kinds of information about themselves. He enjoyed analyzing people; his style was very much like the TV detective Columbo. Dad called him, "the smart dummy."

Ralph Pepino: The father was tough, that was his way. I respected him for what he believed in but I felt a little bad for Maria Elena. You know, Al came from Italy and that was his way. He always wanted to control his daughters and he wouldn't release them on several occasions. A couple of times they wanted Maria to make movies in California but the father didn't like the parts too much so it never worked out. It was Al's rules and they followed them, that was it.

Linda: Maria worked extremely hard to earn the beauty titles she accumulated. She was completely devoted to working out and eating healthy. I liked all the new experiences she was having in the pageant world, but I realized I didn't have the intense level of dedication she had. After all, I was in school and had to stay focused on that as well as helping my mom around the house.
Maria's notoriety started generating a lot of publicity for the family. Our family was different, having nine healthy, well-adjusted vegetarian kids. The press was drawn to that.
Eventually, the heads of some contests saw me in the newspaper or with Maria when she was making beauty queen appearances. They sought me out and asked me to enter their contests. Wow, I never foresaw that happening.
I was a little bit uncomfortable with the idea of competing in beauty contests but my eagerness to get out of the house and have an adventure of my own, helped me to swiftly overcome my insecurities. Besides, I knew I should broaden my horizons. I won the title of Miss Delaware County

"I saw the angel in the marble and carved until I set it free." - Michelangelo

and I was also crowned Miss Maryland for the Miss Hemisphere Pageant. As a result, I learned about politics, business, fashion and poise. This gave me the confidence to move forward in my passion for singing.

Maria: One of the prizes I won in the Miss Pennsylvania World contest was a part in a major motion picture starring Robert Mitchum, *Going Home*. I didn't really have any lines, I was basically a background player, but I got to see how a movie company worked on location and I had some close-ups and danced in a night club scene.
They cast Linda too, my father liked us to be together when we were away from home. The filming was done in Wildwood, New Jersey, a beach town where we used to vacation as kids. They put us up in a hotel overnight and I guess my father must have slept in the car to keep a watch on us. He told me the next morning, "I saw one of the girl actresses going into Jan Michael Vincent's room last night. She was in there a long time!" It was like he was checking out the whole scene like Columbo, "What was she doing in there?"
He went to the bar later that evening to talk with Robert Mitchum while I waited in the car. He came back looking very disappointed and told me, "You know, it's a shame this business. Everyone drinks after work." He told me he spoke to Robert Mitchum and he said, "This isn't the kind of life for a clean-living girl like your daughter." Of course, I didn't want to hear that. My father found out co-star Brenda Vaccaro's room number and he made me knock on her door with him. She had this very loooow voice. My father was trying to look into her room while he talked; what does she have in there, booze, cigarettes, just checking it all out, you know? He told Brenda Vaccaro what Robert Mitchum had said to him and she agreed that being an actress was a tough life. My father did not get the feeling that he wanted me to go into the movie business after that.
I never did see *Going Home*, I was only allowed to watch G-rated movies.

Ralph Pepino: I took Maria Elena to a gym and trained her for bodybuilding contests. I put her in two big shows in New York. We didn't train long and she won both shows, Miss Body Beautiful USA and Miss Americana all in the same year. Arnold Schwarzenegger, Mr. Olympia, was one of the judges. She beat all the girls in there, who had been training for years. She knew how to eat, she ate raw foods and exercised.
Maria Elena could not be beat. She made the *Strength & Health* magazine cover. The first time a girl was ever on the cover by herself. The sisters were good, clean-living girls. That's the way the girls should be today.

Ben Weider, International President, I.F.B.B., Muscle Builder magazine: *On September 16th, 1972, bodybuilding aficionados from all over the East Coast jammed their way into the Brooklyn Academy of Music in New York to witness one of the greatest bodybuilding events ever held in the United States. Highlight of the gala spectacular affair was the tremendous battle for Mr. World which saw a much improved Mike Katz barely edge popular Ken Waller for the crown. Ed Corney won the Mr. America title going away. Beautiful Maria-Elena Alberici outclassed her rivals to win the Miss Americana in a breeze.*

The Miss Americana winner, Maria Elena Alberici, was one of the most popular beauty queens to ever win this event. She was outstanding and far outdistanced the competition. She is beautiful, with a sexy but regal figure. We were told that she has several sisters at home that are just as beautiful. Right On!

Maria: We knew women in those days whose main ambition was to win pageants but that was never my ambition. I just wanted to get into show business so working out was naturally a good thing. Then I heard that one of the women was using steroids and I thought, if this is where these kinds of contests are going, this would be my last one.

Unfortunately, I was not business savvy at that time. People told me there were posters of my winning the contests all over New York City, but we never cashed in on the publicity.

My father realized the hullabaloo I was getting and said, "You should enter the Miss America pageant because that has a talent competition." So we did. I thought it would be like the other contests, you know? I didn't realize the Miss America contest was all about fitting a mold.

You know how you would fold a piece of paper, cut out the silhouette of a doll, unfold the paper and you had a whole row of dolls that looked the same?

In those days the Miss America pageant had a certain image and we were not the normal family. Being in the Miss America pageant was far different—it was not about being fit and healthy, it was more about fitting the image they were looking for.

My father talked to an Italian judge at the Miss Philadelphia contest and the judge told him that Miss America was more of a political thing. The pageant was more concerned with the girls and their parents that were involved in the club. The club put on the local pageant and you could tell the club girls were treated with kid gloves. I was an outsider.

The Italian-American judge told my father, "Listen, off the record, your daughter is Italian and, no offense, but there's never been an Italian to win Miss America." My father said to me, "Why would he say that, an Italian girl never won Miss America? There's always a first time."

I guess there is a stigma attached to being Italian, that you might be related to gangsters in the Mafia! I didn't realize this until I saw the first *Godfather* movie. I was really upset at the way the movie depicted the Italian family, because I wasn't raised that way at all. Of course, *The Godfather* is a classic movie with great acting; a date took me to see it and he thought it was the coolest movie he had ever seen.

Jan Kubicki, Drama teacher Marple Newtown High School:
She was definitely the best girl in the contest but she was too ethnic and that wasn't 'in' then. It was futile to even try at that time but she gave it her all and she was just amazing. It was still WASP, protestant America that was the mainstream.

Linda: I watched the pageant and Maria was the prettiest and most talented but she was so different from all the other girls. The other girls were like debutantes and Maria was a free spirit, she had this natural animal sexuality.... she was 'whole wheat bread' and the pageant wanted 'White Bread.'

Maria: After that experience, I felt my beauty contest days should come to an end. It was time to move in a different direction.

I had a big argument about that with Dad after that. He wanted me to continue in contests but I was adamant; there was no way! It was taking too much time away from what I really wanted to do: sing, dance and act. I didn't know which way I should go because Linda, by that time, was all absorbed in music in college and not paying any attention to our act. She used to come home from school with trumpets, drumsticks and violins. For her homework assignments, she would have to learn how to play them so I'd hear these weird sounds coming out of our bedroom.... "Honk, Honk" and "Sqweeeek!"

I'd say to her, "Do you really want to do this; don't you just want to sing together?" It seemed like she was spinning her wheels. I felt that she was being held back from what we were building together as a sister act.

***Variety,* February 1973:** *Golddigger auditions at TV studio on Eighth Ave. N.Y. The girls were to be 18 to 22, able to sing and dance.... Only the "spectacularly beautiful," need apply....*

Linda: I was a voice major at Westchester University, studying to be a music teacher. I was not enjoying it all that much and I was growing restless, expectant for change, looking for adventure. It wasn't long after, I happened to be in the college library one day and picked up a copy of *Variety*. I don't know, it was very random, like God drew me to it. I read about this national audition for The Golddiggers, a group of vivacious singer-dancers who appeared on *The Dean Martin Show* and thought, "That sounds like fun." I shared my find with Maria and we excitedly talked about going to New York, one of the cities where auditions were being held. It was just a two or three hour drive from our home in Philadelphia.

Maria: Linda and I showed the audition notice to our parents. If we were chosen, we would have to perform and travel around the world. We loved the idea but Dad most definitely did not. He began to spurt out pointed questions and stern warnings.
"I don't like the fact that...."
"What if...?"
"How about...?"
We just knew this could be the chance of a lifetime but now, after hearing our dad's dire predictions, we began to have our doubts. What else could I do? Should I continue my education in theater? I felt imprisoned. Our Dad was strict, very strict. He always kept an eye on us, which was good, I guess, but I felt like climbing the walls sometimes. Why study voice and dance if I was never going to have the opportunity to express my talents to the world?

Linda: Well, Dad finally gave in and drove us to the audition. He decided beforehand that he wouldn't separate us. We both had to be chosen or he wouldn't let us go to Hollywood, as if the odds weren't already big enough for even one of us to land a network TV gig?

But no matter, I was ready, I'd had enough of college after two years, so we headed for New York. It was a cloudy, drizzly day and we practiced our voice in the car on the way up.

When we arrived, I thought to myself, "Wow, this is it." There were lines of gorgeous girls circling the block, pushing to get inside, and the press was busy taking pictures. It was astonishing. Hundreds of girls showed up for the audition, so what chance did the two of us have to get into the group? You know, New York has the best talent anywhere.

Maria: It was like a cattle call with herds of girls trying to gather into a huge dance hall with a wall to wall mirror. This was our first New York audition and we were green. We didn't even bring a leotard, we wore stylish street clothing similar to what beauty contestants would wear. However, I made sure I could do a high kick in my slacks and brought dance shoes to change into.

Each girl sang with a piano player in a private rehearsal hall. It took a while for each girl to sing. I sang Carol King's "I Feel the Earth Move." Although the song didn't show off my vocal range I chose it because I could show personality and groove to it in the style of The Golddiggers. When it came time to learn the choreography, they split us into teams but Linda wasn't in my group. Greg Garrison was the executive producer of the Dean Martin television shows and he ran the audition along with Lee Hale, the program's musical vocal director. I knew Greg was someone important because at the dance audition he told me to go to the front of the line and directed all the other girls to perform it like me. I was flattered but scared because I was following the girls dancing in front of me. As I moved to the front of the line, I quickly caught the attention of the choreographer and with begging eyes asked him to do the steps in front of me. Little did Greg know, I was just faking it.

Linda: First, Greg Garrison looked at you and, if he didn't like your look, you were out. He actually took hold of my face, by the cheeks, and looked at my teeth like I was a horse. He raised thoroughbred horses and he was very much into teeth. He wanted good teeth and a homespun, natural kind of beauty. Next you had to dance and if they didn't like that, you were gone. Those who were left got the chance to sing and then dance again for the final cut.

Maria: After all the singing and dancing, the producer called us in and told us that he wanted to see Linda and me in a leotard. There happened to be a dance supply store across the street so we rushed over to buy one. We had to try them on quickly. Did we look good enough? We had no time to decide. We rushed back to show him how we looked in it. Whew! That was a little awkward.

After a long day of auditioning, all the girls that had survived so far squeezed into the rehearsal hall. Greg pulled me aside and asked, "What if I pick you and not your sister? What will you do?" And I said, "I don't think my parents would let me go by myself." Which was true!

Greg began eliminating more girls by putting his hand on their shoulders to say, "Thank you very much…." After he had chosen me and another girl, Greg stated, "Only three will be chosen from this audition."

Linda was in a line with the other girls and Greg continued to put his hand on their shoulders to say, "Thank you very much" and they would leave dejected. He was going towards Linda to do that motion and he was watching me. I was desperately trying not to make any expression.

I really wanted to go to Hollywood and Linda would have to be chosen in order for my childhood dream to come true. He put his hand on her shoulder and said, "You're going to Hollywood!" just like they do in the movies. He did that on purpose!

Linda: As it turned out, Greg Garrison was playing with our minds. I could tell right away, he liked to do dramatic things just to see how people would react.

Maria: Our father used to test us in the same way so when I saw Greg Garrison, I recognized my father in him. I thought, "I'm leaving my father for a new father; look at his tactics." I was definitely not looking for a new father figure so I decided to keep my distance and leave everything business-like.

Linda: I could hardly comprehend it. We were leaving home? Our parents were extremely protective so it was a little strange that they would even consider letting cross the country and beyond to be part of the Golddiggers group. We weren't even allowed to date except for our school proms. That meant I had only been out on two 'dates' in my whole life and now I could possibly be living on my own in Hollywood.

> **Lillian Alberici:** It certainly did concern me that they were leaving for Hollywood but we knew it was a wonderful opportunity. My husband talked to Greg and he told him, "Oh, they would be well chaperoned at all times." So we thought they would be okay.

Linda: We were big hometown news, queen for a day, pretty much, even photographed for the newspapers. I remember my father going through the motions, "should you go, shouldn't you go?" I think he always knew in his heart that he would never keep us from this opportunity. Mom and Dad always believed it would happen for us and when it did, it must have felt right to them; even though it was the wildest thing they ever let us do. I guess Maria and I going together and being able to watch out for each other helped ease our parents' mind.

Maria: Dad had some opportunities too. When he was younger he was asked to be a part of the singing group on *The Perry Como Show* but it would have taken him away from his family, so he didn't do it. For my parents, this was like a dream they once had but couldn't pursue. We were going to pursue the dream now.

Linda: Our family gathered at the airport for final goodbyes and prayers. It would be our first time on an airplane. We were a little nervous but my father was more anxious about it than we were. It was hard for him to finally let us go to board the plane.

Maria: I was filled with anticipation, in Hollywood there would be more auditions and another chance that one of us could be cut. Would we be put on the spot and forced to choose staying or leaving? I was glad Linda was by my side, she could hopefully keep the stars in my eyes from blinding me. As the plane lifted off into the air, we gasped and held on to each other's arms. We leaned towards the window and watched the world we knew slowly diminish from our sight. The sky was vast and misty, like an empty canvas waiting to be painted.

on our way...

While the truth about Martin's habits is hard to come by, certain facts about his career are crystal clear.
Once considered en route to oblivion as the lesser half of the sundered comedy team of Jerry Lewis and Dean Martin, he is now America's highest-paid entertainer. And he is the only star who is a consistent draw at the theater while also appearing on weekly television.
His defiance of traditional taboos and his obvious virility (liquor+golf+an eye for girls) have made Martin a hero with the male audience. His Italian good looks, his suave manner and his way of cuddling up to a romantic ballad are enormously appealing to women. Thus, he is one of the few stars who seem to be liked equally by both sexes.
-*Good Housekeeping*, 1967

STEREO

reprise
RECORDS
6233

Marilyn Monroe: *Hollywood's a place where they'll pay you a thousand dollars for a kiss, and fifty cents for your soul. I know, because I turned down the first offer often enough and held out for the fifty cents.*

Linda: We touched down safely in California but I was still flying high with the anticipation of meeting the winning ladies from all the big cities that held auditions. It was a beautiful spring like day when we arrived, just glorious. The mountains were so incredibly striking against the clear blue sky and I was very impressed by the majestic palm trees. It was the first time I ever saw one other than in pictures.

Maria: In February we went from cold, freezing, icy Philadelphia and stepped off the plane to palm trees, warm weather, everything green. Paradise. February can be like spring in Southern California.
My last view of Philadelphia on the way to the airport was not pretty. The snow was melting and turning to slush. The trees were bare and any remaining snow on the road was covered with a dark residue from the traffic and car exhaust.
Taking the cab ride from the L.A. Airport was vastly different. Everything looked so crystal clean and colorful. I felt like I had arrived in the Emerald City, 'somewhere over the rainbow.'

Deborah Pratt, Golddigger 1973-1974:
I had just gotten a job as the swing girl in a show called *Don't Bother Me I Can't Cope* in Chicago. My mom had come to see me and was blown away, she said, "Oh my God, I didn't know you could sing and dance and do all this other stuff." So she called me maybe two days later and said, "The Golddiggers are in town."
I said, "Oh no. I saw them, I don't like their shows."
And she said, "Well, they're auditioning, you said you wanted to do TV, you should at least go check it out."
"Oh yeah, I did say that." So I packed up my little bag and went and

five hundred girls were there!
I got there at ten, I think it was six o'clock and it was between myself and one other girl and I had to go to work. I had a curtain call, I had to be at the theater in a half hour.
And so I said, "It was really, really wonderful doing this but I've got to get out of here. And thank you so much." I started to pack up my stuff to leave and I saw them all hubbubing to themselves and Greg Garrison came over to me and said, "Who the f**k do you think you are?" And I said, "Excuse me, who the f**k do *you* think you are?"
He said, "I'm the producer."
And I said, "Yeah, well, I'm the talent and I've got a job and I gotta go to work."
He said, "You know what, I'm going to bring you out to Hollywood and I'm going to break that 'f**k you' attitude you have." So I told him, "Bring it on, send me a ticket! I'm coming!" And I'm thinking I'll never hear from him and walked away.

Linda: The day I met the rest of my competition, I had dressed carefully, choosing my most slimming dress. There were ten of us assembled in the rehearsal studio. I was very impressed with the gals, especially Deborah. When she told me the story about how she handled Greg during her Chicago audition my mouth was hanging open; I couldn't believe her strength and self-assurance. I was nothing like that. I wasn't sure about anything but I was willing to ride the wave as far as I could.
We spent a week together rehearsing an entire show. It was one of the most grueling weeks I ever spent in my life. Having to learn music, dialogue and choreography for an hour-long show was exhausting.
We were told that only eight of the ten would be chosen to be a part of The Golddiggers, they were purposely being tough. One girl didn't even make it through the week, she couldn't handle it. She wanted to go home and then there were nine left.

Maria: After a few hours of rehearsal we would get a break. I needed a snack to refuel but what would I eat? Down the block I saw a 7-11 store that carried a few food items, sodas and drinks. I didn't drink sodas so I bought what looked to me like fruit punch.
"Hmm, Apricot and Peach Sangria, oooh, this sounds tropical. I never saw this before, I'm going to try it."
I drank almost the whole bottle. I think I only had a yogurt or a cottage cheese with it, not much to eat because we had to be thin. And this was the afternoon that Greg Garrison, Lee Hale and company were going to pick the final girls to be in The Golddiggers.

I was saying, "I don't feel so good, I feel a little dizzy, nauseous right now. I don't know if it's nerves or what."
Patti, one of the girls, said, "What are you drinking there?"
I said, "Just some juice, some fruit punch."
She said, "I think there's alcohol in there!"
It was Sangria. I didn't know Sangria had alcohol in it. From then on, the girls called me, 'Maria Sangria.'

> **Mark Jones, *Los Angeles Times*, May 8, 1973:** *To the winners Garrison was all smiles and congratulations but he asked for strict attention as he recited a list of no-no's for all Golddiggers.*
> *No dating on the road, no smoking in public (or use of marijuana or drugs at any time), nor could the girls marry during the duration of their one-year contract.*
> *And, said Garrison, "Don't come to me May 1 and tell me your head hurts and you want to go home or you've fallen in love and you want out." He said that quietly, matter-of-factly, then added, "If I'm crossed I'll keep you from working anyplace else."*

Patti (Pivarnik) Gribow, Golddigger 1973-1985: I was in my junior year as a musical theater major at the Conservatory of Music at the University of Cincinnati. During one of my dance classes a friend asked why I had not gone with my sorority sister to Dayton, Ohio, a neighboring town, to audition for the Golddiggers. The reason? My gal pal ripped the notice off of the bulletin board, hoarding the opportunity for herself.
When I found out, my dear parents gave me the airfare money to the next audition in Boston to meet the producers and they liked me! The only caveat was that I would have to put my education on hold, give up sorority life as a Tri-Delta and leave Cincinnati. Yikes, the roll of the dice.
That March in 1973, Patti from Cincinnati left Ohio and traveled to Los Angeles for ten days of training.

Linda: The last day of the week-long audition they put us in the costumes of the previous Golddigger group. There were some glittery sequined hip-hugger outfits with bare midriffs and matching boots. I saw the name

Rebecca written on the inside of one of my costumes. I tried to remember the face of the girl I was possibly replacing but I couldn't.

We ran through the entire show for a very select audience and, after some discussion, one girl was eliminated. It was sad to see her go because she was so talented. That left Maria and me as part of the final eight with Robin Hoctor, Patti Pivarnik, Deborah Pratt, Susie Buckner, Lee Nolting and Colleen Kincaid—The Golddiggers.

Patti (Pivarnik) Gribow, Golddigger 1973-1985: On the tenth day, Greg came to Moro Landis Studios in Studio City to watch the nine of us rehearse. We knew from the beginning one of us was going to be cut but did not know when. We

Photo: "The winners" - Clockwise from the bottom: Patti, Linda, Robin, Maria, Colleen, Deborah, Susie, Lee

were told to take a break and we all went into the dressing room but one of the girls wasn't with us. It was then we knew *we* were the new Golddiggers.

I was feeling weepy, I cry at the Pledge of Allegiance and this instance was no exception. Greg came over to me and gently touched my face and asked me if I was sad that she was cut or upset that I couldn't go home to Cincinnati. I told him I was sorry for her. Later that year I was in the Garrison office in Burbank and, in a meeting with Greg, he came over to me and motioned to the cross I was wearing around my neck. He said, "Never forget this or where you came from."

Maria: We hardly knew each other and now we would be spending most of our time together. There were many more rehearsals and solos were given out for our show.

Patti sang the song she auditioned with called 'I Got Love'. It was a light-hearted song and she expressed it with lots of pizzazz and a bouncy strut. Patti was a perky, petite brunette with fair skin and twinkling blue eyes. Each girl had something special to do in the show that accentuated their unique talents and personality, that's the way we first got to know them.

Lee Nolting, Golddigger 1973-1974: I loved the feeling of having seven beautiful, older, talented big sisters to look out for me off-stage and onstage. I was a strong dancer but not as strong in singing so Linda and Maria would swap with me, giving me a singing lesson for a dance class every now and then. Susie and Deborah took me under their wing when it came to worldly advice. I wasn't even 18 years old when I auditioned but I had already been doing professional work and had my Equity card. Now, I would be living my dream of performing and traveling around the country and abroad.

Greg Garrison, Lee Hale, and Ed Kerrigan put our Golddigger group and shows together and made us feel like we were a higher caliber of talent than the former group. Linda and Maria both had amazing voices and never pulled any diva attitude. I liked hanging with the two of them because I was very curious about being a vegetarian and they were always so positive.

Maria: On a performance level, our group was jelling well together but

I have no doubt that Linda and I seemed most unusual to the girls because of the way we ate. It was difficult to eat healthy on a budget because we couldn't eat fast food. Our paycheck wasn't a lot but to us it was enormous. I was thrilled when I could buy a bean burrito with shredded lettuce for less than a dollar. I ate that a few times until I learned it was made with animal lard. Yuk!

On our day off, some of the girls baked cookies or prepared an entrée in one of the rooms that had a kitchen. Linda and I decided to bake something healthy, our mom's nut loaf. We found a health food store to buy some ingredients…. yippee! We didn't have the recipe so we improvised. The girls must have thought we looked like mad scientists. They usually loved eating the samples but, needless to say, no one tried our Frankenstein creation that day. Oh well, more for us!

Linda: When we weren't rehearsing we all stayed at the Starlight Motel in Burbank on Alameda, maybe a mile from the NBC studios. The rooms had beds with metal boxes attached to the side, if you put in a quarter in, the bed would vibrate. The motel was pretty old. It was not shabby but it wasn't chic either—far from it, it was just a place to sleep. Most of the time, we were busy training and rehearsing at the studio.

We had a very tight schedule. Our group was specifically equipped to be able to tour as an act but also do television. We had a ton of musical dance numbers to learn in a very short time.

After a week or so of intense rehearsing, we had enough numbers to do two different one-hour shows. Then we were shown sketches of the designs for our new costumes. One had circles in the artist's rendering going all the way down to the crotch that were labeled 'nude panels.' Maria and I were looking at each other with our mouths open, we're saying, "Oh no, we can't wear that! Is that going to be see-through?" It wasn't actually nude, what they had in mind was flesh-colored fabric for the 'nude panels' but we didn't know that.

Then we saw our first G-string. They said, "This is what you have to wear under the costume." We're dying a thousand deaths.

Maria: We thought, "Oh my God, we're really going to Hell now if we put on a G-string." It doesn't sound like a big deal now but back then I had never seen such a thing. Actually, we almost quit.

They had told us earlier, "We're going to make you more sophisticated and glamorous than the previous group." We didn't know what that meant. Are see-thru costumes their definition of sophistication and glamour? They had Bob Mackie, who fashioned costumes for Raquel Welch, Carol Burnett, Mitzi Gaynor, Ann Margret, and Diana Ross, design a couple of Golddigger outfits and I think that one might have been one of his.

Even with the nude panel fabric it was a little too see-through so the costume designer doubled up that material for us. It was a little more bulky but we thought that was better than seeing through the fabric.

Linda: There were other original costumes designed for us: a black corset style outfit for our 'Cabaret' number, silver lamé hot pants and a beautiful satin gown that went over it which fastened at the side so it could be removed for a quick change.

Now that our new costumes were ready we would be prepared for our first photo shoot. My heart sank when I saw the intimidating figure of Greg Garrison stride into the studio. As he checked us out in the new outfits, I felt so insufficient. I tried to stay toward the back of the group thinking if he got too good a look, he might change his mind and send me home. He peered straight at me and said, "There are three blondes, who wants to be a redhead?" Before anyone could speak up, Greg selected me to be a strawberry blonde. I gulped, I couldn't believe it. I was terrified but went along with it. I had never been to a hairdresser before so I didn't know what to expect. A team of hair stylists went to work on me and a few of the other girls. One had her hair lightened, another had a fall added to blend in with her hair. When the transformation was all over, I was pleasantly surprised. My hair color was very subtle, the same strawberry blonde as Ann-Margret's hair. Later we were all expertly made up and told how to maintain our new "look."

Robin Hoctor-Horneff, Golddigger 1973-1974: Greg Garrison was a businessman building an enterprise and he wanted things done a certain way and he usually got what he wanted. All of us became The Golddiggers because the previous girls made demands and said if they weren't met that they were going to quit. You don't mess with Greg. We were like, "How are they replacing an entire group of Golddiggers?" Then we found out. I guess the former group started to feel like they were important and deserved more credit, more money, whatever.

Lee Hale, Musical Director, *The Dean Martin Show*: I'll tell you how the Golddiggers started. In 1968 we were going to do a summer show for Dean and we all wanted to do something different; we thought about going back into the 1920s but then we said, "Everyone's overdone the twenties why don't we do the 1930s?" To me that meant the old Warner Bros. movies, *The Gold Diggers*. When the producer Greg Garrison's secretary wrote up the notes of the meeting she put those two Gold Diggers words together and it became one word instead of two.

We decided we should have a line-up of girls like they did in the movies. We auditioned girls from eighteen to twenty-one with no previous experience because we wanted to create our own talent. We had a massive audition at NBC and over five hundred girls showed up.

The *Golddiggers* show was number one for that summer and again the second year, too. Probably because of Paul Lynde, who was the guest host on both of those shows.

The third year we went to London, it was *The Golddiggers in London,* and that got big ratings too.

Then Chevrolet liked the girls so much so they offered them a half-hour show for two years in syndication.

After the syndicated show the girls were on the road all the time and some of them were not happy with it so they quit, they didn't think they were making enough money. So we changed girls and hired a whole new crew.

Neil Daniels, former NBC VP and founder Dean Martin Fan Center: When the Golddiggers were first started there were twelve girls, actually there were thirteen girls, one was an alternate. To get the money out of having twelve girls on stage you had to work them a lot. So when they first started out they were going all over the country doing fairs and Vegas and everything. It got to the point where they were shipping them out of the country but things got really confusing when it got up to about the fourth year.

They would go across the border to Mexico and perform at some big casino or some huge auditorium and they would try to get back into the United States and realize they didn't have their passports. Or they weren't getting paid what they were supposed to.

I can't tell you whether Garrison just wanted to hog all the money or whether things were just falling through the cracks. So Greg whittled the group down from twelve to ten then to six. He started the Ding-A-Lings which was four. He started whittling them down so he could have the TV girls and some that were out there performing, that way he could make money on both ends of it.

It got to the point where it was too expensive to have so many girls. And things weren't really jelling for the girls, they weren't being treated very fairly. They did their own syndicated series in 1971 and were taping multiple shows in one week which was not what the union required. They were only getting paid once instead of being paid for the individual shows. It was getting really bad for all the girls so they all got together and said, "We're not going to do this anymore" and they all quit.

Francie Mendenhall, Golddigger 1971-1973: I had been with the Golddiggers for two years and others had been there longer when the group decision was made to leave. It really happened so fast it would make your head spin.

I really think that a combination of factors played a part—road weariness, biological clocks, girls wanting to settle down and have families. The place where we were when it was broached was Mexico City. There was an altitude problem, some of us were unhappy because we felt we needed a new act and fresh costumes. The end came when we were scheduled to close in Mexico and, lo and behold, we were told we'd been held over. The people there held back our passports and it was felt that we'd been abandoned and kept there against our will. Well, an attorney was contacted and then a meeting was called for us all to get together and call Greg after he'd received the papers to cut our ties. It was very upsetting.

> **Susan Lund, original Golddigger, *Fanfare* magazine:** *That was the end of the line for us. We had a little party. We all put our false eyelashes in a pile and burned them. Then we put all our falsies in a pile and we burned them. Then we all hugged each other and talked about how wonderful it had been.*

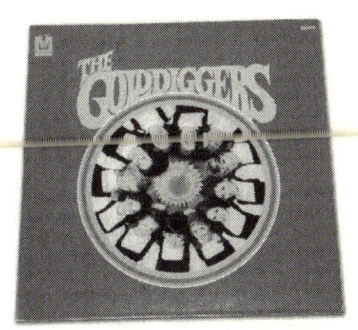

Robin Hoctor-Horneff, Golddigger 1973-1974: It was Greg's creation, The Golddiggers, it was his idea, his thing; you don't want to do it he'll find somebody else. He replaced the entire group and in one fell swoop all of us came in. I guess nobody believed he would do that. It definitely taught us not to step out of line because nobody was irreplaceable.

Maria: New costumes, new choreography, new girlfriends, new bosses.... I thought,somebody help me, please!'
Robin Hoctor was our dance captain. If you didn't get a step right away, she never made you feel like she was better than you, instead we would laugh about it. During one rehearsal we were trying to learn a syncopated dance move, "Pelvis Rock, Pulse and Drop." I never did a dance step like it before. I didn't want to appear vulgar so I felt awkward doing it. The choreographer, Eddie Kerrigan, threw his hands up in the air in a flamboyant gesture, told us to practice then left the room.
Some of the girls who had a lot of dance training, like Robin, looked so confident doing the move, so I asked her to help me. She tried but I still wasn't getting it. I was so frustrated. Then Susie and Deborah circled around me to help. That was a funny scene, all of us girls learning and teaching each other, "Rock your pelvis, not your hips.... Not side to side,

forward and back.... Pulse it.... Bend your knees.... Sit into it.... Now rock it.... Not so big.... Relax!"

Linda: Robin was very sweet. She had show business parents, they owned a dance studio and came from generations of great dancers, yet she was a family girl all the way. We related to Robin a lot. As a dancer she was in a league of her own. Lee was also an accomplished dancer as were Deborah and Susie.
For our first ever gig in Hot Springs, Arkansas The Golddiggers were the headliners. We played the Vapors Club, the site of the very first nightclub in the United States.

> **Robin Hoctor-Horneff, Golddigger 1973-1974:** The Vapors Club in Hot Springs had a very small stage, it was a little strange dark club and here we were these eight girls dancing and strutting all over the place. Being the tallest girl in the group, I felt like a big geek.
> Lee Hale, the music director, and the choreographer were there. I had a solo number and I completely forgot the lyrics, I was making it up as we went along hoping they didn't notice.

Maria: Robin wasn't confident in her singing but her dance solo was nothing less than outstanding. Even so, I worried about her dancing on this particular stage. They actually had to build an extension on the stage at the Vapors Club. The stage was in two pieces and it moved while we were performing so we had to watch that we didn't get our heels stuck in the crack.
The first show went well for me. It was like a whirlwind, there was so much to think about. It's like, you know the hurricane is coming and then it's there—but you're prepared.

> **Colleen Kincaid Jackson, Golddigger 1973-1975:** One of the worst nights of my life was dealing with "microphone spaghetti" as we graced the stage in the midst of our 'Cabaret' choreography. All of us were dancing and singing on chairs when the audio cable intertwined and oh the calamity! Like dominos the microphone stands that were lined up behind us fell to the ground one after another. I was mortified, embarrassed and fearful; I knew the domino effect

started with my microphone cord but I kept it a secret.

Linda: Our choreography was very difficult. All eight of us were working with microphones that had very long cords. It was scientific the way we had to cross the stage. If someone made a wrong cross there would be a tangled mess but I don't remember anyone making a mistake.
We had just finished our first show as The Golddiggers in Arkansas and we were exhausted. We had two one-hour shows to perform with numerous costume changes and different boots or shoes for every outfit. That was so exhausting, the zipping and the changing.
We were sleeping in the next morning, my father must have called about nine o'clock, that was still the middle of the night for us.

Maria: Dad asked me, "Are you going to church?"
"Oh, is it Sunday? Oh, yeah, I guess we'll have to look in the phone book and find a church."
Dad said, "Okay, well, don't forget to go to church now."
"Okay." I hung up the phone and tried to go back to sleep. Then we hear a knock at the door. I yelled, "Go away, we're sleeping!" In a mumbled voice, behind the door we hear, "It's the maid." The knocking didn't stop. "Go away, we're sleeping!" My sister was closest to the door so she got up to answer it. One by one, each of our brothers and sisters appeared in our room with a sheepish smile on their faces. My father was the last one to enter and said, "I thought you were going to church!"
They drove most of the day and all through the night, from Pennsylvania to Arkansas, just to see us.

Linda: After our first gig we flew even further south to New Orleans and The Fairmont-Roosevelt Hotel, where we were again headliners in The

Photo: Going to a press luncheon.

Blue Room. The historic hotel was built in the 1800s and had a wonderful vintage feel to it. I was fascinated by the decor and I couldn't wait to see the famous French Quarter just outside the hotel.

Bourbon Street at night was packed with people, Southern girls in risque costumes were swinging on fancy swings from the balconies of the Creole style townhouses where brass bands were playing the blues and Dixieland jazz. Music was everywhere; it was a party every night. The festivities carried on for blocks. That night, standing in the French Quarter on Basin Street, the song Maria and I sang with our mom, 'Basin Street Blues', came alive for us —"Down in New Orleans, land of dreams...."

> **Keith Spera, music writer, *The Times-Picayune*:** *Back in the day, the Blue Room hosted all manner of marquee entertainers: Louis Armstrong, Frank Sinatra, Sonny & Cher, Tony Bennett, Ella Fitzgerald, Marlene Dietrich, Jimmy Durante.... It was the place to see and be seen.*

Linda: The locals still called The Fairmont by its original name, "The Roosevelt." It was renowned for the Sazerac Bar and the Sazerac Room for the finest dining in the region.

In the restaurant at the Fairmont there was a dessert carousel in a glass case, we had never seen anything like that. We started to realize how strict our father was, he never let us eat birthday cake or anything at parties, so we really went to town. We wanted to taste everything. His extremism made us rebel a little bit.

Maria ordered about three desserts to try, something we were never allowed to do. Of course, I helped her eat some of it. The other girls' minds were blown because they would never do something like that; then again, it was always available to them.

One thing we never tempted to do was eat red meat. It still looked pretty gross to us.

> **Robin Hoctor-Horneff, Golddigger 1973-1974:**
> Maria and Linda were such characters because they were vegetarians, they had the most beautiful skin, the most beautiful faces. They were just bubbly and happy and they definitely ate way differently than we did.

Sun & Fun!

***TV Radio Mirror Magazine*, December 1973:** *"You can't go home again." Frank Sinatra takes exception to Thomas Wolfe's infamous words. Frank practically lived in Las Vegas in the days of the legendary Clan (or Rat Pack). Then a series of punch-ins with various hotel officials made Frank so angry that he vowed he'd never appear again in the gambling spa that he helped put on the map. Maybe the years have mellowed the star but he's planning a Las Vegas comeback. He's set to resume his nightery career at Caesars Palace, certainly a fitting place for the "King of Singers."*

Maria: After our week in New Orleans it was on to Las Vegas and Caesars Palace to open for Steve Lawrence and Eydie Gorme, also known as the husband and wife team Steve and Eydie.
The hotel gave us a beautiful dressing room filled with fragrant flowers and an exotic fruit basket. Delicious! The whole room was delicious!

Pat Cooper, comedian:
I opened for Sinatra, Ella Fitzgerald, Nat King Cole, Perry Como, the list goes on and on and on. I played everything in Vegas. Everything. I played the Riviera, I played the Caesars, I played the Flamingo, I played the Sahara, I played them all. At that time Caesars was the best. The Sands started to collapse when that guy hit Frank Sinatra. Frank quit the Sands and went to Caesars and he brought all his people over to Caesars and it hurt the Sands.
When I went downtown after working with Sinatra they would make fun of me. "How can you leave Sinatra and go downtown with Joe Williams?" I go, "Because when I work with Sinatra I get a thousand dollars. I work with Joe Williams I get five thousand dollars."
They all made fun of me. A few years later Frank goes downtown, if Frank went to a sh*t barrel youse'd all follow him. All of them went downtown because Frank was there.

Linda: We arrived in Vegas the night before our show so we got to see the act we were replacing, the Ding-a-Lings, who also appeared frequently on *The Dean Martin Show*. They were a spin-off of The Golddiggers, a sophisticated and sexy quartet, they had a wonderful show.

Frank Sinatra: *Steve and Eydie represent all that is good about performers and the interpretation of a song— they are the best.*

Eydie Gorme: *I learned my phrasing from Frank. I loved him so much.*

Steve Lawrence: *In those days when we were here doing two shows a night and they had high rollers that they used to take care of on every level and you couldn't get into a showroom unless you had a shirt and tie on, and a jacket; and the women were dressed, even some of them with gloves. It was really quite a town then.*

Maria: We loved Eydie Gorme's records. My mom had all her albums and we would sing along to her songs. 'Gypsy in my Soul' was one of my favorite numbers from her old albums. Both Steve & Eydie had fabulous voices. His was a mellow, velvety voice and she had a belting pop sound, especially in the high register.

Bob Mackie, *Dressing For Glamour*: *Eydie has an opening night tradition. Her husband, Steve Lawrence, never sees any of her gowns until she walks out on stage. It's her way of surprising him, and she gets great pleasure out of making him proud of the way she looks.*

Linda: Steve was easy going but it looked to me like Eydie ran the show. There was a little bit of an uptight vibe to her. There was something going on but I didn't know what.

Robin Hoctor-Horneff, Golddigger 1973-1974: I don't think Eydie liked us very much. We were not allowed to have anything to do with Steve. She kept us far away from her husband.

Lee Notling, Golddigger 1973-1974: Eydie Gorme was very insecure. She wouldn't let her husband Steve come backstage until all of us had left. The tech crew told us she had them working for hours and at the end of the session, the levels were exactly the same as when they started. Shortly after, I saw her in the casino playing Twenty-One and was surprised when officials arrived to escort her out of the casino. It was rumored that she had been cheating. I never told my mom about it because Eydie Gorme was her favorite singer.

Maria: Eydie Gorme actually cut our show down. We had a fifteen-minute act that we were supposed to open with but she cut it down to eight minutes. Her attitude towards us was, "We're the stars and you're just a little bit of fluff to get the audience warmed up. Do your little bit and get back in your dressing room." Our dressing room had all the trimmings fit for a star but we were being treated like the hired help. Oh well, I guess I'll peel *myself* a grape.
After we were finished with our portion of the show, we would sometimes watch Steve and Eydie's performance from the back of the showroom. Individually they were wonderful song stylists but we particularly liked when they sang together and their interaction. They had great comedic timing and related to each other more like brother and sister, rather than husband and wife. Linda and I could identify with their duet, 'Together, Wherever You Go'—"Wherever we go, whatever we do, we're gonna go through it together…."
There was still a hint of romance during the Gershwin song, 'Our Love is Here to Stay.' Steve and Eydie paid tribute to Frank Sinatra by singing a few of his songs. In this segment Steve Lawrence took the lead but it was Eydie Gorme's 'Blame it on the Bassa Nova' that got me and the audience all riled up. They had a bombastic act and even won a Grammy in the early sixties as a duo.
The next time we appeared at Caesars we were with Petula Clark, who had over a dozen top 40 pop hits and won Grammy's for 'Downtown' and 'I Know A Place.' She also co-starred with Fred Astaire in the musical movie version of *Finian's Rainbow*. We were given more time to perform which allowed us to do our solo spots too.
Compared with the entertainers who also graced the Caesars' stage, we were just babies strutting our stuff. The main showrooms in Vegas were home to the top performers in the world. Elvis. Tom Jones. Nancy Wilson. Carol Burnett. Wayne Newton. Johnny Carson. Frank Sinatra. What a rush! Would we measure up?

"You're not drunk if you can lie on the floor without holding on." - Dean Martin

Deborah Pratt, Golddigger 1973-1974: The first time I turned around to a full house at Caesars Palace it was an out of body experience. I turned to sing in 'Cabaret' and all of a sudden I was in the back of the room watching.

Linda: Some people used to look at us like a lightweight act so we always wanted to prove ourselves as legitimate entertainers. For us it was enough to keep out of trouble and mind our own business. We were very concerned with doing our job to the best of our ability.

> **Alan Hess, Las Vegas, *After Hours Architecture:*** *The model prototype used for most Las Vegas resorts since 1941 called for buildings to be arranged casually on the site. A sign or facade was likely shifted to face oncoming traffic. Caesars faced the strip with a royal presence and bulk that established its own organization in its own domain. It disdained accuracy in favor of vigor. Technically speaking, the wings that marked the entry were more Baroque Rome (they took the parabolic shape of Saint Peter's Square) than Imperial Rome. The statues and fountains evoked the Villa d'Este and other summer villas of Baroque cardinals in Tivoli. Such lapses have to be excused; a resort more accurately named Popes Palace would not have drawn as many gamblers.*

Maria: I didn't like Caesars Palace at all. We called it 'The Tomb' because you didn't know if it was day or night inside, there were no windows or clocks. It was like being in an altered reality state. I just thought, "Where do you relax?" I'm a nature girl, I like trees with birds singing.
One of our first days at Caesars we were walking back to our rooms and some businessmen asked us, "Are you working girls?" Linda and I looked at each other and we go, "Yes, we're working."
"Well, there's a party upstairs...."
We had no clue. I was toying with the idea of going, I was thinking maybe they'd have some food to eat. We told the other girls about the party and they told us, "Working girl means a prostitute!" And Linda was like, "I don't think that's a party we want to go to...."

Patti (Pivarnik) Gribow, Golddigger 1973-1985:
Vegas was a culture shock. We had no idea what defined a call girl. I went to the bar right outside the showroom at Caesars Palace between shows to say hello to my folks because, of course, my parents traveled to see me perform in Vegas for the first time. A man came up to me and said, "Are you a working girl?" I said, "Yes, I am a working girl. I'm working in that showroom right over there." You know what he meant by working girl.... hello!

Deborah Pratt, Golddigger 1973-1974: Some famous hockey player invited Robin Hoctor over to the big gambling table and he lost like fifty thousand dollars in ten minutes and she started to cry!

Linda: We were deathly afraid to party because we were so out of our element and we didn't want to expose ourselves to any kind of situation that we couldn't handle. Typically, we went right from the show back to our room.
That environment was weird for us, we spent most of our time out by the pool during the day. Caesars had a spectacular pool with towering columns and Romanesque marble statuary.

Photo: Postcard of Maria at the pool.

Some of us girls struck up a friendship with a couple of the guys who worked at the pool. The pool manager had a speed boat and he took us out on Lake Mead. It was extraordinary, a huge body of water in the middle of a parched desert. You could boat around for a whole day and not even see a quarter of it. I learned how to water ski; it was a good time.

Maria: Lake Mead was a most welcome break from my routine of swimming and baking in the sun by the pool. Cruising the lake at a slow speed was like floating in nature's majestic cathedral with nothing around but mountains, water and sky. It was so peaceful.

Robin Hoctor-Horneff, Golddigger 1973-1974: We were all so young, I think at the time I was eighteen or nineteen. I had never been to Las Vegas before. It was a whole different world—the casinos, the way everybody dressed, it was a little bit overwhelming. A lot of the other girls had a great time in Vegas meeting people, going out and networking. I was definitely not one that went out and partied very much, Maria Elena and Linda weren't either. I had a reality check. I turned on the TV once in Vegas and there was news about the Skylab space station and I had no idea this was happening. I realized how out of tune you become with the world because you live in this little bubble performing, rehearsing, sleeping, performing, rehearsing. You really lose your bearing about what's going on in the outside the world.
After that I wanted to get up in the mornings and not sleep until one in the afternoon to try to have a semi-normal life.

Maria: Deborah and Susie were loving the Vegas vibe and night life.
I learned not to call their room until after 2:00pm. Together they were a team and watched out for each other. Linda and I did the same thing. Susie was all personality, we called her "Susie Cheerleader." She was a very fun loving person and a great showperson. She could play cute and sexy to the hilt, she had it down.

Linda: Susie could make something out of the smallest part but everybody had something that made them stand out. Deborah was a statuesque, regal beauty, reminiscent of Lena Horne. She had it all, a wonderful sense

Photo: Deborah Pratt & Susan Buckner.

of identity, a great education, amazing talent, and she knew it. She wouldn't let Greg play his games with her and belittle her.

Maria: Colleen had a natural, country girl essence about her but was wise beyond her years. When we weren't performing she carried her guitar almost everywhere and would strum out a folk song nonchalantly. It was comforting to see her remain down to earth in this neon casino world.

Patti (Pivarnik) Gribow, Golddigger 1973-1985: Those were the days when people were paged over the casino intercom, "Will so and so please call the operator." You would hear, "Maria Golddigger or Linda or Patti Golddigger please call the operator." We thought it was hysterical.
Showtime was all glamour and business. I remember never leaving the dressing room in casual attire but rather dressed to the nines.

Linda: We were fascinated by Patti Pivarnik's people skills. She was very impressive, with sophisticated networking and social abilities. She would hang out and have a drink with the adults. Maria and I knew nothing about that kind of thing. We felt socially awkward.

Maria: Every place we traveled to we would have newspaper interviews or local TV and radio shows to do. We had to be up at five or six in the morning with all of our makeup on!
Early in the morning Patti would have our signature false eyelashes on, I thought that was going way beyond the call of duty. I wore mascara, lipstick and a little make-up but there was no way I was going to play around with false eyelashes first thing in the morning.

Top photo: Patti and Dean backstage.

Patti aimed to please; that was her way. The office said wear your makeup so she wore all her makeup. This is how Patti got the nickname 'Patti Perfect,' she was always looking like the perfect Golddigger.

Robin Hoctor-Horneff, Golddigger 1973-1974: Somebody from the front office told us that at all times we had to be wearing our lashes and we had to be fully made up. I wasn't going to do that. I was just going to wear the Golddigger makeup when I was on stage. A lot of us didn't want to have to go around pretending we were Golddiggers twenty-four seven.

Linda: I didn't mind having to wear makeup. I like the artistic part of applying it. I did have something to learn about the way I carried myself, though. I was barely out of my tomboy phase. In fact when we started, Maria would tell me I was still walking like a softball player at times. Like I forgot people were looking at me on stage!

Maria: My sister would do the choreography and look fantastic—then, when she would stride back to her microphone stand, she would be walking like an athlete. What a difference a few months made! Now, in Vegas, all the aspects of the ideal "Golddigger" image had become more natural to her.

Linda: Our first TV show taping was *The Wacky World of Jonathan Winters,* a variety show which featured a spot where the comedian would rummage through his 'attic,' pick up some random object and do a whole monologue on it. We were on for something like eight shows, we shot two a day. It made sense that the Golddiggers would be regulars on Jonathan Winter's show since this Chevrolet sponsored production basically replaced The Golddiggers' syndicated series that ran for the two seasons before we joined.
We appeared on the show with some wonderful stars like Glenn Ford, Jim Backus, Charlie Rich, and Charo. Twice we guest starred with Bill Cosby.

"Three F's; faith, family, food" - Al Alberici

A few of us even got a chance to do skits but they're all a blur to me. We had the occasion to perform new material and also songs from our act. We were "shaking our money makers" in 'Tamborine,' playing the coquette in our dance routines and spreading peace and love in 'Hands'—"Hands joining together, hands can't tell what color they are so let's join hands and sing...."

Patti (Pivarnik) Gribow, Golddigger 1973-1985: Music would be handed to us on a Monday. We would then record our individual parts and lyrics that we were expected to have memorized by the next morning. On Tuesday, we'd be on our feet blocking. This process continued through Friday when we taped two full episodes, seldom being given the opportunity for a second or third take. Talk about pressure!

Maria: *The Wacky World of Jonathan Winters* series was produced and directed by Greg Garrison so the production shared most of the same staff as Dean's show. Dean's son Craig was an associate producer. Our musical numbers were staged beautifully; the crew really took their time to get everything right. Greg made sure the way we were photographed for the TV shows was top notch—the lighting, the makeup, the scenery, everything. We did a very stylized bluesy ballad in authentic cabaret outfits called 'You'll Remember Me.' Only a few girls sang solos in this number and I was one of them. The set was dimly lit with a spotlight on each singer. This was a rare occasion for me to put away my teasing smile and wear the theatrical mask of melancholy as I sang, "Remember me, I taught you how to find love, first love, happy love and blind love. Now you're leaving me behind love but part of me will always be part of you." This number led directly into the ravishingly rowdy 'Cabaret,' where we danced on chairs doing kicks and back bends while singing our hearts out.

Most of our numbers were highly choreographed so the singing was pre-recorded and we lip-synced to our voices. Linda and I were a little apprehensive about appearing too sexy for the folks back home so we held back a little during all the choreography.

Deborah Pratt, Golddigger 1973-1974: Jonathan Winters' mind was just so explosive, he was in his own world. My favorite part was to come and watch the ending where he would take nothing and make it into fifty things just with the sound effects he did with his mouth while his hands were doing mime.

Linda: There was not much interaction with Jonathan Winters on the set but our trailers were side by side so I would talk to him outside the soundstage. I had pleasant conversations with him, he was very approachable, very mellow and warm when he wasn't on stage.

One day when I was talking with Jonathan he invited me into his trailer. If it had been someone else I would have had second thoughts but not with Jonathan. In spite of his zany TV characters he was pretty normal, super nice and very intelligent. We talked about our mutual November birthdays and *The Twilight Zone* episode he did. I was a big fan of *Twilight Zone*.

Jonathan was an incredibly talented, funny guy. He invented lots of crazy characters, I adored his old lady character Maude Frickert. Every time he became her, everyone was hysterical with laughter. As Maude he stole every scene he was in. The other guest stars didn't have a chance except to go with the flow and let whatever happened happen. That's what was so great about his show, the improvisation and spontaneity.

Maria: Jonathan Winters as Maude Frickert was also a guest on *The Dean Martin Comedy Hour*. Dean would try to hold his own as Maude flirted shamelessly, his reactions were priceless. One smirk would say it all. Dean was the perfect straight man—although his TV persona could not walk a straight line.

From *The Dean Martin Show*: Jonathan Winters as Maude

Frickert: *Well here we are again. Hi Deansie. What do you want to do?*
Dean Martin: *I don't know. What's your pleasure?*
Maude Frickert: *Well, if I told you that we'd be off the air! Oh, my dress is caught on this funky little stool. I thought maybe you got me Deanie.*
Dean Martin: *No, I never touch old ladies…*
Maude Frickert: *Oh really?*
Dean Martin: *Actually it's the station break announcement time, we'd better read it, huh? Oh card person?*
Cue Card Girl: *Here I am Mr. Martin.*
Dean Martin: *Isn't she graceful?*
Maude Frickert: *Not particularly. When she walks it looks like she's got two kids fighting under a blanket.*
Dean Martin: *Why don't you tell the people where the announcement is written, honey?*
Cue Card Girl: *All over my body.*
Maude Frickert: *Poor deformed creature.*

Maria: We toured almost the entire summer of '73 with the legendary Italian crooner Jerry Vale. He was someone that would fit in well with our family. I personally loved listening to his show because in my teens I used to sing along with his albums at home. Now, as The Golddiggers we shared the co-star billing with him.
Jerry Vale opened the show with a few songs like 'Lonely is a Man Without Love' which had a lilting melody and built into a dramatic ending. Jerry Vale's songs were brilliantly arranged but the orchestrations were crisp and not overpowering. His clear, cultured voice was always the focus of your attention, with tasty tempo changes which usually led the way to a flawless high note soaring above the orchestra. After he engaged the audience, he would introduce us for our portion of the show.

Linda: We did a wide variety of music. 'I Want to Be Happy' was done in a campy Marilyn Monroe style then the tempo would swing during 'Black Magic.' 'In the Mood' stretched our vocals while the 'Torch Medley' gave each girl a featured song. That medley led into a short tap dance solo by Robin, during which the rest of us had less than sixty seconds to run backstage and whip off our gowns to reveal the silver lamé short shorts we had hidden underneath and quickly put on tap shoes. Our 1930's tap dance climaxed with a high kick-line reminiscent of the Busby Berkeley movies and the Radio City Rockettes. The crowds cheered us on with enthusiastic whistles and applause.

We had lots of novelty numbers with distinctive choreography using waving tambourines and hats. The duet, showcasing Maria and me, brought in the sounds of contemporary pop music, segueing into a foot-stomping, hand-clapping gospel version of 'Time and Love' where the lyrics playfully warned, "Don't let the devil fool ya…."

Maria: Jerry Vale flirted with the audience as he sang his sophisticated version of the Tom Jones hit, 'Help Yourself'—"Just help yourself to my lips, to my arms…." then turned the mood with the romantic, 'My Love Forgive Me.' His specialty was smoothly combining Italian lyrics with the English translation to the delight of his fans.

He was tender when he sang, 'For the Good Times'; I think all the women in the audience believed he was singing to them. Jerry would lighten it up with some Italian jokes and stories, keeping everyone in the palm of his hand as he sang the classics, 'Return to Me,' 'Mala Femmina,' 'Mama' and 'Al-di-la.' As soon as he opened his mouth to sing those Italian standards there would be thunderous ovation. I secretly hoped he would sing his rendition of 'Maria Elena' but I was too shy to ask him.

Jerry Vale, *Las Vegas Visitor:* What's it like working with the Golddiggers? I love it. What's not to like? They're eight beautiful young ladies giving the audience all they have. I watch their show almost all the time. I enjoy going to work just to see them. They wouldn't have to do anything, just stand there and let me look at them.

Maria: We played a lot of the Music Fairs with Jerry Vale, some of these theaters were shaped like circus tents, some were open to the outside and some were enclosed. The Valley Forge Music Theater and the Cape Cod Melody Tent were humongous theaters in the round that seated three thousand or more.

Another stop on our way was the Westbury Music Fair; this time we were with the wonderful Italian tenor, Enzo Stuarti and comedian Myron Cohen. Myron was known worldwide for his brand of Jewish humor and his knack for storytelling, Borscht Belt accent and all. Speaking to him in passing, though, I noticed he did not have any trace of an ethnic accent. It was so very humid that summer on the east coast, I was sweating bullets and my hair would be drenched because we'd be singing and dancing and the air conditioning couldn't keep up.

During our summer tour, Jerry Vale's five-year old daughter visited him. She was adorable and was in awe of our sparkling costumes. With the help of the staff, we had a modest little Golddigger outfit made for her birthday. She looked really cute in it. We gave her the finishing touches by fixing her hair and applying a touch of make-up. One night, she surprised her dad by coming out on stage in the outfit. The audience loved it, especially her dad.

The people who ran the music theaters were all family oriented, very down-to-earth people. Because of this, our family was raring to

Top photo: Backstage with Jerry Vale.

come see us perform in this environment as compared to the nightclubs. My dad enjoyed singing the Jerry Vale songs at home and called it good, clean entertainment that the whole family could enjoy.

Al Alberici: I didn't throw my daughters to the wolves! Greg Garrison doesn't want them to run around, either. After all, they might see a millionaire and get married! I'm most concerned that my daughters be nice people.

Darlene (Alberici) Cianci, our younger sister: Keeping the family connected was very important to our dad. He wouldn't let too much time pass without paying Linda and Maria a surprise visit. We usually didn't stop at places to eat on those trips except to buy produce or go to health food stores. Mostly we would eat in the car as we drove along rushing to the next destination.

Of all the stars The Golddiggers worked with, Jerry Vale was a standout to me. His voice was everything our family loved. He was a dramatic Bel Canto tenor and there were my two sisters on stage with him.

It was all quite amazing to get to know the other girls in The Golddiggers and see their relaxed backstage personalities compared to their dynamic onstage personas. My family was continually dazzled by the updates in their act. It was a real treat to see these performances but traveling on the road to get to their gigs was not.

My father was always losing things. Things were always falling and flying off his body because he was nearsighted and was always moving really fast, always living in the moment. Once, he dropped over a thousand dollars in cash in a trailer park where we stopped. My father didn't believe in credit cards so that was all of our travel expense money. We were scrambling around looking for it. My mother frantically started knocking on doors asking if anyone found any money in the area.

Eventually someone said, "Yes, I found your money." It was a great relief since my father and mother scrimped and saved all the time for our large family. It always seemed that God protected and helped them in their efforts.

My mother would build a makeshift bed in the van when we traveled. She figured out how to place a board above our suitcases and then put thick foam rubber on top so we could take turns driving and then sleep in the back. I don't know how in the world we did this but three of us at the same time could sleep on it as we drove along.

One night, after we had stopped, I had fallen asleep in the car and, when I woke up, nobody else was around. When I got out of the car the place was deserted and I'm looking for everybody but didn't have my contact lenses in. I could see someone at the edge of the pier about ten feet away and I thought it must be my father in his big jacket. I started going over toward him and somebody began yelling, "STOP, it's a bear!" I couldn't tell my father from a black bear at ten feet away! When we would arrive at places we would be like dirty rags in our travel clothes. Then we would put on our fancy outfits, fix our hair, and polish up like silverware to see the show.

Maria: The way our family traveled was rough so Linda and I would try to make sure that they were given the royal treatment when they would arrive to the show. We would have a reserved table set aside for them. Of course, no one in our family drank alcohol or soft drinks, only fruit juice. After the show our mom sometimes gave us performing advice and Dad would offer us vocal tips, "Remember to increase the falsetto." They would bring food and always had some

Photo: The Alberici family.

supplies to give us like vitamins, freshly squeezed vegetable juice, homemade protein candy or a special nut and dried fruit mix. It was most welcome after being on the road in an atmosphere of junk food. Sometimes we squeezed in the car with them and went for an outing to see some nearby sites. Right before they left Dad usually slipped us some money and told us to buy something healthy. It was always sad to see them drive away.

Patti (Pivarnik) Gribow, Golddigger 1973-1985: When the sisters' family came to see us, I was always amazed how those young, gorgeous, sexy, powerhouse performers on stage could immediately after a show become nurturing caretakers, bouncing their younger siblings on their knees and changing diapers.

My diet was mostly healthy due to my parents being raised on family farms, but the sisters' nutritional knowledge of health and well-being raised my awareness to another level. Maria and Linda were way, way, ahead of their time as experts in the field of nutrition. Their entire family walked the talk, if you will. Who knew in 1973 that weight lifting was key to a beautiful body? Maria, Miss Body Beautiful U.S.A., sister Linda, and Arnold Schwarzenegger, that's who!

It was always a pleasure when meeting the family of my fellow performer's or co-star's. Jerry and Rita Vale took us under their wing. They were and are amazing and wonderful people, always watching over us and often inviting us to join them for dinner. Jerry is a true family man.

Maria: Spending time with these remarkable, seasoned performers was one of the perks of being in The Golddiggers. After the show all of us would get together for a bite to eat and sometimes Jerry Vale and his manager Carl Victor would join us. We found out that Jerry was a gourmet Italian cook.

That's something we missed when we traveled on the road, good home-cooked meals so Jerry offered to cook for us. Having the Vales prepare dinner for us was beyond the call of duty.

Unfortunately, most of the dishes that they made had meat in them so Linda and I couldn't eat them. Everyone else was in hog heaven.

Linda: Jerry Vale had a beautiful home, it was very humbling the way he embraced us like part of the family. Rita, his pretty blonde wife, was charming but a little guarded, as some women were around us. An Italian feast was served with a fabulous array of dishes.
After dinner we traded road stories and talked about taking care of our vocal chords in the dry Vegas air. We all used humidifiers. For a singer the desert was the worst, drying up the nasal passages, causing all kinds of vocal mayhem. Performers called it 'Vegas Throat.' Jerry's voice was better than ever at this time of his life, even living in the Las Vegas climate most of the year.
I told Jerry about being sick and experiencing sinus problems during one particular Vegas gig. For some relief, I ran the hot water in the shower to steam up the room. The next thing I knew hotel security was banging on my door, I had fallen asleep and flooded the room under mine.

Susan Buckner, Golddigger 1973 -1974:
Jerry cooked for me a couple of times. He was pretty good at it. Jerry and his manager, Carl, were a lot of fun.
Sometimes, Deborah and I would stand backstage and watch Jerry's show. We could be mischievous. While he did his act, we would dance around in the wings and try to crack

Photo: Deborah, Jerry, Susie and Linda.

him up. Oh hell, we were always dancing, we danced whenever and wherever we could.

I was good at entertaining myself. "No" was not in my vocabulary. To me "no" meant "do it!" I lived to push the envelope and push it I did. Why not? I was good at it.

At one point during our tour, while we were all flying to the next city, Carl Victor smuggled me into first class. I got away with hanging out there with Carl and Jerry for the rest of the flight. And the winner is...!

Robin Hoctor-Horneff, Golddigger 1973-1974: I didn't date at all when I was in the Golddiggers but when we were in Ohio with Jerry Vale I met a gentleman from the Cherry Hill area and we started going out in September 1973. I knew the first night I went out with him I was going to marry him.

His family came to meet me for the first time at our Latin Casino show. Susie Buckner used to wear a hairpiece extension and we did a dance number together, '2001 A Space Odyssey.' We did this contraction where we threw our heads forward quickly and one night her blond hairpiece went flying off on to the table in front of us where a family was eating. She just leaned over, picked it up and continued dancing. I was laughing so hard inside, I thought I would die.

At the Latin Casino the customers definitely got more than they bargained for when we were performing.

Patti (Pivarnik) Gribow, Golddigger 1973-1985: We had the front hook bra type of *I Dream of Jeannie* outfits and one night I was singing "When the moon is in the second house" and my bra popped open for everyone to see. Embarrassing!

The Graduates

TV Guide, **September 8, 1973:**
The Dean Martin Comedy Hour is the new title for Dino's weekly revels, which will put a greater emphasis on laughs this season, bringing in new comedy acts each week.

Linda: At the end of the summer we returned to Los Angeles to tape our first *Dean Martin Comedy Hour*, we received personalized parking spots at NBC next to Zsa Zsa Gabor's. The show was given a new name and moved from Thursday to Friday nights for the fall of 1973.

Greg Garrison: *Women adored [Dean] and guys looked at him and went, "Hey, he's a real guy."*
Somebody once said to me, "What's Dean like?" and I went, "What you see is what he is." He's a real guy. There's no baloney, there no phony little pretenses, and "Hey, I'm a big movie star." He never liked being called a star. Somebody once said "Hey, you're a big star." He said "Hey, I'm a personality. I'm not a star. I'm a personality."

Bob Mills, comedy writer, *Dean Martin Show, Bob Hope Specials*: Greg Garrison was a piece of work, I'll tell ya'. His headquarters across from NBC resembled a former motel so every team of writers had a pretty good sized office. I got to meet some of the giants, some of those guys had come from radio; they were so good. They always hired the best around on that show. That was a pleasant show to work on.
Greg made a lot of friends on the variety show, one of whom was Orson Welles, who used to drop by the office. He was an amateur magician and he used to do tricks for us. He weighed about four hundred pounds, he was just huge. You'd see other characters dropping by, the Golddiggers among them.
Greg was a guy that, if he liked you and thought that you had talent, boy, he would bend over backwards to promote your career. Harry Crane was the head writer, he was very much like Greg. They were tough guys. They had come up in that era, they were kids from New York's rough streets.
We'd hear stories. Sometimes Greg would get mad at somebody—he actually threw a writer down the stairs one day. "What, my Greg?!?"

Maria: We didn't have any desire to go hang out at Greg's office. Some of the girls did; they had social skills where they could schmooze and network but we didn't and we knew it. I figured, Greg Garrison knew I was talented and that's all he needed to know.

Neil Daniels, former NBC VP and founder Dean Martin Fan Center: Greg Garrison came out of live TV, he did *Your Show of Shows* in New York; he was in such demand at that time because he could do things so inexpensively, he would direct a program in one studio and would have thirty minutes to run down the street to jump into another studio and direct another show. The guy was super busy but he knew how to make things just move.

When he got to Dean's show, everything was recorded on two inch Quad tape so everything took a long time to do by the time they got the videotape machine going and everything else.

People like Perry Como, they would rehearse all week long and have it down pat because, when taping time came, it was very expensive to stop that tape and start it again.

There was a different look to Dean's show. Greg, because he came out of live TV, didn't want it to look like a rehearsed, videotaped show. So everything was done pretty much fast, quick, just get it done, and Dean liked that.

Greg actually geared the show around the premise that Dean was like a little boy in an adult world. They put a fire pole in his living room. When the camera would come up they'd catch him messing around with the wine bottles and he'd flip it around like he was caught. You never saw him drink. There were tons of gorgeous girls that would flaunt around, it was like a little boy looking at the girls but no, no, you couldn't touch. That kind of thing. I think that was part of Dean's personality, he liked simple fun.

Pat Cooper, comedian: See, Dean had an individuality about him that people really, really liked. He was one of a kind, he just had a tremendous charisma, very macho, more so than Sinatra. If you talked to any Italian man, they'd say, if you hadda be born again would you like to be Frank or Dean? They'd all say Dean. He had that kind of a hop, a kind of a skip and a jump that was just very charismatic.

He was one of the great crooners. A lot of people didn't give him that credit. He was a great crooner but he was not a singer. Frank and Vic Damone were singers.

Linda: Dean was a pro at playing the innocent naughty boy. Greg Garrison, on the other hand, was a real mischief maker. He periodically amused himself by making the people around him squirm. Greg had a great deal of power and he would use it. If he knew a girl wanted fame and would do things for it, he tested them. I was told he said to one of the girls, "I have this friend, he's big in the business and if you want to fly over to this place to be with him...."

Anyhow, she didn't take him up on it; she wasn't even sure Greg was serious. Maria and I wanted success but only under the right circumstances. We weren't buying into the facade. Don't get me wrong, we were in awe of everything but we were observing, learning. We were sheltered, this was a whole different world. There could predators anywhere and we knew we could be eaten alive.

On the oposite end of the spectrum we had Lee Hale performing and writing music for us, he wrote for radio and TV programs in the sixties and seventies working with Bob Hope, Tony Bennett, Count Basie, Joan Crawford, Jimmy Dean, Pat Boone and Carol Burnett. I felt blessed to be working with the best talents in the industry.

Lee Hale, Musical Director, *The Dean Martin Show*: Greg was always good to me because he kept upping my salary every year. I didn't have any problem with him, he made it easy as far as *The Dean Martin Show* went because he never came around to rehearsals. Basically I put that show and the Golddiggers' show together myself, just myself and the choreographer.

But Greg liked to take credit for everything himself, even when he was doing interviews with newspapers or magazines he would say he did everything, that he rehearsed everybody and wrote all the material which was not true. And I would be sitting there hearing him say this. But, since he paid me, I didn't care.

Neil Daniels, former NBC VP and founder Dean Martin Fan Center: Lee Hale was working on the Carol Burnett series *The Entertainers*, a New York based production, when he was called out to California to see if he wanted to work on Dean's show.

Here's a guy who started out doing special material for Dean, all the musical bits that tied the music and the comedy together, then he morphed into musical director, then went into editing and producing. He produced the Roasts. So many talented people came out of *The Entertainers*. It only lasted one year but Ruth Buzzi, Bob Newhart, Dom DeLuise, Caterina Valente, Lee Hale; all of those people were pulled over to *The Dean Martin Show* from *The Entertainers*.

Lee Hale, Musical Director, *The Dean Martin Show*: By the ninth season we were shooting on Saturdays. I would start on Monday putting together all the music for the show and deciding who was going to do what.

Then on Tuesday we usually got our first guests in for rehearsal and they would rehearse Tuesday, Wednesday, and Thursday.

On Friday we had a run through with all the staff, the cameramen and everybody involved in the show who hadn't

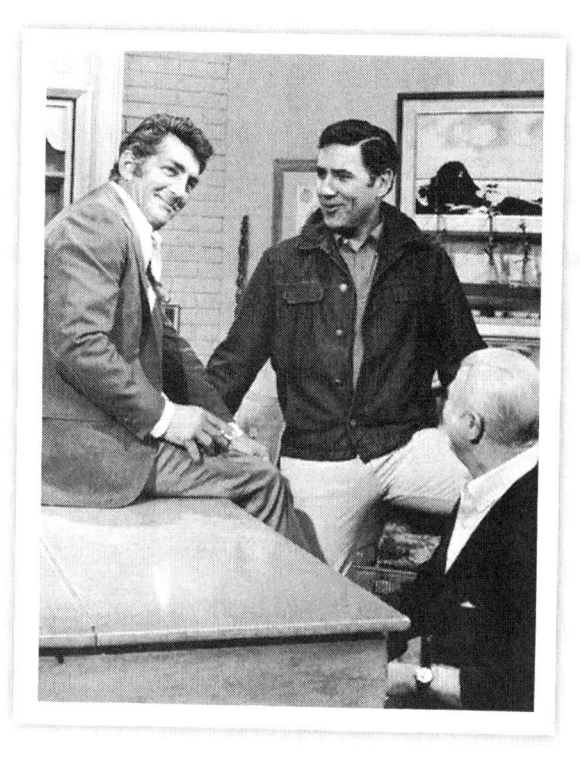

Photo: Dean, Greg Garrison and music director Ken Lane.

seen our rehearsals. And then on Saturday we were in the studio and we did all the camera work ahead of time and then the orchestra rehearsal was three hours in the afternoon. Greg's motto was "We're not making records" so we couldn't go past that three-hour period. And I don't think we ever did, we had to rush things along. It was great for me because Greg never came to any of the rehearsals so the choreographer and I, usually Bob Sidney, would do the whole show. The best part of it was, the writers and any agents or managers were not allowed at rehearsals so we just had the guests and us.

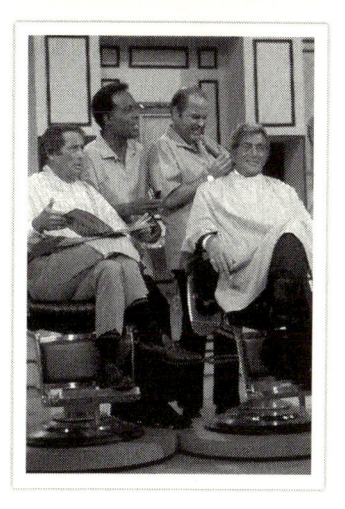

The guests were always on their best behavior because they wanted to be part of a hit show so they didn't give me any trouble. It was very easy for me.

Tape day was the first day Dean worked with any of the guests. We were all in awe of him because he could do this. He would come in and all he relied on was the cue cards. Even as far as the music's concerned, we had one orchestra rehearsal with him and that was it. He'd watch the rehearsal on a monitor in his dressing room and the next thing he's in front of the audience and we taped the show. We

Dean with Petula Clark.

couldn't believe what he was doing. Of course, he made mistakes but that was part of the fun. He didn't know who the guests were going to be on his show, he didn't care, Dean liked everybody.

The first original Golddiggers were not as good singers as the Maria and Linda group. This new group of Golddiggers did what we called the country medley every week, about a ten minute hunk of music. Dean was really into country at that time so we had all the big country stars on.

That particular year half of the show was the comedy roasts and the other half was a country medley with a couple of sketches and that was it.

Maria: Our special musical numbers for Dean's show were rehearsed at NBC or Moro Landis studios in Studio City. Lee Hale would sometimes stand in for Dean, he was responsible for organizing and rehearsing our musical numbers during the week. Lee was very creative and wrote lots of thrilling musical medleys and specialty numbers for us too. Later in the week we had a rehearsal at the NBC soundstage that was set aside especially for Dean's production. After a round of golf in the morning, Dean would arrive on Saturday, tape day, where we anxiously awaited Dean's arrival, as would the guest stars.

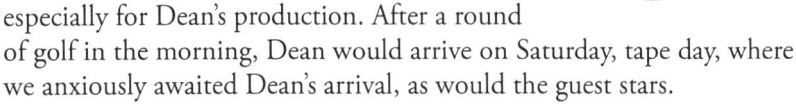

Lee Hale, Musical Director, *The Dean Martin Show*: I was not a fan of Dean Martin's before I got on the show. Martin and Lewis were not that funny to me, what I'd seen on television was a little crazy. So I wasn't thrilled to start with *The Dean Martin Show*.

But then when I understood what was going on and that I was responsible for what Dean did on camera it got to be a real challenge for me. I had to come up with things he could do that he would not have to rehearse.

The lucky thing for me was that Neil Daniels gave me a list of every album Dean had made and what songs he'd sung. I thought if he learned a song for a recording session he must have some memory of it. And there were a lot of them.

Dean would know a song but he wouldn't remember the words so if I changed the lyrics he just read what was on the cue cards, he didn't know the difference.

I never had any conversation with him before the show, he trusted me to not overdo it and not make him look bad. Sometimes after the show he'd say, "Was I all right? Did I sing in tune?" something like that. Who else could come in and wing it like he did? Nobody else.

Maria: My first impression upon meeting Dean Martin was that he was very, very charming. He looked the same in person as he did on TV. I can't say that about all the stars I've met. It was a pleasure to watch him interact with all us girls. He never made a vulgar or cheap comment or anything like that. He was fun loving, good natured and made you feel comfortable.

These were the days of the Women's Liberation Movement and Greg Garrison was feeling pressure from the network. Instead of revealing outfits, the Golddiggers were clad in long gingham dresses to do our country music numbers on a segment called 'Dean's Music Country.'

I absolutely loved it. We danced and sang with the top country stars like Lynn Anderson, Conway Twitty, Ray Stevens, Buck Owens, Loretta Lynn, Crystal Gayle, Mel Tillis and Mac Davis.

> *Well, I guess you're all dyin' to know why I drink. Well, I'm goin' to tell you. No, this ain't funny. I mean this is not being funny. I just want to say I drink because I'm insecure. No, I mean it, I can not accept the fact that I'm Dean Martin, movie star or somethin'... So I must drink to believe I'm Dean Martin. Without booze I'm Eddie Fisher.*
>
> *- Dean Martin, from his nightclub act*

Linda: The country set was like a breath of fresh air equipped with a barn, a plow and a miniature horse. We would sing a sweet ballad on stacks of hay, our colorful prairie gowns draped around us and then skip to the other side of the set to sing the next song to some guitar picking and fiddle playing.

I grew to have a greater appreciation of country music singing songs like 'I Was Raised on Country Sunshine', 'You Got a Friend', 'Tie a Yellow Ribbon', 'Houston', 'Jambalaya (On the Bayou)' and 'Country Roads'. Maria and I were ecstatic when we saw in the script that we would be singing 'I Believe in Music' with Dean. We sang the verse while Dean joined us for the chorus and then the whole cast extended their harmonies for a reprise as the scene peaked for a big finish—then cut to commercial.

Maria: Another scene, another set, was the spot where Dean flirted with the girls at the bar. It was an on-going feature. He would make a suggestive comment with a little song like, 'I'm in the Mood for Love' and we would shoot him down with a funny comeback. Then Dean would try another line with the next girl. He had great comic timing, Dean could be subtle and just raise an eyebrow and we all got the joke. He was the 'King of Cool.'

My very first TV taping.... I blew it. I decided I was going to use the Stanislavsky method of acting, so I was thinking of the motivation of my character and the back story. Well, when Dean walked up to me at the bar and gave me my cue I forgot my one line! This was in front of a live studio audience. Greg shouted, "Cut!" and I thought I would be fired for sure but he laughed and gave me a hug and told me to do it again. He put the mistake and the retake on the show. Greg liked to keep it loose. So did Dean.

Linda: That was Maria. It didn't matter how small her part was or how big. She was always on, all the time, giving one hundred percent.

Sometimes she was too much. Once Greg had to tell her to stop moving around so he could give her a close up. Performing in front of the camera required different techniques than what we had learned from being in musical theater and doing live shows.

Robin Hoctor-Horneff, Golddigger 1973-1974: I was so nervous for the first taping because we never really saw Dean Martin. We hadn't rehearsed with him. It was strange because we were regulars; it was like you were a part of it but you really weren't part of it. We prepared everything, we were involved in different skits, musical medleys, but Dean showed up to shoot the show and did everything right off the cuff, just did it right then.

> **Greg Garrison:** *We're the only live show on the air. Of course, it's on tape, but we rarely alter a thing—maybe we 'blip' a word or two once every ten shows. People like Dean the way he is, mistakes and all.*

Patti (Pivarnik) Gribow, Golddigger 1973-1985: My mom and all her friends were in love with Dean and, of course, his good looks. The persona, Dean Martin, appeared to be a cad and a real 'player' but in reality Dean was one of the nicest and genteel men I have ever met. He was exceedingly humble and once told me, "It's so hard to be mean and so easy to be nice." I will always carry that memory with me.

Lee Notling, Golddigger 1973-1974: Dean was shy, quiet, polite and, of course, very handsome. His special guests were kind and welcoming. Loretta Lynn was so very humble, she waited in line to get her make-up done and talked with any of us who started a conversation with her. She was a legend in country music but very unpretentious.

Maria: We had to make sure we knew our blocking and all of Dean's and all the blocking of the guest stars too.
It was a big responsibility. We were basically singing and dancing party hosts. We were like moving scenery that would guide Dean and his guest stars from one scene to the next. We had to know what stars went where and in what scene. The director would be talking to the stars because they were doing it for the first time for the cameras so all the attention was on them on tape day. That's why we had to know everything ahead of time.
We didn't hobnob with the guests because we had to keep our focus but there was a definite air of playfulness on the set between takes. We would hear jokes going back and forth with laughter, lots of laughter.

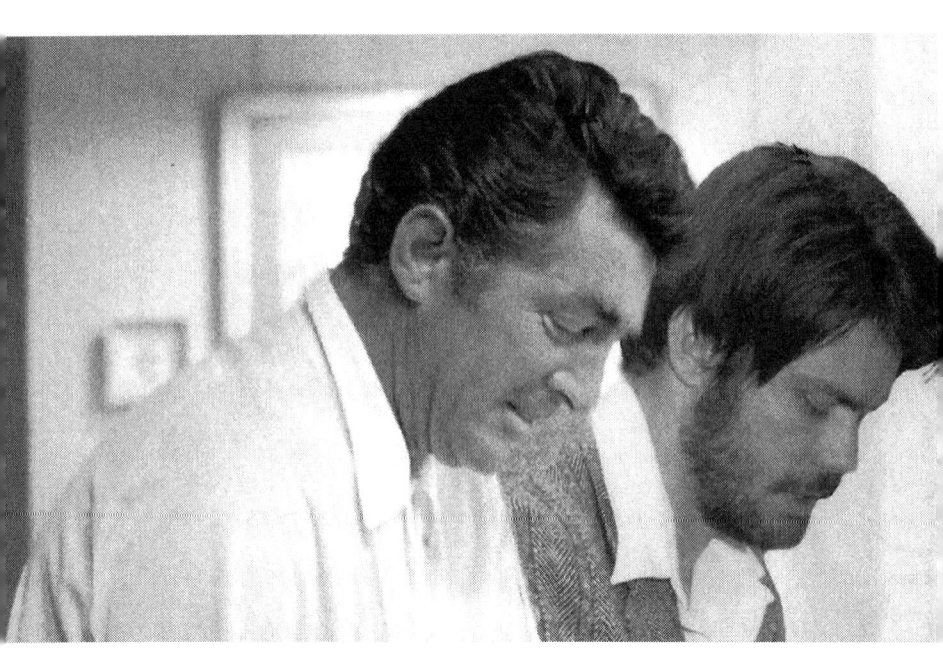

Neil Daniels, former NBC VP and founder Dean Martin Fan Center: There were a few problem guests. Linda Ronstadt was one. She was surrounded by a whole lot of people who decided she wasn't going to do a duet with Dean, wasn't going to do this, she wasn't going to do that. With what she was trying to do with her career, singing with Dean Martin was not exactly where she wanted to go, she wanted to be more "with it." You couldn't talk to Linda herself so Greg just said "Screw it, she's off the show."
I know Raquel Welch was a little bit tough at one point. Kate Smith was hard at one time but in a funny way.
But there weren't many problems. Dean's show was always in the top ten for so many years and Dean was such a big star, everybody wanted to be on that show. When you look back and see all these actors that appeared—Jimmy Stewart singing or Orson Welles—it just shows you the magnitude of what Dean could accomplish.

Maria: On tape day we started early. We would have to be at the NBC studio about five in the morning for hair and makeup before the stars arrived. We'd have to wear that stuff all day long. I hated it. The make-up artists kept putting powder on our faces until we finished taping, which was usually well into the evening.

Peggy Lee: *Dean Martin was a devil for having his guests rehearse until they're blue in the face—and then appearing without*

Photo top: Dean with Neil Daniels.

a single rehearsal himself. I told him when I accepted to do the show that I couldn't rehearse because I didn't have the time. So both of us went in and did the whole thing off the top of our heads. It was great.

Linda: On *The Dean Martin Comedy Hour* our production numbers were pre-taped the day before with a full orchestra. Part of every week was spent in a recording studio where we would put down our group vocals. We would leave spots for solos that would be captured live, in front of a studio audience, on tape day.
I loved recording because of the amazing sound; every harmony was crystal clear. When it came to the bigger cast production numbers, Lee Hale brought a few professional studio singers. Together, with Lee, they formed a quartet. I was in awe of them and completely absorbed in how they performed their craft. Their vocal artistry and musicianship was an inspiration to me.

Deborah Pratt, Golddigger 1973-1974: Les Brown was conducting, we had a full orchestra, it must have been thirty pieces that we were standing in front of singing.
We did what we were supposed to do, we each had our little solos. I guess maybe on the third show we came back for Dean walked in, saw me, and went, "Oh, oh—the riff! You're the one that does the riff. Come stand by me." He pointed me out and brought me over so we sang together,. He liked my voice, he liked the fact that I had some soul going.
We were standing there at the bar where we did the little jokes and they brought Dean what looked like a glass of ice water and I said, "Is that ice water?" He said, "Why don't you taste it?" It was straight gin. Not even vodka, gin. I said, "It's eleven o'clock in the morning." He goes, "Not everywhere in the world!"

Robin Hoctor-Horneff, Golddigger 1973-1974: Dean was very pleasant. He was very sweet, very nice, he ran through the show once and we were done. There was no effort, it seemed like he was never stressed about anything. It was, "Hey, that's okay, don't worry about it." He was laughing all the time, he seemed to be having a great time.
I remember thinking, "Is he really drinking?" He used to keep glasses at different places all over the set, one on the piano, another over there. Out of curiosity I went over to smell one of the glasses and it

really was booze. At least the one I smelled, I don't know if they all were. I thought it was supposed to be all faking, but no, he was really drinking. To my knowledge anyway.

Don Cherry, singer, professional golfer: I tell you something, for eleven years Dean was the dearest friend I ever had. He was Italian. I told him one time, if I could have just been Italian think of how much more famous I'd have been. Dean said, "Let me call Chicago and I'll call you back in thirty minutes." Like he was going to make me Italian.

We played golf every single day at the Country Club, he was about a ten or twelve handicap, he was that good a player. We played golf everywhere he went, if he would go somewhere like Lake Tahoe or something, they would book me up there. I worked at the Riviera, I worked at the Sands, I worked everywhere when Dean was there. Vic Damone and I did the summer replacement show for Dean in 1967 and I did Dean's show about six or seven times myself. I can't tell you how much he meant to me, really.

It was so simple, they didn't have much rehearsal but they had the cue cards so you'd know what you were doing. I enjoyed it more than anything. I guess Dean did more for my career in those days than anybody else ever did.

I'm on the show one time and Dean looks at me and says, "That's the worst hairpiece I ever saw. You go over to Max Factor and get you another hairpiece." Well, I went over there and found a good looking hairpiece and I wore it back to the show. They told Dean, "That hairpiece used to belong to John Wayne."

Dean was singing and had a great sense of humor but I think the thing he'd rather do was play golf.

Maria: The country guest stars we worked with were a different kind of show people. I remember, Lynn Anderson was very down to earth and was on the show quite a bit. She had a big hit, '(I Never Promised You a) Rose Garden' a couple of years earlier. Lynn was pretty as a picture with her blonde hair perfectly lacquered in place. I just stood back and watched her be the center of attention, while cracking jokes and looking so confident. It made me wonder if I would ever be able to feel so at ease on the set.

With our busy schedule we didn't have a lot of opportunities to explore Los Angeles but we got out when we could. Susan Buckner had driven down from her home in Seattle, she had the only car among the eight of us, a tiny Toyota Corolla. We used to squeeze six girls into it. It was kind of like stuffing people into a phone booth, we'd be sitting all over each other hanging out the windows trying to get somewhere.

> **Patti (Pivarnik) Gribow, Golddigger 1973-1985:** None of us had wheels because we were all from different parts of the country. At one point Susie and Deborah had a dog named Tizz and the dog would pile in the car with us.

Linda: We used to cruise up and down Sunset and Hollywood Boulevards at night, just looking at what was going on. We became night owls, our bodies' time clocks were wound up to exercise or put on a show.

We walked down Hollywood Boulevard toward Vine Street along the Walk of Fame reading the names of entertainment legends on stars embedded in the sidewalk. Hoping to soak in an atmosphere of Hollywood glamour and success, we were instead blindsided by a lackluster ambiance, projected by shabby stores selling drug paraphernalia and shady characters congregating in the alleyways. We passed by an old woman muttering to herself, her face overly made up as if she was still an ingenue ready to appear on stage; this gave me pause. Her red lipstick was crooked, drawn high above her lip line, and her eyes told the story of a woman lost in a world from her past. Gazing at her was like confronting my darkest fear.

I quickly looked away and then we came across Ann Margret's star on the Walk of Fame. I felt an odd connection because I was told that, with my strawberry blonde hair, we looked similar. Was I expected to live up to her fast and loose image? I stared at her star almost wishing it had a secret to confer—but all I saw was a wad of chewing gum stuck on one of the star points. Dean's star of pink stone and brass was not too far down the street. It was pretty but cold, lacking any stellar appeal.
As I looked around I thought "note-to-self; fame is all just smoke and mirrors."

"February 14th, Valentine's Day, Dean Martin legally filed his case for the dissolution of his marriage to Jeanne Martin. For Cathy and Dean, it was a double celebration. Their fiery affair was no longer 'just another Dean Martin fling.' He was more than serious. They would marry.

"Dean Martin's marriage will only be the beginning of some turbulent days ahead. At this moment, Jeanne will not re-marry and Dean's own wedding to Cathy is of her choosing, not his! This is hardly the way to begin a new married life."
- Movie Mirror magazine September 1972

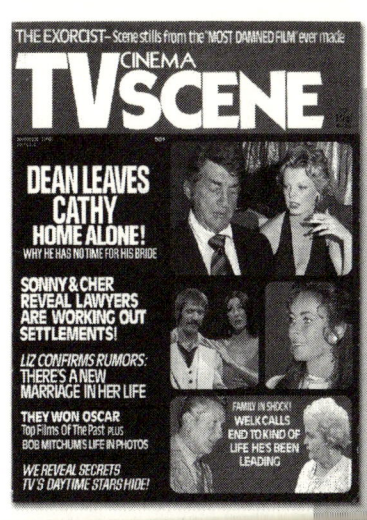

"It didn't matter that Cathy had been married once before.

"He wanted to get it over quietly," a close friend explained. "But Cathy refused to be married in Las Vegas, and she fought bitterly with Dean about it. She wanted a ceremony she could remember with fondness, not some tacky Vegas marriage done in the back corner of a hotel room. Dean agreed," the friend went on. "But he began to resent Cathy. He told her a long time ago not to ever make demands on him and there she was, wanting all kinds of things."
- Motion Picture Magazine November 1972

Dean's Queens

Don Rickles: *"Dean Martin, rest his soul, he was a good friend to me. I was at his wedding when he married the nine year old."*

Maria: Pretty much everybody on the set thought that Dean had lost his mind when he married a twenty-six-year-old hair salon receptionist. There were a lot of arguments going on between Dean and his new bride Cathy, she specifically wanted our numbers cut because she didn't want him spending too much time around us. We were told by Greg Garrison to stay away from Dean because she was jealous of us.

Well, Cathy certainly disturbed the vibe on the set. We were cordial to her but she had no interest in developing a friendship with us. When you think about it, we were closer in age to Cathy than Dean. Other than that we had no common ground, except for our proximity to Dean and she was very territorial with him. You could see that she didn't like us girls buzzing around the set and would give some of us the evil eye, especially Linda.

Linda: I could understand Cathy's insecurity but to go so far as to have our number cut, I couldn't comprehend it. I was very hurt that she would deliberately try to harm us by making our part in the show less significant. To me, her actions were proof that she was out of her league and she knew it.

Maria: Greg always gave Linda a lot of close ups on TV. I heard that one of the girls asked Greg's assistant, Janet Tighe, if she was doing her part okay. Janet told her not to worry, "All they want to see is Linda's face anyway."

Linda: I was totally clueless about that, I was busy worrying that my hips might look too big. I mean, they weren't too big for normal people but television makes you look ten pounds heavier.

Our Hungarian grandmother used to always tell us growing up about how she was known for her "big beautiful butt." And I used to think she was crazy. She used to tell us she had "the best butt in Budapest" and that's what she was known for. "All the other girls had to put padding on their butts," she would tell us with great pride. It's a cultural thing. When we were on television it was important to have a small butt. I was worried about not being thin enough.

During one of our rehearsals at Moro-Landis Studios Bob Sidney was running our choreography rehearsal. Ed Kerrigan usually did this but he was busy doing a show for some big star. He was very much in demand. Bob caught me checking out my butt in the mirror and said sarcastically, "Yeah, your butt is big."

That was the last thing I needed to hear. I was always watching my weight. Needless to say Bob was cranky and caustic, he didn't act like he really wanted to be there rehearsing us.

Maria: Dean attracted the biggest stars in show business. Every week was star-studded with a wide variety of entertainers like Joey Bishop, Lou Rawls, Bob Newhart, Phyllis Diller, Petula Clark, Norm Crosby, Foster Brooks, Ruth Buzzi, Rowan & Martin and Audrey Meadows. County artists like Buck Owens, Doug Dillard, Tom T. Hall, The Statler Brothers and icons Ronald Reagan, Jack Benny, Donald O'Connor and Gene Kelly dazzled us with their talent. It was a lot to take in, I dared not think about their celebrity status for fear my performance would be affected.

> **Deborah Pratt, Golddigger 1973-1974:**
> Everybody in California was very, very nice. This was the way to come out to California if you're going to be a performer in the sense that you're not stepping off a bus and you don't know anybody. We stepped into NBC, that's where our rehearsal facilities were for the show. It was a whole other world at that time because variety was still very, very big. So Sammy Davis and Cher and all these other people were walking around in Bob Mackie costumes.
>
> I'm from a big city—Chicago—but still, this was Hollywood royalty.

And we would just kind of hang out with them. When Gene Kelly walked into rehearsal I did that knee slide up to him like he did in *Singing in the Rain*.

Robin Hoctor-Horneff, Golddigger 1973-1974:
I was so excited, we were going to be doing a tap number with Gene Kelly! My father and mother were both professional dancers so I was a really good tapper and Gene immediately picked up on that.
Some of the girls could fake it but most of the girls were primarily singers. I was the token dancer.
The number didn't turn out the way Gene wanted but he called me a few years later and I ended up working with him.

Deborah Pratt, Golddigger 1973-1974:
I could tap but not like a hoofer. Gene Kelly did the most intense tap routine so I went to Susan Buckner and Robin Hoctor, who were really good tap dancers, and I made them work with me until my toes bled. The next day we went in to do the number and Gene cut it because everybody couldn't do it. He was a taskmaster, he was tough and I wished I had been a better tap dancer because I was such a fan of his.

Colleen Kincaid Jackson, Golddigger 1973-1975: We practiced those special tap steps in our bikinis next to the pool at the motel. We were efficient; practice, practice, practice while we got a tan at the same time. When it got too hot to continue, we jumped in the pool!

Maria: We furiously rehearsed but tapping wasn't our thing. That's a whole different craft. Gene Kelly had certain steps and a definite style that he tried to teach us. He did this little sway from side to side when he tapped.

He wanted us to be more in sync with him but we weren't that technical. We were disappointed that we didn't do a tap dance together but we did get to tape some other musical numbers that he made famous at MGM. In one routine we wore beautiful costumes while he sang and danced around us. In another number we joined him to sing 'Count on Me' from *On the Town,* a musical Gene Kelly originally starred in with Frank Sinatra.

Linda: Gene Kelly was very much a perfectionist. Dean's program was fifty percent fun and fifty percent craft. It was apparent Gene wasn't looking for fun as much as he was

interested in giving a highly precisioned performance.
Besides doing our number with Gene the Golddiggers had their own spot on the show singing 'Open Up Your Heart.' We also performed 'Banjo Man' with Bluegrass Banjo legend Doug Dillard. Bob Fletcher, the show's costume designer, created adorable outfits for us and Van Alexander wrote some clever arrangements. The production was a uniquely talented team of seasoned artists that mostly came out of the motion picture industry.
After several weeks of taping television shows we wrapped it up and said our goodbyes to the cast and crew. I asked Dean what he was going to do with his time off. He replied with a grin, "Relax."

> **Joyce Haber, October 22, 1973:** *The latest big star to sneak in and out of Los Angeles' Midway Hospital for some kind of minor cosmetic surgery was Dean Martin, who used the pseudonym David Miller. Dean has been on a two-week hiatus from his TV show. Martin, who has had eye lifts several times before, was unavailable for comment.*

Linda: After a few weeks in L.A. we were back on tour again, I think we were on the road 40-45 weeks that first year. We had to do two separate one-hour shows so we had dozens of costumes, loads of music—we had solos, duets, group numbers, dance numbers, singing numbers.

Maria: At this time, we traveled with a road manager Frank, our drummer Barry Brysman, and Charles Sanford, our conductor. Charles used to be the orchestra leader for *Your Show of Shows,* he shared fascinating stories with us about Sid Caesar and Imogene Coca. He raved about Sid Caesar's comedic timing and what a pro he was. Charlie had a great smile especially when he talked about the good old days.

Linda: He loved being on the road with us, so much so that I think his wife may have been a little envious of the time we spent with him, maybe even threatened. As a matter of fact, she said something to one of the girls about "getting too close to her husband" but that was completely far-fetched. Charlie had a saying for the musicians playing the opening number, "Play it like a bat out of hell!" It was so fast one reviewer said we were, "High energy to the point of frenzy." Charlie believed an opening act should hit the stage hard and fast. Every once in a while Charlie would get into heated arguments with Barry, our drummer, about the tempo of the show. Otherwise, he was pretty easy going.

Barry was a fun-loving guy who got along well with all the girls. He was like a brother to me. Maria and I bonded with him the most because he ate healthy foods. Barry used to make us laugh. He would fool around, entertaining us with his drumming gymnastics, twirling the sticks and then pretending he dropped them like a goofball. He was a body builder so he had a lean muscular body which made his antics all the more funny.

Patti (Pivarnik) Gribow, Golddigger
1973-1985: I loved Charlie Sanford, he was our chief cook and bottle washer doing everything and anything for us. As our confidant he took care of us like a father, watching over us and making sure we were all in good health and eating properly. Can you imagine how he kept eight estrogen filled young women in line? You know we all had our moments, both individually and together. What a guy!

Deborah Pratt, Golddigger 1973-1974: Barry was all of maybe twenty-five. Charlie was seventy so he had to crack the whip to make sure we got home safely and behaved and acted relatively sane. But we were pretty good girls, I think that's one of the reasons why we were chosen, there was something wholesome about the way we looked. I remember Greg saying, "From the neck up you're the girl next door only ten times more beautiful. From the neck down you're everybody's fantasy." Thanks, Greg.

Maria: Besides Charles Sanford mentoring us on the road, he instinctively knew how to pace a show and when to milk an audience. We gained a lot of insight but, most of all, we felt safe traveling with him, even to foreign countries.

Linda: The Casino Royale in Mexico City was a mind-blowing experience for us. They idolized us there, more so than in the states, it was like we were superstars. We were treated like royalty. They went crazy for us. Every night it was flowers galore, all kinds of gifts. For a small town girl suddenly thrust into that situation there's a lot you have to take in. A fan ran up to me after the show and said, in his heavily accented English, "Oh my, you have such beautiful teets." I was horrified, the look on my face must have told it all. He started pointing to his mouth, "No, no! Teets, teets!" meaning teeth. He was an innocent, sweet guy, I just misunderstood him. Like I said, Greg picked us for our teeth.

Maria: The Latin guys are not afraid to tell you how they feel. They were very exuberant. I was on stage singing and a man rushed to the stage

Photo: Deborah Pratt and Susie Buckner

calling my name, "Oh, Maria Elena, bonita señorita…." He was carrying so many bouquets of flowers that I could hardly see him.

After we performed in Guadalajara we boarded a private Lear Jet to Puerto Vallarta where we stayed at Jorge Loera's mountain top home. This was a side trip, a rare chance to relax. Each girl was given their own room, the enormous house had many maids and butlers with a spectacular pool. For dinner we had our own private fiesta with a Mariachi band.

Linda: It was a spectacular mansion high up in the cliffs; up on the roof I could see snipers strategically placed on all corners. Jorge was a high profile guy with bodyguards everywhere. Despite that, we had the time of our lives. Jorge went all out to make us feel pampered; but then again, this was probably all normal to him so he wouldn't dream of treating guests any other way. He was always the gentleman with impeccable manners.

One morning the cooking staff made us juice from fresh squeezed strawberries for breakfast. It was one of the most heavenly drinks I had ever tasted. We were served outside on a terrace in a beautiful tropical setting. The only thing that marred the experience was the high humidity. The air was so heavy, I felt like I was breathing water droplets.

Deborah Pratt, Golddigger 1973-1974: We found out much later that Jorge Loera was the son of basically the Godfather of Mexico. He owned a bull ring and he invited us down for the day to enjoy the arena.

Maria: I had no desire to go to a bull ring because it seemed so cruel. I decided to stay up on the balcony at a specially prepared table to munch on chips and salsa and sip Sangria. All of a sudden I heard someone say "Susie and Deborah are in the bull ring!"

"What?!?" I jumped up to see. They must be crazy! One of the bodyguards assured us it was safe because this was a baby bull but it still looked big to me! Susie and Deborah definitely liked to live on the wild side.

Barry and Charlie were all along for the trip as well, Charlie was the grandfatherly type and was highly concerned while the girls were in the ring.

Deborah Pratt, Golddigger

1973-1974: They put us in the ring with a baby bull and, you know, a baby bull is still four hundred pounds. They were teaching us how to bullfight, pass the cape—if you commit to the left stay to the left, if you commit to the right stay to the right.

I was standing in the middle of the field and they let this new, young bull out and he was feisty, you could see he was feisty. And I did one pass and Susan was out there and she did a pass. I did another pass and we were being funny, people were shouting, "Toreadoria! Toreadoria!"

At one point the bull was coming at me and I was doing my pass to the right and the bull did like a two step, it went to the right and then to the left. It threw me off because it was so close. And I went to move the cape to match it—which you never do—and the cape ended up in front of me.

I've got this bull charging straight at me and I'm in a mini-dress and platform high heels. I somehow managed to throw the cape forward and vault over the bull. It missed me, I literally vaulted over it, legs spread, and all I heard was everybody yelling, "Run!!!"

And I'm running in the high heels and all I hear behind me is bar-ump, barump, barump, and it's catching up to me! I see this five foot block wall in front of me and I put my hands up to vault over it, I was so grateful I was a dancer.

I heard right beneath my feet as I cleared the top, "Bam!" and this bull slammed into the wall. He would have broken my back. He hit so hard he broke his horn and everybody was upset because this was like a prize baby bull and I said, "A—it didn't kill me. B—I'm glad its horn is broken because it'll never fight and never be killed."

Linda: We worked Mexico quite often and had some hairbrained escapades. Jorge Loera developed a relationship with Susie and, during one of our breaks, she was flown down to Mexico to be with him. Almost as soon as she got there, Jorge was called away on some important business, so Susie asked him to fly me, Maria and Deborah down to keep her company. For him that was no problem and it sounded like fun to us. We stayed at an exclusive hotel bungalow in the city, very posh.

Susan Buckner, Golddigger
1973-1974: Jorge was young and so good looking. We had a flirtation going. I wasn't happy with him for putting business before me but since he let me bring a few of my friends down, I forgave him.
We each had our own rooms. The place was huge. We were supposed to meet Jorge for dinner the next night but he was detained with business another night. Now I was mad. How dare he keep us waiting!
After a few days Jorge still hadn't showed up and the girls had to leave for various reasons. I couldn't believe that they had left me alone.
The hotel desk called me wanting to know how long I would be staying. They wanted a deposit on the bill! I told them I didn't know how long I was staying and Jorge would take care of the deposit. I don't think they liked my answer because a security guard was placed outside my door.... Oh goodie, someone to play with. I told the guard my sad tale and had him feeling really sorry for me. Eventually, I talked him into taking me out. I got dressed up and stuffed a wig and change of clothes into my big purse. While we were in this amazing disco, I excused myself to go to the *cuarto de bano*. I quickly changed and slipped by him in my disguise. I stayed at a distance and entertained myself for about forty-five minutes watching him frantically try to find me. I eventually turned myself in and we went back to the hotel.
Jorge finally returned the next day. I was relieved but still he got an ear beating from me.

Maria: Susie would find that Jorge was a little hard to train. Through the years, I noticed that most multi-millionaires were.

"There is a very easy way to return from a casino with a small fortune.... go there with a large one."
—Jack Yelton

"[Las Vegas is] a place where the promise is everything and the payoff elusive, a place where the level of frustration and nervous boredom is so pronounced that a crowd will form around the search for a dropped dime."
—Joan Didion

"It's a corny old gag about Las Vegas, the temporal city if there ever was one, trying to camouflage the hours and retard the dawn, when everybody knows that if you're feeling lucky you're really feeling time in its rawest form, and if you're not feeling lucky, they've got a clock at the bus station."
—Michael Herr

VEGAS & BEYOND

Linda: On December 5, 1973 we were back in Las Vegas, this time to appear with Dean opening night at the brand new MGM Grand Hotel. I felt like a princess, the taxi that delivered us to the door could have been a carriage. It was all so glamorous.

Opening night was one of the most fabulous nights of my life. It was such a huge deal, a big event for the city of Las Vegas and for us. Vegas was so different then, it had that old Hollywood magic. The city had style, everybody dressed up in those days. I usually wore long, slinky gowns in the evenings, before and after the show.

Newsweek, **December 17, 1973:** *"Las Vegas' newest, biggest, and most expensive pleasure palace—MGM's Grand Hotel. The 26-story sybarite's dream premiered last week amid floodlights and a progression of vintage cars that disgorged celebrities including Fred MacMurray, Jane Powell, and Barbara Eden. But the real star was the massive T-shaped hotel itself. And Las Vegas was revved up in a fashion it hasn't seen for years."*

Dr. Gene Moehring, Professor of History, UNLV: Raquel Welch was the one that set off the bomb that started the construction of the MGM Grand.

You didn't have any high rise hotels in Las Vegas until the Riviera in

1955 because there's water under the valley and no one knew if the aquifers would mess up the high buildings. All the early hotels were two and three stories, that was it; they were like ranches that went on for fifty rooms but they weren't high rises.

Vegas was the first place to give deluxe, using the French word, luxury rooms to the middle class for a low rate. When they ran the place in the fifties and sixties the mob would give you a nice room for ten dollars a night. They'd get it all back in the casinos.

Very few hotels opened in Las Vegas in the seventies but in the sixties you had Caesars Palace open in 1966, Kerkorian had opened The International which is today the Las Vegas Hilton in 1968, and the first MGM Grand, today Bally's, in 1973. So you had all that growth but it slowed down in the seventies.

The Governor in those days, Paul Laxalt, was very impressed by Howard Hughes, who had come back to stay at the Desert Inn from 1966 to 1970, and he wanted a clean corporate image for Las Vegas and to get the mob out.

Baron Hilton and his father Conrad, who was still alive at the time, were saying that they wanted to get into Vegas but the problem was, the laws in those days stated that every stockholder had to be investigated by the gaming control board and, you know, Hilton has thousands of stockholders.

What the 1969 Laxalt law did was change the rules so that only the key executives had to be investigated. Once you had corporate gaming, those corporations had access to billions of dollars in capital from Wall Street, the banks, money that people like Bill Boyd, Sam Boyd, didn't—even Del Webb couldn't raise that kind of money. That more than anything else drove the mob out.

> **PBS, The American Experience:** *Kirk Kerkorian surpassed the size and scope of the International when he built the MGM Grand. The hotel had 2,100 guest rooms, five gourmet restaurants and the world's largest casino. At 26 stories high, the MGM Grand was the tallest casino in the free world.*
>
> *The completion of the MGM Grand led to the corporate revolution in Las Vegas. In order to have the funds required to finance the $106 million MGM, Kerkorian sold his International and Flamingo Hotels to the Hilton Hotel Corporation, marking the first time a publicly owned conglomerate was in charge of a Las Vegas casino. By 1976, 63% of Hilton's earnings came solely from its Las Vegas establishments. The success of the Hilton Corporation spurred the interest of other businesses; soon, Sheraton and Holiday Inn were investing in Las Vegas and buying casinos.*

Maria: I thought the MGM was incredibly gorgeous, I liked it much better than Caesars because that place was so dark inside. Everything was a lot grander, so to speak, at the MGM— more open, and it was all about the Hollywood experience so I loved it. The movie star pictures beside the rooms were so glamorous. I thought, "Oh, what star's picture will my room be next to? Maybe some of her magic will rub off on me."

Dean Martin, on stage: *"I work in Vegas at that new big hotel, the Megum. The MGM. That's a big mother, I'll tell you. They even got a theater there and you can see a picture and it's open in the afternoons for some of you guys who want to knock off a matinee. Ain't too many of us old guys left.*
And they have beautiful suites upstairs named after the great stars, they have the Clark Gable suite, the Jimmy Stewart suite. I always stay in the Raquel Welch suite—no doorbells just two knockers."

Ichiro (Masatoshi) Mitsumoto, Sands Copa Room Cellist: Antonio Morelli, the bandleader at The Sands, asked me to join his band in 1967. Dean Martin's show was my first, it was my introduction to show biz. Dean was one of my favorite stars. His routine was perfect in balancing and pacing the show with talking and singing. I played many, many shows with him and it was always the same, identical show but each time he made it sound so natural, like it was spontaneous, and I never got tired of it. There was no room to improve it.
Except he once tried a change in the routine and it didn't work. I think he changed some songs and also some jokes but it happened only one time.

I was sitting at the end of the stage on a high rise; as Dean walked offstage I was right there. At the end of the show when he exited the stage he used to tap my shoes lightly with his fist. I liked that, most stars don't interact with the musicians.
Except Sammy Davis. He loved us and used to hang out backstage and he often joined us for poker games between shows. We played in a very inexpensive way, our ante was five cents but we made him up the ante to twenty-five cents. We usually played five card stud. He wasn't very good but he didn't mind, he enjoyed being with us. He considered himself a musician.
Sammy was very, very generous to us. An engagement lasted two or three weeks and just about all performers would give us a closing night spread after the show with little finger food and drinks. But Sammy did it every week he was there.

Sammy Davis Jr.: "*The main point in the game of life is to have fun. We are afraid to have fun because somehow that makes life too easy.*"

Deborah Pratt, Golddigger 1973-1974: We were backstage in Dean's suite one night when the Rat Pack walked in. I'm sitting between Danny Thomas and Sammy Davis, Jr. and Danny Thomas looks at me and says, "Well, you're the highest yellow black woman I've ever seen in my life." And Sammy hit him! It was really funny, and I turned around and said, "It's nice to meet you, too." I wasn't intimidated by them because they were nice. They weren't bullies. Well, Joey Bishop was maybe a little bit of a bully.

Maria: The MGM was certainly grand in every sense so I wanted to spend as little time in our dressing room as possible. Our call time to be in the dressing room was an hour before the show. It was a long time to hang around backstage with a bunch of dynamic personalities, all chattering, borrowing make-up and spraying clouds of Aqua Net. Usually, I would zone out the noise. I much preferred to get made up in my hotel room where I could do vocal exercises.
When it got closer to showtime I relished the adrenaline rush of walking through the casino and seeing the crowd still waiting to be seated for our show. Outside the Celebrity Room, the excitement of the gamblers in the casino and the bells and whistles of the machines shooting out coins energized me.

Linda: We would be chastised if we were even a minute late, they would threaten to dock our pay. It was very, very strict. Dean gave his big dressing room to us along with the flowers and fruit that were meant for him. Dean would show up fifteen minutes before the show in a special room built for him on the side of the stage. He liked to come by private elevator directly from his hotel room to the stage, dressed and ready to go. I don't think there was even a door on his little room but we all gathered there at a certain time every night to say hi to Dean before we went on. He had his water, snacks and drinks in there; all he had to do was stroll on to the stage a few feet away when it was time for him to make his entrance.
For Dean we did twenty minutes ahead of his act. When we worked with different artists the time would vary.

Patti (Pivarnik) Gribow, Golddigger 1973-1985: Before the shows with Dean at the MGM we would often hear his wife, Cathy, stomp

In 1973, the MGM Grand was the largest and most expensive hotel in the world.

into his dressing room, scream at him, and then stomp off. We knew she was most unhappy that he was performing with the Golddiggers. Dean once commented that he didn't understand her anger, saying, "It's just my image!" The truth is that our relationship with Dean was platonic, yet caring. Traditionally, prior to the performances, we would each give Dean a hug and a peck on the cheek for good luck. Both Dean and "his girls" looked forward to these innocent and special show biz moments.

Linda: After they split up Greg was hinting around how much Dean liked me and how he wanted to set us up. Or he could have been testing me just to see what I would do. I never got back to Greg about that but I was kind of flattered. I wondered what Dean and I would talk about if we were on a date. Hmm.... I couldn't think of much so I put it out of my head.

Maria: Dean was funny. He was like my dad, in that he liked to have the girls fuss over him. I guess Italian men are that way.
His entrance on to the stage got me. I thought, "Whoa, this guy is a superstar." His persona, his look, he had such charisma, even before he opened his mouth. He just had it without saying a word, like he had the world on a string and he didn't have a care in the world.

Linda: We were appearing with Dean in Vegas so we dropped in one night to see Don Arden's *Hallelujah Hollywood,* an extravaganza that played nightly in the Ziegfeld Room, the other big showroom at the MGM Grand. It was our first time seeing topless girls, our eyes were popping out.

Maria: I kind of felt sorry for them in a way. They were beautiful and statuesque but I was uncomfortable watching them. I guess I found it a bit demoralizing but I didn't let on. Instead, I put on an air of sophistication like the rest of the spectators. I have to admit the production numbers were spectacular. The showgirls would glide down an enormous staircase and would cover the stage with glitter and feathers. It was magnificent. Later, I talked to one of the showgirls and she told me she developed spinal problems from the heavy headpieces she wore.

Because we were Dean's opening act, we were invited to the celebrity shows on the Strip and all us girls dressed to the hilt. We were given the VIP treatment, escorted to a special table and sometimes we were introduced to take a bow. This is when we could play the starlet role. Before we left the dressing room, we would freshen up a bit. We had a vigorous show and would perspire, sometimes our false eyelashes would be slipping off our eyelids. I would just take them off, minimize my make-up and smooth down my hair a little. Stage makeup is not pretty when you're meeting people face to face.

Lots of times, I would just chill after the show in the coffee shop with a few of the girls for a light snack or stroll back to the room to watch Johnny Carson.

Linda: Some people believed the Golddiggers were created for the fantasies of men. We believed we were picked for our talent. We were under the illusion, I guess, that we were basically a group of talented young ladies and for some people that was their perception. But for others we were just mindless sex objects. We could see that everybody was staring at us in the casino or on the way to the show. It was an ego boost to know we had that kind of allure but it was a game not our reality. It was important to us that we work hard to develop and prove our talent.

Jan Kubicki, teacher Marple Newtown High School: I visited Maria Elena in Las Vegas one time. I was walking with her through the hotel and it was a horrifying experience because every sleazebag guy that we saw looked at her like he wanted to do every disgusting thing he could imagine. They looked at her like a piece of meat and I was horrified because she wasn't a piece of meat to me.

She didn't understand the power she had over men. She was aware of it but she didn't understand it, she just thought it was a kind of a joke. She never took it seriously.

If she'd had the right exposure, the right experience and opportunity, she would have been a big star. But she didn't fit in anywhere, there was no place for her.

Maria: When it was time to do television with Dean we would get word from Greg Garrison's office warning us, "Okay, better start going on your diets, watch what you eat because the camera adds ten pounds." I also noticed that sequins pick up the light and can make you look larger. Sometimes, to get ready for television, I would go on a liquid fast and that would shrink my stomach. It gave me an opportunity to be introspective and calm and balance my energy. Usually, I was running in high gear so it was a nice break. I routinely dropped about three pounds in two days, no problem. Whatever I did to lose a few pounds, I always kept nutrition foremost in my mind. I was also very aware of my posture; standing correctly automatically makes you look thinner. That was a secret I learned from the beauty contests.

Linda: There was a particular Dean Martin show we did where Colleen had a co-starring role with Dean in a comedy skit. She was supposed to wear a bikini in the scene. This was right before Thanksgiving so when we had Thanksgiving dinner together, Colleen didn't eat a bite of food. We were amazed at her self control but felt bad feasting in front of her. I know I was grateful I wasn't chosen to sacrifice myself for the show. The day of the TV taping, Colleen looked fabulous but it was soon announced that her scene had to be cut. Talk about feeling someone's pain, we all felt horrible for her.

> **Deborah Pratt, Golddigger 1973-1974:** We worked hard but we had a great time because Dean made the set fun. He did what he needed to do but basically he never came in and learned the choreography, it had to be simple enough for him to pick up in thirty minutes. Then the choreographer would dance out in front of camera and Dean would just follow him. We had to know what we were doing behind him.
> It was fantastic because the people around us were such professionals that we learned from the beginning what was expected of us and I thought we gave it.

Maria: You never knew what big name celebrity you were going to see when you walked on the set. Dom DeLuise was often requested by Dean to be on his show. He was always in high gear and would do zany pranks that had us howling with laughter all day long.

Linda: Foster Brooks was another one who always had us in stitches. Sometimes we could hardly breathe we were laughing so hard from his drunk routine.
Part of our job was to sit in the audience while

they shot the *Dean Martin Roasts*, at least the segments that were filmed on Stage 4 at NBC. They also made a deal to film some portions of the Roasts at the MGM Grand in Las Vegas. We did them back to back, we shot the variety show segments in the afternoon and the Roasts later that night. It was a pretty long day but the Roasts section was hardly work and it gave us time to unwind. Waiting around in between takes I had some pleasant conversations with Howard Cosell. He was pretty cool. I was too shy to talk to most people but I felt safe and at ease with him.

Greg Garrison liked to have sports stars on the show every now and again. On one show they roasted Wilt "The Stilt" Chamberlain. We were shooting the breeze after the show with Audrey Meadows, Ken Berry and George Kennedy when Wilt strode over toward us. Wow, he cast a large shadow. Even in my highest heels I wasn't as high as his chest. Wilt had a sensational personality but I had to strain my neck to have an eye to eye conversation with him. A couple of the girls kept in touch with him and a few months later Wilt took some of us to a club in Beverly Hills. He picked us up in his white station wagon. When we got in we couldn't believe what we saw. There wasn't a front driver's seat. Wilt drove from the back seat! The inside of the car was completely gutted and remodeled to fit his gigantic frame.

Maria: The *Dean Martin Roasts* were great entertainment, it was a big party loaded with laughs and we were invited! To think, we were getting paid to sit in the audience to enjoy this banquet of talent, a buffet of comedy. The jokes and kidding around was a delight.

Dean's relaxed manner made him the perfect host to balance the humorous exchanges. Between takes everyone would still be loose and the ribbing would keep going on, unscripted.

Phyllis Diller was broad, loud and fantastically funny as you would expect. In all of this hullabaloo sometimes there would be serious moments from regular Bob Newhart. He was on Dean's show quite often and seemed like such a genuine person, a regular guy.

Some of the roastees were rarified old Hollywood veterans like Zsa Zsa Gabor, Bette Davis, Betty White, and Jack Benny. It was awesome to see Zsa Zsa up close bedazzled with diamonds, Jack Benny's deadpan expression, and Bette Davis' incessant cigarette puffing. It was like being transported to another time.

I ran into Zsa Zsa Gabor a couple of times, once in the ladies' room when we were out to dinner in Beverly Hills. She was lovely to talk to but I almost had to pinch myself. Here I was nonchalantly applying my make-up with the queen of glamour, Zsa Zsa Gabor! I was with the most famous "gold digger" of them all, a major part of the Beverly Hills elite.

> **Dean Martin,** *Dean Martin Roast of Zsa Zsa Gabor*:
> "Well, tonight we salute Zsa Zsa, the most famous of the Gabor sisters.
> You all know the Gabor sisters, the original Golddiggers? Doesn't Zsa Zsa look great? It's a wonder she's still alive with all the blood tests she's taken for marriage licenses."

Patti (Pivarnik) Gribow, Golddigger 1973-1985: We were able to see everyone from Lucy to Michael Landon to President Reagan—you name it, the list goes on and on and on.

Henry Fonda, *Dean Martin Roast of Bette Davis*: *In all fairness I must say this about Bette, she'd never do a picture if cheapness and vulgarity were written into the script. She felt it was up to her to bring that to the role.*

Bob Mills, writer *Dean Martin Roasts*: That show was a big break for me. We worked in teams, I had a partner. We would go into

Harry Crane's office to get the assignment and there would be a bunch of three by five cards on the bulletin board and you'd look, pick out a name that you wanted to write for and you had about two days to write the routine.

When you first started you were at the low end of the totem pool so you would start with people like Dr. Joyce Brothers, I think we had to write for her the first day we arrived. That's a challenge, to do a routine that sounds like Dr. Brothers would sound.

But as you worked your way up, pretty soon you'd go in and they'd say, "Who do you want?" You'd look, "Do we have Orson Welles?" You'd do a spot for Orson Welles, finish that, turn it in and maybe the next assignment would be Zsa Zsa Gabor. Well, the material you can write for Orson Welles and Zsa Zsa Gabor is not even close in attitude and idiom, they just speak differently. So you learned how to put words into real people's mouths that already had an image with the public. That's the key to professional writing, really. You are creating the illusion that people speaking to each other are doing it spontaneously and yet you've written it down. It's a strange feeling at first. But then you find out there's money in it.

Neil Daniels, former NBC VP and founder Dean Martin Fan Center: Orson Welles started out doing live radio, I think the feeling of it being like a live production was what drew him to Dean's show. There wasn't all that much rehearsal, you knew if you made a mistake it would be no big deal, you just got to be yourself. I think when he first appeared on Dean's show he was a little bit hesitant about doing things but after a while he loosened up.

He was also a good friend of Greg Garrison's from the earlier days. Orson didn't drive so Greg would say, "Lee, why don't you go pick up Orson?" And Lee Hale would go over and pick Orson up, drive him around town and then bring him to the studio. It became

Dean, Milton Berle, Abe Vigoda, and the Woman of the Hour Betty White

fun, like he was doing it with his friends. Orson had a good time and I think he learned he could do other things, like comedy, that maybe he never knew he could do.

Orson Welles, *Dean Martin Roast*: *I now direct my remarks to Dean Martin, who is being honored here tonight for reasons that completely elude me. I'm not being fair to Dean because—no, this is true—in his way Dean, and I know him very well, has the soul of a poet.*
I'm told in his most famous song Dean offers a lyric which is so romantic, so touching, that it will be enjoyed by generations of lovers until the end of time. Let's share it together.
"When the moon hits your eye-like a big pizza pie-that's amore."
Now that's what I call touching, Dean. It has all the romanticism of a Ty-D-Bowl commercial.
"When the world seems to shine like you've had too much wine, that's amore." What a profound thought. Should be inscribed forever on a cocktail napkin.
Wait, there's more.
"Tippi-tippi-tay, like a gay tarantella." Like a GAY tarantella?!? Apparently Dean has a side we know nothing about.
"When the stars make you drool just like pasta fazool, scusami, but you see, back in old Napoli, that's amore."
No Dean. That's infermo, Italian for sickening. Lyrics like that ought to be issued with a warning: 'A song like that can be hazardous to your health.' Ladies and gentlemen you are now looking at the end result.

Demond Wilson, co-star *Sanford & Son*: I used to see Dean coming down the hall everyday and I'd say, "How you doing, Dean?" He'd say, "Hey, Pallie." I'd say "What'd you do today, Dean?" He said, "I did the same thing I did yesterday and the same thing I'm going to do tomorrow. I played golf."
When you get a bunch of comics together there's always a fight for the top banana, who's going to be the top dog. It was like every-

body trying to top everybody else's line and giving little behind the scenes ancedotes about things that happened in Vegas, about who schtumped and who didn't schtump who.

I mean, it was like old, old, old school. You had Foster Brooks, you had Phyllis Diller, who I think died twice and came back. Muhammed Ali was on there. You had Howard Cosell, you had Bob Hope, you had John Wayne. It was like the last of a dying breed, it was like the paleolithic age.

These were hard core show business people. This was their life. And they were polite to me because Redd Foxx and I were the kings of NBC so what were they going to say to me? They were talented beyond belief, they were famous and they were iconic but it wasn't my element.

Deborah Pratt, Golddigger 1973-1974:
Sometimes the roasts were very funny and sometimes they were just acerbic. Don Rickles—if he was on he could be hysterical. If he was off he was just mean. Dean was always gracious but he just walked through it, I think.

Don Rickles, *Dean Martin Roast*:
This is one of the great all time thrills I've ever had. This is a bigger thrill than watching Pat Boone autograph hockey pucks during the Ice Follies.
My wife Barbara summed it up best earlier this evening, she said to me, "It's going to be an exciting evening." But don't go by her, she said that on our wedding night. By the way she'd be with us tonight, my lovely wife Barbara, but unfortunately she swam in our pool today with her jewelry on and drowned.
Tonight we're honoring our man of the hour, Dean Martin— you heard the applause Dean, I'd worry!
Look at these beautiful people here to pay tribute to you. The senator, Rich Little, Paul Lynde on the end. Sorry about your seat Paul, why don't you get a pillow so you can see us?
Orson Welles, ladies and gentlemen, has been a great star for so many years. This man was married to a great many women in his life. They're all flat now.

Maria: We hung out a lot with Nipsey Russell between the tapings. He was like Dom DeLuise, always cracking the jokes. He was so funny with his limericks.

Nipsey Russell, *Dean Martin Roast*:
It is said that the Lord made woman last....
A divine and wonderful plan....
'Cause he didn't want anybody talking
him to death....
While he was making man.

Linda: We started meeting some other stars and realized they were not like their TV identities. I would come across Johnny Carson in the hallways of NBC a lot and make small talk; he'd ask us who was on Dean's show that week. He was not as tall as I thought he was going to be but he was every bit as charming as he was on television. In general the celebrities we met were smaller in stature than they appeared on TV.

Deborah Pratt, Golddigger 1973-1974: We saw Johnny Carson at NBC and I thought, "Oh my God, my whole life I've wanted to be on the *Tonight* show." I got up and as soon as I got up everybody joined me. We walked over to him and I said, "Excuse me Mr. Carson, we're the Golddiggers and we want to be on your show." He sucked in his gut and kind of puffed up his chest and went, "Yes, of course, we'll take care of that." Whoever his secretary was at his side said, "All right, we'll handle that, when are you going to be in Vegas, and blah, blah, blah."
They put it all together for us and the night we were on the show Joey Bishop was hosting!
We came out and performed and then we were brought over to sit around Joey, the way that we, as The Golddiggers, sat around all the guys. Whether it was Dean or whoever, that's what we did.
Robin was designated as the spokesperson with Susie sprawled across his desk in the front. I was mad because he wasn't Johnny Carson.

Maria: We did 'Shake Your Tambourine' and we all got to say something. Here we are two sisters from Newtown Square doing the *Tonight* show! I didn't care if Johnny Carson wasn't the host. Joey Bishop was from our hometown area, so that was cool; plus he was a member of Dean's fabled Rat Pack.
After a year traveling and performing together, The Golddiggers became like

sisters. We learned each other's idiosyncrasies— of course, not as much as Linda and I knew each other.

Sometimes Linda and I would argue, especially in the dressing room when the adrenaline was pumping. Don't ask me what we argued about, probably something silly like my borrowing her hair spray with Linda remarking, "Buy your own," and then my retort and so on and so on. The other girls probably thought to themselves, "Watch out for flying hair spray!" But that was just typical sister stuff.

Robin Hoctor was the girl I got closest to right away. She was a part of the New York audition we attended so we shared a lot of the same views on things. Eventually, we all got to know each other and most of us became lifetime friends.

Linda: Several of the girls in the group were Christians, all of us were brought up with strong family values. We continually had to wrestle with the values we grew up with versus the standards of Hollywood and the rest of the world. This may have been the hardest part of working in show business; deciding which road to success was the right one, not the quickest. There were so many temptations and offers presented to us. Every day was a test.

Maria: On our days off, we would be at the airport catching a flight to our next destination. Our schedule was precise, well-timed and organized. After the flight we would be picked up in a limo or a couple of town cars and whisked to our hotel. Again, we would have to get ourselves together to look like the image of The Golddiggers for the entire trip. Even when we weren't working, we were working it.

After we checked in to our hotel, Linda and I would try to find out what kind of food was served in the nearby restaurants. We could usually find something at breakfast because we ate dairy. So there were no late nights for us, we had to get up early. If there was a grocery store close by that was a bonus because we could buy some snacks like trail mix made of raw nuts and raisins for our stay.

In those days if you asked for vegetables at dinner they would come out of a can so it wasn't appetizing, I really couldn't eat it. When you got green beans in a restaurant they weren't even green or crisp, they were soggy and pale. Most of the time our group would go to a steakhouse and all Linda and I could order was a baked potato with a salad.

Being on the road was a big change from the healthy atmosphere Linda and I had known. Often times our rooms would reek of cigarette smoke and the windows wouldn't open. In those days people smoked everywhere, in the airplanes, elevators and in the showrooms. Sometimes the smoke would be so thick that it was hard to sing and dance in it. I could feel the affects on my lungs. It was a dilemma for all of us.

Lee Notling, Golddigger 1973-1974: We were all very independent and not wallflowers. I felt that we were able to get along really well and as the time went on we really became comfortable with each other which made for a better show.

Every day I had a chance to learn something new, be in a new city, get to know myself better and learn so much about everything.

I still had things to learn. I had been struggling with my weight and Greg Garrison's office gave me diet pills. The pills kept me up at night and did not help me lose weight. It would have been better to talk with a professional nutritionist. I ate a lot of red meat. When I couldn't keep the weight off, I was fired.

Linda: Lee getting fired put the fear of God into me and I immediately went on a diet because I needed to lose a few pounds myself. I cut out all flour products, all sweeteners, snacking and any added fats but still ate two balanced meals a day. I had been into crash dieting in the past and fallen into a yo-yo dieting syndrome which usually left me worse off than when I started so I tried to diet sensibly. I had in my mind that I would never be model thin but the Golddiggers never required us to look emaciated. Many people liked the fact that we were "real women" with natural curves.

We had been looking forward for some time to our upcoming job in a tropical paradise, Puerto Rico, but I was very disillusioned on the drive from the airport to see so much poverty. I wasn't expecting that. The Helio Isla, where we would be performing, was opulent, such a contrast to the town.

We were the headliners there with Dick Capri as our opening act. He was known as the "devastating comedy master," his act was a mix of stand up and Kung Fu moves, very unique.

> **Newspaper review, March 15, 1974:** *Wow! Those incredibly beautiful and superbly talented Golddiggers are gorgeous sensations in their blazing show at the Helio Isla Hotel's Theatre restaurant in a scorching combination of singing, dervish-like dancing and delightful costumery that is smash entertainment at an unbelievably fast pace. Each and every one of the delectable Golddiggers is a star performer as a dancer and singer.*
>
> *Ah, the luscious Golddiggers are blonds, redheads, brownettes and magnificent of face and figure—a veritable flower garden on the stage. Linda and Maria Alberici, Susie Buckner, Robin Hoctor (lead dancer), Deborah Pratt, Colleen Kincaid and Patricia Jane Pivarnik are all diamond-bright performers, individually and collectively, in their dazzling production.*
>
> *But even The Diarist was not prepared to see such vivid versatility and showmanship for a solid hour, not counting Dick Capri's hilarious stance. The Golddiggers, clad in brief see-through white costumes with glitter, are terrific in opening on Hands, with rhythmic rock vocals and scintillating choreography to serve notice that they are just about the greatest act of their type on the stage today. The Golddiggers blister the stage with their slow, sexy, hip-swaying version of I Want To Be Happy—a visual and vocal fiesta.*
>
> *When all the flash-dancing dolls sing and swing on That Old Black Magic their show skyrockets and never comes down until the final curtain. Lithe and lovely Robin Hoctor, lead dancer, appears in a beautiful red outfit to burn up the stage with her Terpsichore while the other Golddiggers sing in sparkling harmony Ain't No Sunshine When You're Gone.*
>
> *The crowd rocks the rafters with a thunder of applause for a show that builds and builds with excitement. Patricia (Patti) really turns on the vocal fireworks on I Got Love and it is readily apparent that each of these beauties is an accomplished singer, not merely adept at blending voices. After a brilliant glimpse of the future on the hard-driving 2001 rock number, stunning*

Colleen Kincaid in a pink gown sings a haunting version of If You Go Away; then Maria offers a fine What Now My Love; Linda is dreamy on The First Time Ever I Saw Your Face; Patti chimes in with a poignant Good Morning Heartache; the unit sings Where Is The Love; Deborah solos on Killing Me Softly (backed by the group), followed by a reprise of If You Go Away by Colleen. This is simply great and highly creative vocal styling. The girls in those gowns make you think of moonlight and roses.

The Golddiggers hark back to the 1930s and Robin Hoctor turns on a sizzling tap-dance session to the tune of Forty-Second Street and The Golddiggers revive the unforgettable chorus line of another era with their precision dancing and singing of We're In The Money. Another wow!

Colleen takes the vocal lead on Bill Bailey and her sister Golddiggers are delightful with their straw hat skit. Moving into the 1940s (the time for lovers), The Golddiggers do that Boogie Woogie to the Chattanooga Choo Choo beat for a wild segment. Launching into the 1950s and '60s The Golddiggers throw everything into their Elvis bonfire on Heartbreak and the crowd loves it. Bringing it all down front to the 1970s, The Golddiggers let it all hang out on their rocking Shake Your Tambourine. The young dolls have so much energy that they hardly perspire—and they work!

Maria: From the moment our show got underway we never had a moment to relax. In our dressing room we would be changing furiously for the next number or blotting the sweat off our faces.

Our show was non-stop and displayed the variety of talents we had as a group and as individuals. Each girl possessed different qualities—something for everyone. The pacing of the show built into our audience participation number, which was the sister contest. "Who do you think the two sisters are?" Hardly anyone in the audience ever guessed. After we had our 'Ah, ha' moment Linda and I sang 'I Believe In Music'. It became a high point in our performance as the audience joined in on the last chorus, clapping and singing. We topped off the number with a high kick into a semi-back bend as we hit our last notes.

Newspaper review, March 15, 1974:
There is a cute contest in which the audience is asked to identify the two sisters in the group. No one is ever right and we won't give this delightful bit away here. But Linda and Maria Alberici sock over I Believe In Music and the entire audience gets into the act.
The girls keep swinging on I Feel The Earth Moving, Eli's Coming, and Time and Love and you never saw such pretty legs as The Golddiggers whirl about the stage.
Delectable Deborah Pratt is superb on her soulful styling of God Bless The Child (from Lady Sings the Blues*) for another golden vocal solo. The grand finale is still another wow. Colleen takes the lead singing You'll Remember Me, using a chair with devastating effect and she is joined by the other Golddiggers with chairs for super sexy choreography that should be filmed.*
The Golddiggers really go to town on Come To The Cabaret to climax a spectacular performance in every department. The Golddiggers can stay at the Helio Theatre Restaurant forever— and ever! All hail to Robin Hoctor, Colleen Kincaid, Deborah Pratt, Patti Pivarnik, Susie Buckner and Linda and Maria Alberici—golden girls indeed.

Linda: In Puerto Rico we spent our free time out by the gorgeous pool during the day. That's where I met my first con artist. This man was a nice, friendly, regular kind of guy so we struck up a conversation. I saw him again out by the pool the next day. After I talked to him for a while, he explained that he listened in on people giving their names and room numbers when they charged things. He would charge all his food and drinks to those rooms, then move on to another place before anyone found out. He confessed this in a very matter of fact way as if it was normal and I would think nothing of it. I thought, "Am I in the Twilight Zone?" How very odd it was that he didn't feel any guilt about it. I realized more than ever that I had so much to learn if I was going to make it out in the real world.

Deborah Pratt: During our stay in Puerto Rico, I had been using a product call Sun In and went to the store to get some more because I ran out. The woman working in the store told me they didn't carry it but she had another product that would do the same thing. Her bad English, my bad Spanish, I said "okay." I went back to the room and put the liquid in my hair starting on one side and working it to the other, by the time I'd done half my head the first half was Bozo orange. She had given me bleach!

I was in tears. We had a show in two hours and Linda was the only one who knew what to do. She threw me in the shower to wash the bleach out, used the rest of the bleach, diluted I think, to balance the hideous color across my head as best she could and sent someone down for a box of hair color to dye my hair. My fall didn't match so we chucked that and I wore an afro. My hair came into this amazing copper color that perfectly matched my suntan –I was looking like an Aborigine but at least I didn't resemble Bozo. Was I ever grateful for Linda's quick thinking.

Robin Hoctor-Horneff, Golddigger 1973-1974: We were headlining in Puerto Rico at the Helio Isla Hotel when Tom Jones dropped in to see us perform, he was there in the front row so we all got together at an afterparty.
He left and a bunch of us girls stayed behind to grab something to eat. All of a sudden these three or four men came down, actually one of them was Tom's teenaged son, they came over to me and said, "Tom Jones wants to see you up in his room."
And I'm like, "What do you mean he wants to see me in his room?"
"He's inviting you up to his room."
"Well, if he wants to see me he can come down here and see me with

Tom Jones and The Golddiggers.

everybody else."

They left and I thought, "You've got to be kidding me, you're sending your son and a bunch of men down to pick up a girl to bring to your room? Oh my God, that is so unbelievable." The girls were all laughing and cheering that we totally turned Tom Jones down! He was so hot then. If Tom Jones wanted to see you, any girl would have jumped at it, but that definitely was not my style.

Maria: We couldn't believe it! Tom was sitting in the front table throughout our show like he was the King of Sheba and we were his dancing girls. Then, he summoned the one he wanted and expected her to appear in his room. I thought, "Yes, you are Tom Jones, a great entertainer with sexual energy but really! Who do you think we are?" All of us came from small towns, Robin and I talked about how we'd like to get married some day and have a normal life. We weren't 'party girls' with our eyes fixed only on stardom; we were entertainers with a soul. Was it too much to ask for people to like me for who I was, not the 'Golddigger' persona?

Linda: We performed at a couple of big state fairs that summer, one in Great Falls, Montana and one in Pueblo, Colorado that drew 10,000 excited people to see us with Rich Little.

Deborah Pratt, Golddigger 1973-1974: That was awesome. That was when I decided I should become a rock star because that energy from 10,000 people focused on me was intense.

Robin Hoctor-Horneff, Golddigger 1973-1974: I was the first one to quit the group, in April of 1974. I was going to be married and I'd also met Gene Kelly when he was a guest star on the show and he asked me to be assistant choreographer on a film he was making with Fred Astaire, *That's Entertainment*. As a dancer, to get to work with Gene Kelly and Fred Astaire was amazing, I couldn't have wished for anything more.

I worked with Gene on quite a few projects up until he got sick. He was going to do a Broadway show about Louis Armstrong and we worked on that and I was supposed to do *Xanadu* with him but at the time I was pregnant.

Maria: Robin's future husband, Van, was very handsome. He used to lead us in Bible studies and we got very involved in the church with Pat Boone. Pat used to conduct baptisms in his pool at his home in Beverly Hills. The Boone's were a closely knit family in show business so we were drawn to them. We thought they had the right perspective as far as family values were concerned. We weren't in town a lot but when we were, we went to Bible study because I think you need to ground yourself.

Linda: We did go through a charismatic period. We were led into it by Van and some of his friends who were really nice people. We thought about becoming Christian recording artists and looked into that for a little while but at the time we didn't see God moving us in this direction.

Susan Buckner, Golddigger 1973-1974:
Something did change in us, something good. We were filled with love, especially love for each other, and it showed. People began remarking about that and some even noticed my voice was different—better, stronger.
Before long, we were interviewed by the *Dayton Daily News* and the whole article turned out to be about how each of us came to Jesus and how it changed our lives. When Greg Garrison's office read it, they went through the roof. They were horrified. We were told not to do that again because it might be offensive to some people who carried influence in show business.

Bobby Goldsboro and the girls at The Thunderbird in Las Vegas.

Maria: These were disruptive times for us. When Lee Nolting left we did a few shows with seven girls but now Robin was leaving the group. We were happy for her because she was going to marry a nice guy. Now, there was six of us.

Linda: Lee and Robin leaving the group was bittersweet. Lee was a bit of a surprise but it was most likely for her best. Robin's exit we saw gradually coming but still it was painful to see each of them go. We continued on as a group of six. An executive decision was made not to replace Lee and Robin and that was fine with us because it gave each of us a raise in pay. In July of 1974 we joined Bobby Goldsboro at John Ascuaga's Nugget in Reno and at The Thunderbird in Las Vegas. Touring with Bobby Goldsboro and his band was enjoyable because they would engage us with their southern sense of humor. Most of them were married and would flirt with us but they were harmless.

We were co-headliners so we both did a full show and a number together as well. During our first week at the Thunderbird's Continental Theater we made headlines when we "broke all attendance records for that Las Vegas institution."

Maria: Our two acts jelled well together on-stage and off. Once, we all went for an excursion to a ghost town not far from Reno that had an old cemetery. For fun, Deborah laid down in front of a gravestone that was engraved 'Unknown' and everyone started taking pictures. That was our dynamic together, fun and down-to-earth.

Before I joined The Golddiggers, I briefly dated a newspaper publicist from my hometown and we got engaged rather quickly. He didn't like me being on the road and didn't like the idea of me spending time with the guys from Bobby's show either. What was I supposed to do…. be anti-social? I assured him that I was always with the other girls in my group but my fiancé wouldn't believe me. We spoke on the telephone almost every night and I would end up crying because he would give me a hard time about this or that. This began to take the joy out of my job. The phone conversations with my fiancé became more and more toxic so

I decided to end the engagement and I gave him back his ring.

We needed to move on with our lives; the heartbreak wasn't doing either one of us any good.

Next stop, Vegas. The Thunderbird had an intimate showroom and I liked the people that stayed there. It had a funky style about it, not as glitzy as the other casinos on the strip.

One morning I saw Cyd Charisse lounging by the pool there so, of course, I had to nonchalantly pass by her and say hello. She was inspirational to me; after all she danced with Gene Kelly in *Singing in the Rain*. I could relate to her dark hair and her long legs. When we met her hair was colored lighter but she was still the epitome of womanly beauty and grace. Every inch a star.

Linda: Cyd Charisse was married to singer Tony Martin, they played a lot of the same places we appeared, like the Executive Inn. Since we were on the same circuit, periodically they were coming in after we finished someplace or going out before we arrived.

During this gig at the Thunderbird, my family paid us another one of their impromptu visits. I had started dating a man who worked at Caesars Palace, we were about to go out after the show when, without warning, my father appeared in the hallway. Boy I was surprised.

When Dad saw my date, he got pretty upset because this fellow was drop-dead gorgeous, dressed in a white three-piece suit. There was no way dad wanted me getting involved with anyone. We abandoned our plans for the evening and, after my date left, my dad chased me through the hotel lecturing me about taking my career seriously or start thinking about coming home.

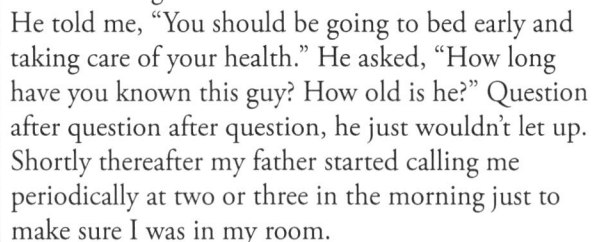

He told me, "You should be going to bed early and taking care of your health." He asked, "How long have you known this guy? How old is he?" Question after question after question, he just wouldn't let up. Shortly thereafter my father started calling me periodically at two or three in the morning just to make sure I was in my room.

Bottom photo: Dad with Linda.

Stronger

Lee Hale, musical director, *The Dean Martin Show*: NBC gave up on our variety show in 1974, Carol Burnett was the only one continuing on and then, a couple of years after we stopped, she did as well.
The public didn't like variety anymore, I think they'd seen enough of it. It was so saturated in the sixties and seventies, there were so many variety shows on the air.
The reason people liked variety shows was that they were seeing the big stars in their homes that they couldn't pay to see in theaters and nightclubs. That was what variety was all about. But then we exhausted it, nobody knew what to put in there. The roasts were very popular so that took over for Dean. Plus he was losing his energy, too.

Ed Robertson, entertainment journalist, host of *TV Confidential*: This was the tail end of the variety show era. The fact that Dean switched from the standard musical comedy skits to doing the celebrity roasts each week showed things were changing. And it was the last vestiges of the Rat Pack era.

Neil Daniels, former NBC VP and founder Dean Martin Fan Center: To clear songs, to produce a variety show, is way more expensive than creating one set and having people walk up to a microphone. Greg Garrison came out of comedy, he wasn't a person who knew music very well. With the Roasts he had more control over that. Dean's ratings were starting to decline, times were changing. There was a Smokey Robinson special that Dean appeared on and he was so out of place on that special because it just wasn't his element.

Maria: We were disappointed about the format change. Greg's office told us we would be doing musical specials in the future but first they were focusing on celebrity roasts—comedy, without the musical numbers. Our group didn't seem to fit in with this new direction of television.
We missed doing the weekly TV series but we had so much touring on our schedule that we kept very busy. In the meantime, we opened for some big stars in some glamorous

venues and that was very gratifying.
During this period Susie and Deborah announced that they were leaving the group to pursue other goals. Linda and I were also wondering if we should stay with The Golddiggers or branch out and do different things.

Linda: I couldn't wrap my head around continuing in the group without Susie and Deborah, so soon after losing Lee and Robin. They were street smart compared to Maria and I and they showed us the ropes. Both of them added so much to our lives with their bold and fearless spirits. We had bonded and shared the deepest part of ourselves with one ansother and now Maria and I felt a little left out that they were moving on.

Maria: We had heard stories growing up about Philadelphia natives Frankie Avalon and Fabian being discovered by Bob Marcucci in the 1950s. He started Chancellor Records in Philly with Peter DeAngelis. Who could ever forget Frankie Avalon's recording of 'Venus'? It was one of the biggest selling hits of our youth.
Marcucci also signed Fabian and the hype Bob created before Fabian's appearance on *American Bandstand* helped launch him as a teen idol. Later on, allegations that his recording voice was enhanced caused a bit of a scandal. That just wasn't done in those days, it was considered cheating if you can imagine that. Bob Marcucci's incredible success, launching the careers of these South Philly guys, was the subject of the movie *The Idolmaker*.
Could he do the same for us?
I found out that he had an office in Los Angeles so I gave his office a call and Linda and I went to meet him. We sang an original song that I wrote called, 'Music of Earth.' He liked our blend and we talked about our experiences and musical directions for recording. Then we told him that we had a beautiful sister at home who sings and we showed him a picture of our family.
He pointed to our brother John and asked, "Does he sing?" and we said, "Of course, everybody in our family sings!" He told us he would be interested in hearing him. He thought our brother was good looking and told us to prepare a song with him.
Tony Orlando and Dawn were very big at the time, Bob Marcucci was interested in doing something similar with us. He thought it was easier

Photo: Fabian.

for a guy to become a star because girls are more loyal fans than guys. We told our parents about our meeting and they told us to come home. They were always telling us to come home but this time it was to get our brother ready for show business. We weren't sure what we were getting ourselves into but then again, we never were.

Linda: Our brother John was tall and good looking, that's for sure, but we hadn't heard him sing much. When we got home and told him about the interest in our becoming a singing trio with him, he was not at all interested. Maria and I persuaded him into learning one song with us, a Hall and Oates song, 'How Long Has This Been Going On?' It was like pulling teeth getting him to rehearse but he turned out to be a very good singer. We had a fantastic blend but after a few days he just gave up on the idea.

Maria: Linda and I decided to go back to LA and stick around a while longer with The Golddiggers. Our two year contract was ending. We were glad because it had stated that we couldn't make any personal appearances away from the group. From this point on, we made verbal commitments to take part in the tours ahead of us. We didn't necessarily trust Greg but we had a business relationship of integrity with him and with Lee Hale. The fact that we had the option to walk away, also gave us a sense of liberation. Greg Garrison seemed to lose interest in the group, so Lee Hale took over the casting and picked two new girls primarily for their talent.
I felt good about this transition and Lee's artistic control of the group. He used to perform himself and could understand our need to grow as artists. I could sense his enthusiasm when he wrote special material for us. He always looked satisfied as he watched the choreography unfold and our act take shape. This gave me a sense of pride too.

> **Lee Hale, Musical Director, *The Dean Martin Show*:** Greg was always there but if I insisted Peggy be in the group because she had a great voice he probably did take my word for that. Wendy had a great voice too but she was kind of cute. She was a bit shorter than the other girls. Both of them, I think, got Greg's approval and mine but I probably pressed a little for both of them.

Photo: John Alberici & Dawn - (sisters Darlene, Maria and Linda).

When Greg would say, "Okay, you can have a new arrangement and have a choreographer stage it," he'd put up some money for that. That didn't happen very often, I have to say, but when it did it was fun to rehearse.

Wendy Kimball, Golddigger 1974-1976: My audition was held at a very famous New York studio, it was in the summer. I'd gone to the beach that day and when I came home there was a big ad for the Golddiggers in one of the trade papers. I almost didn't go, I never thought I stood a chance but my mom said, "Oh, go in, you never know."
I was hired on the spot—that was the very first and last time that ever happened to me. That never happens, it's very rare.
Deborah Pratt and Susan Buckner were leaving, two very tall girls. When Lee Hale hired me, he was certainly hiring against type. I was a ninety-two-pound blond, very small, about five feet and a half. I'm the shortest Golddigger they ever had. I was shocked I was hired. I'm sure the other girls were as well.
Three days later I was at the NBC studios watching the California auditions. I watched Peggy Gohl get hired. I knew the minute she walked in the room that they were going to hire her. She's a comedian, she's adorable. She's like a combination of Mitzi Gaynor and Carol Channing.

Peggy Gohl, Golddigger 1974-1991: I'm about five years older than Linda, I was actually told not to give my age when I joined. I was twenty-four. I had been in the business for about nine years; I'd done Ellie in *Showboat* with Mickey Rooney, I was in *Damn Yankees* with Gwen Verdon and Ray Walston. To make a long story longer, I was on *The Dean Martin Show* in 1969 when I was nineteen years old with a group called The Kids Next Door, they were a derivative of The Young Americans. We did 'This Is My Once a Year Day' to this whole choreographed number on Hoppity Hops, those big, inflatable balls that kids bounced around on. There were fifteen of us and Dean came out bouncing on a ball at the end of the bit. His ball popped and he reacted to it by saying, "Oh, those are my wife's jewels!" And the censors cut that out!

Wendy Kimball, Golddigger 1974-1976: Peggy and I became new friends because we had just been hired. We went to see the Golddiggers' show at the Thunderbird prior to learning the routine. I was just blown away. How could you not be blown away by six stunners who could sing and dance? I couldn't believe I was with this group!

Maria: Greg and Lee told us that they were going to give us new numbers to perform that would highlight our individual talents. We didn't know if we should believe them or not until we saw the music. Lee Hale had written us a sensational 'Showstoppers Medley,' a salute to the leading ladies of music, past and present. The song selections were some of my favorites. Listening to them woke up the musical comedy part of me that had been stifled.
When Wendy, our new tiny beauty with the mighty voice, sang 'Over the Rainbow' she sounded just like Judy Garland. It was unbelievable. Peggy sang the song, 'Everything's Coming Up Roses'—"Curtain up, light the lights..." and she was just as dynamic as Ethel Merman. We said, "Okay, things may be changing for the better." I appreciated Peggy and Wendy's sense of humor, they had that New York gypsy persona. They could get down a little bit and that made rehearsals more fun.

Peggy Gohl, Golddigger 1974-1991: Wendy had the talent to become a big star. Her voice was incredibly unique. She could imitate Judy Garland, Barbra Streisand, and could have been a Broadway star or a great recording artist.

Linda: Peggy and Wendy both had big voices and big hearts. I liked them right away. Peggy was so funny. She was self-deprecating when it came to her looks, which was charming at first, but she sometimes took it a little too far. When it came to her personality and talent, though, Peg seemed very self-assured. She belted out her songs with abandon and played up her comedic skills to the hilt.

Peggy Gohl, Golddigger 1974-1991: I had two faces, on and off. The other girls were beauties when they woke up but I had to work at it. My face was in my makeup bag. I think my legs were my best physical attribute.

Linda: We were all excited about the new focus for the act. There was a sophisticated gown made for each of us and some great music was added. Lee Hale was very creative, he was in his element. He wrote a spectacular medley of country hits for us in addition to the showstoppers medley of songs from Broadway and Hollywood. There were two versions of that medley, an eight minute and a twelve minute version. The best part was, Lee had several solo spots picked especially for our voices. He gave me a Julie Andrews number and gave Maria a Barbra Streisand song. We started getting rave notices for the new act and the reviewers were starting to pick us out individually as singers. That's what we had been working toward. If you want to have longevity in the business you have to grow your talent.

Some people were a little taken aback by the newly revamped Golddigger group and wanted the old dancing in 'go-go boots' group back but we had to get with the times. There was still plenty of choreography and movement in the show but now we were primarily a vocal group.

Maria: From that time on, reviewers were calling us the showstopping Golddiggers. We were finally being respected for our talent and showmanship. That was something I was proud to represent and a good reason for Linda and I to stay in the group a little longer.

Sylvia Bangert; The Golddiggers, Sparks Nugget: *The dynamic Golddiggers burst on stage doing 'I Am Woman' with all the spirit and sparkle anyone could ask for. Costumed in glittery outfits with a faint harem flavor, they swirl around on the stage with smooth vivacious choreography while they sing away, taking turns as lead vocalists. But it's not just tinsel. They have good voices and good material as a solid base for* *all this eye appeal. The first routine is a country medley, well done and enjoyable. It's followed by a series of songs associated with prominent Broadway heroines, covering 'Lullaby of Broadway' to 'On A Clear Day,' and tributes to femme singers, groups like the Andrews Sisters and individuals like Liza and Barbra, and the entire segment is excellent. They sing briefly of 'The Age of Aquarius' and of 'Jesus Christ Superstar.' In short, there is a little bit of almost everything and the show is almost breathtaking, in its fast paced impact. The Golddiggers were loudly acclaimed opening night.*

Linda with Patti Pivarnik.

Linda: We took the new act on the road and returned to places like the MGM in Vegas, the Executive Inn in Indiana, The Fairmonts in Dallas, Atlanta and New Orleans, The Queen E. in Montreal, the Beverly Hills Supper Club in Kentucky and the Sparks Nugget in Nevada. We enjoyed new venues in California, Texas, Atlantic City, New York and North Carolina. It was a whirlwind of touring. In the middle of all this, it was nice to land in familiar territory with our friends Bobby Goldsboro and his group at the Nugget. Watching his show and hearing his soothing vocals always mellowed me. His repertoire included 'Honey,' 'Watching Scotty Grow' and my favorite, 'Summer the First Time.' When Bobby sang this toward the end of his show some of us would go into the wings and watch. The sensuality of the song, the arrangement and the lighting were incredible. We couldn't get enough of it. Bobby knew how to set a mood, most people didn't realize what an amazing musician he was. Our dynamic opening act was a good balance to his warm, personal style of show, giving the audience a nice variety of entertainment.

We stayed pretty busy on the road with the new act. At one point our tour brought us close to Los Angeles when we played Magic Mountain billed with Kenny Rogers and the First Edition. We met Kenny in his dressing room after the show and it wasn't long before he was venting to us about the biz. He opened up to us like we were long lost friends about how he had to "break out," take it to a different level. Kenny said, "I've had it; I'm done with this." He was tired of spinning his wheels with the First Edition and wanted to strike out on his own.

When we had time off and we were in Los Angeles, Maria and I would hang out with Susie and Deborah, they had already made some connections in the 'business.' They graciously shared what they had learned. They also shared their apartment with us. One day Susie told me about a commercial audition for toothpaste that she was going to, "You would be perfect for this, come with me." I never would dream of crashing her audition but she was persistent. Commercial auditions were hard to come by and I could have been competition. Susie didn't look at it that way, she wanted to share the experience with me. She was such a beautiful, free, open spirit. She exuded adventure, blessings and love. I loved to be around her. Everybody loved being around Susie; however, neither of us got the commercial.

Sammy Davis Jr. used to like to come around to hang out at Susie and Deborah's apartment. I always assumed it was because of their fantastic personalities, Maria and I were shy in comparison. I was surprised when Susie said to me, "Sammy has a crush on you." He was a gentleman so it wasn't obvious to me. Sammy was a cool, fun loving guy who loved to laugh. He laughed with his whole body; it would move all around. He would sometimes slap his leg too. He was into goofy physical comedy like pretending to trip over some invisible object and almost crashing into someone, or the furniture, whatever. He would have spells of random off the wall craziness. I sensed that Sammy was just looking for friendship, for young people to hang out with. He was very young at heart.

Sammy Davis, Jr., source unknown: *For a long time I didn't like me. I didn't like what I had made up. I became Dr. Frankenstein and the Monster. I was Jekyll and Hyde. I created both. Nobody told Henry Jekyll to go mess with those drugs and mix up this potion. Nobody told Dr. Frankenstein to go put this Monster together. They did it of their own free will, and they created something that they could no longer control, and subsequently it destroyed them. I was lucky that it didn't destroy me.*

Susan Buckner, Golddigger 1973-1974: Sammy would sometimes drop by our place for lunch, he used to grind his jaw and teeth when he talked and sang. It was our thrill but look what he got—our company! I was very comfortable in his presence; he was easy and fun. Quick to laugh. Wilt Chamberlain used to come by quite often too.
Sammy thought Linda was a Kim Novak lookalike. He called me "Buckner" and Deborah "High Yellow." I had never heard of that term before, it meant her skin was fair.
Sammy always brought his appetite. Of course, we were not as skilled at cheffing back then. What would we serve, corn flakes? More than likely it was something out of a box.

Maria: I thought whipping up some fresh Guacamole or dip and chips would make me the hostess with the mostess but that was short lived when I found out how passionate Sammy was about food. He actually packed special

cooking equipment with him when he traveled on the road. Sammy was always positive and very upbeat when he was around us. He loved talking about food and was very enthusiastic as he described his favorite chicken wings. His casual personality made it easy for me to cast away my timid side as we spoke about food, family and friends.
Of course, I was all ears when Sammy told tales about the Rat Pack, especially his close friends Dean and Frank Sinatra. Besides their carousing together, I learned they had another side to them which came from a deep sense of caring.

Linda: Sammy never ran out of stories about Frank and Dean. When he talked about them his face would get soft, reflecting the love and respect he had for them. He painted a picture of the Rat Pack that was different from what I had heard and read about. They were not all about smoking, drinking and hell raising. I never knew they did so many good things for people and for various charities.
As Sammy chatted with us, my mind went to wondering, what's his real story? Why is he here? Is he looking for a date, respect, acceptance? All I can say for sure is, underneath it all, Sammy felt he was never fully appreciated by the powers that be, never given the kind of credit he should have been accorded for his contribution to the entertainment industry. Let me say, I think he was right. To me he was the ultimate triple threat performer, an adept singer, dancer and actor.

Deborah Pratt, Golddigger 1973-1974:
One night after we finished performing, we were invited to see Sammy's late show. He was an incredible showman and knew how to capture an audience and fill them with his light. Seeing him do 'Mr. Bojangles' was one of those entertainment events that you get once in a lifetime. After the show we were invited to his dressing room. It was the first time I remember seeing a real SUPERSTAR dressing room. It was one of the big penthouse suites at the Sands with a winding staircase from the second floor backed by a two story glass window with the Vegas strip stretching out like a galaxy of lights outside.

Helen Costa, wife of Sinatra's musical arranger Don Costa:
I knew Sammy Davis Jr. back when I performed at a club called The Riviera in the early fifties that was just across the bridge in Jersey. It was a beautiful club, they had a top that opened up when the people

danced. That's where I met Don, he was doing arrangements for Connie Francis.

I was in the chorus and Sammy was dating one of the girls in the chorus and even then he liked blondes. She was a real blonde. He was very sweet and very nice then, he was with his father and his uncle at that time.

His personality changed along with his history, every time I saw him he was somebody different. He was terrific, he was nice, and then he was rotten and mean. I remember one incident in the early 1970s where he was on the phone to his wife Altovise and he was being verbally abusive. Who know what goes on? I had the feeling that he really didn't like himself, he was small and not attractive and all that but he had this great talent.

He was always nice to me and Don, very congenial. His biggest hit 'Candy Man' was Don's arrangement.

Sam Kashner, *Vanity Fair* magazine, April 1999: *The late 1960s and the 1970s were unkind to Davis in other ways. He was out of sync with the new music. For the first time, he started chasing trends instead of making them, recording pop tunes far inferior to the velvet standards he had established earlier: 'The Candy Man' and 'Talk to the Animals' instead of 'Hey There' and 'What Kind of Fool Am I?' Sadly, that's the Davis we remember: Nehru jackets, love beads, hugging Richard Nixon, fawning over Liz and Dick on his short-lived television show. He even showed up in hot pants at a formal dinner party given by Mary and Jack Benny, two pillars of Hollywood's old society.*

Maria: Sammy had a magnificent voice that was underestimated by so many. You didn't expect that thrilling voice to come out of him. He wasn't the leading man type, on par with Dean Martin and Frank Sinatra, but his talent was huge, he had a hunger to please his audience and that was very, very engaging.

Linda: Susie, Deborah, Maria and I met a manager who wanted to record the four of us and call us "Fantasy." He had big plans for us. We would be the next big pop sensation! We were so excited. We thought, this was it, our big break. He had promo pictures made of us and meetings set up with producers but when Maria and I told our dad about it, he didn't like the idea or the contract. He didn't want us to do it, so we didn't. Maria and I were disappointed but Susie and Deborah were very upset. Not too long after, though, someone reputable in the industry told them that we had done the right thing, so they were relieved and grateful in the end. God works in mysterious ways—and through parents.

Whenever Maria and I worked near our hometown, it was so exhilarating. We were all over the local newspapers. They made us feel bigger than life. This was especially true when we appeared at the Steel Pier Theater in Atlantic City.

Maria: The Steel Pier was the home of the Miss America Pageant. My mom sang there too, on *American Bandstand* in the early-sixties. The famed boardwalk was hustling and bustling with amusement rides and swarming with vendors. Memories of my childhood came alive with the smell of freshly roasted peanuts filling the air. I followed that salty aroma to a pack of giggling children pointing to Mr. Peanut dancing a jig with a cane in both hands. We stayed in an old quality hotel near the boardwalk where they advertised the Diving Horse. When we were kids that was the big attraction, a horse that dove forty feet into a tank of water. They had been doing it since the 1890s.

John B. Abbott, Jr., *The Voice*: *I remember anxiously getting bleacher seats to see the Diving Horse. As we took our seats, the horse, with a fellow named Arnette Webster (clad in a rubber wet suit) on its back, was about to jump from a platform roughly 30 feet high into a pool.*
I recall staring at the odd sight of a horse standing as calmly as you please on a platform above a pool just like the kind I swam in at my Aunt Anne and Uncle Leo's house. To a recorded drum roll and cymbal crash, Webster urged the horse forward, and the two fell through space to make the biggest splash I'd ever seen— even bigger than the cannonballs my uncle could make in his own pool! Wow! And then both horse and rider surfaced, though for the life of me, I can't recall how they got out of the pool.

Linda: After our show at the Steel Pier I went out the back door, I didn't know that my sister and everyone else was waiting for me in the front. I walked into a mob of fans, for the first time in my life I felt like I was in danger, like I could be crushed. There were people grabbing at me, pulling at me, I felt I had to stay there for almost an hour to sign everything they put in front of me or something bad could happen. I got to experience what some stars must go through and it was horrifying. There wasn't enough money in the world to make me want to have a life like that.

Maria: I must admit, when Linda told me about the fans rushing her for autographs like she was a star I thought it sounded cool!

Louis, Bob, Dean & Mike

Maria: We appeared with the great Louis Prima and Sam Butera and the Witnesses at the enormous Nanuet Theatre-Go-Round in New York.

Mark Glick, Nanuet Theater-Go-Round stagehand: The Nanuet Theater-Go-Round was in the suburbs of New York City, it opened in November of 1973 and closed in November of 1978. It was an exact duplicate of the Westbury Music Fair; it was partly owned by the mob connected comedian Corbett Monica.
The Nanuet had your Las Vegas type of performers there, everybody from Louis Prima to Pat Cooper to Liberace to Sergio Franchi to The Jackson Five. They would perform from Tuesday to Sunday, maybe two shows on Saturday and Sunday.
There were people like Buddy Hackett, who was such a nice guy. One night after a show he took all the ushers and usherettes out to one of the local diners to have a snack with him.
Then there were stars like Jerry Lewis, he was really nasty backstage but I loved his stupid slapstick type of humor. He wasn't doing very well attendance-wise, he would come offstage and say, "I don't care who's out there, I've had enough!" Meanwhile, I thought he was good but he was a really mean guy.
Sammy Davis, Jr. would come in at six for an eight o'clock show, sometimes he'd have the patch over his eye, and the aroma of marijuana from under the door of his dressing room would fill the entire backstage area.
And the Golddiggers—my friends and I were seventeen, eighteen years old and here were these beautiful young ladies just a few years older than us prancing around on stage, it was wonderful. It was a fun place to work, we would have worked there for free. I got to smoke a joint with Cheech and Chong!
A couple of years after Nanuet opened up, about nine miles away

across the Hudson River, another theater opened which was a little more accessible to New York City, The Westchester Premier.

Maria: We loved watching Louis Prima's wild show. Sam Butera and the Witnesses were not the typical band, oh no, they were entertainers. They did one humorous bit after another and were skilled musicians, cleverly putting a new twist on a standard song.

They were a fun bunch of guys that didn't try to hit on you or that kind of thing. Louis, on the other hand, he seemed to be pretty much of a flirt. I don't know if he wanted his flirting to be taken seriously or not but he did give the impression of being on the prowl. Was it just his image? I don't know.

He wasn't a romantic singer, that's for sure. I don't even remember him singing one ballad during his show. Still, Louis Prima was an amazing performer, one of the most exciting Italian-American entertainers of all time and the support of Sam Butera and the Witnesses gave him that extra spark.

> **Keith Spera, *The Times-Picayune*:** "Louis' ace-in-the-hole was Sam Butera," said Gia Prima, the fifth of Louis' five wives and the singer in his band from 1962 to 1975. "That animal attraction that they had, with Sam's honking sax and Louis' jumping and jiving—without Sam, Louis couldn't have pulled it off."
> "Every night before the shows, you could hear Sam in the dressing room running scales and fussing over his reeds," Gia Prima recalled. "He wanted everything to be perfect. I don't think there's another tenor sax man that could touch him."

Tony Horowitz, trumpet player for Louis Prima's band 1974-1975: In the early 1950s Louis Prima had retired from the big band and all that, he and Keely Smith were living in New Orleans and they went out to Las Vegas on a vacation. Louis was looking the town over and he saw what the lounges were all about; basically a lounge at that time was where you sat, had a couple of drinks, bet your keno tickets and the entertainment usually consisted of an accordion, a clarinet, a bass player and that was it. And they were playing music that made elevator music sound like heavy metal.

So Louis had this idea. He called Sam Butera, whose father had a butcher shop in New Orleans, and Amado "Motsey" Rodrigues and some other New Orleans boys. Keely was their singer and Louis paid them to rehearse five or six days a week until they got really tight. He wanted go in there with a jump, jive and wail outfit—nobody was

"There's nothing like walking out and watching the people get turned on."—Louis Prima

doing that. When Louis presented the idea to the powers that be at the Sahara they said, "You are stark, raving mad." So Louis told them, "I'll show you how mad I am, I'll four-wall the joint." That meant he leased the room and took the door and the drinks, everything that was spent in there went across Louis' hand. However, he had to pay rent on the lounge, he had to pay the cocktail waitresses, he had to pay the bartenders, and he had to pay for the booze. This was quite a gamble and it paid off in spades. Louis became an icon.

I first met Louis and Sam in 1963, this was after he divorced Keely and married Gia Maione [the band's new lead singer that he met at the Latin Casino in Cherry Hill, New Jersey]. I was like 17 years old, I was with Jimmy Wakely's band at the time and we swapped sets with The Witnesses at Harrah's in Lake Tahoe so I made friends with Sam Butera, the Italian Troubadour "Rolly Dee" DiIorio, and the rest of the guys in the band.

Now punch your clock ahead to 1974. I got a call from Sam, apparently he remembered me. Trumpet player Morgan Thomas, drummer Jimmy Vincent, bass player Rolly Dee, and keyboard player Bruce Zarka had decided to leave The Witnesses and start an act called The New Goofers. They were an incredible comedy act as well as playing good music—but they would do the routine while swinging from a trapeze.

Sam asked me if I'd like to join the new Prima band. Having just finished playing lead trumpet and recording with Ray Charles I was looking to go with Count Basie's orchestra.

But the opportunity to play with Louis Prima? He was a whole different animal. I knew he wasn't getting any younger, this was a one time shot.

Butera had already booked another drummer; he asked me about a bass player so I told him, "Yeah, I got a kid in L.A. who can fit the bill." He hired a Las Vegas keyboard player and a Vegas guitar player and away we went.

We hooked up with various acts when we were doing the summer theater circuit, whether it was Sergio Franchi, or Jerry Vale or The Golddiggers.

It was a wonderful experience being with The Golddiggers. They held

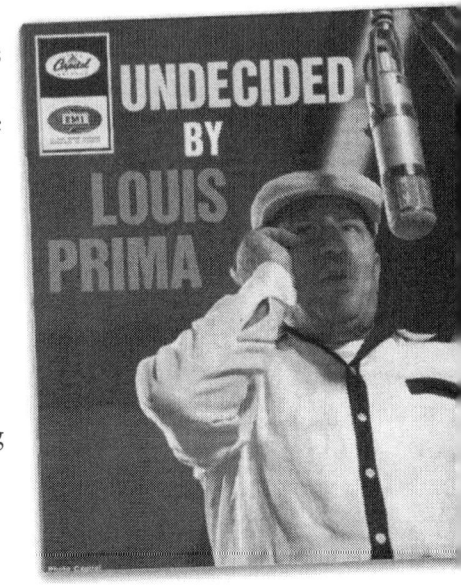

Photos from the Nanuet Theater-Go-Round on 9/24/74.

165

forth like nobody's business, they sang, they danced, they were terrific. You're talking the major leagues here.

> ***Philadelphia Inquirer*, 1974:** *What's all this crazy talk about art? The hell with art, whatever art is. The audience has paid to have a good time. This is the Prima formula. Clearly it works because the audience has a good time.*
>
> **Greg Moore, guitarist for Louis Prima and Frank Sinatra, *Evansville Courier & Press*:** *Sinatra and Prima were very close friends and Sinatra walked into our recording sessions many times. There was an Italian rule back then that good friends did not take musicians from one another. When Prima got too sick to play and eventually died, Sinatra's people called me up and told me that Frank wanted me to tour with him.*
> *Frank Sinatra was like two people. When he was sober, he was the nicest, most friendly guy you could ever want to meet. However, when he wasn't sober, he could walk by you like he didn't even know you.*

Maria: Louis Prima and Sam Butera's show had so much energy that it was contagious. The music coming from the stage and into our dressing room kept us buzzing after the show. I must say, it was utterly delightful to hear Louis and the band chant out the hit, "Oh, Marie!" Louis sang with abandonment and with complete disregard to any sentiment while the audience cheered him on. Even though there was no alcohol drinking during these theatre in the round shows the audience could get pretty rowdy. When Louis humorously sang, "Oh, Mama, zooma, zooma, bacala…." the audience would heat up, which wasn't hard to do on these smoldering summer nights.
Sometimes, after Louis' part of the show, we would all do a little socializing with him and his entourage. A few times, Wendy's mother came down to see us perform. I could see Wendy and her mom were very close, she was classy and attractive. It looked like Louis Prima was interested in her, we had lots of giggles about that.
It's true that music sets the tone. Onstage there was nothing serious about Louis Prima and his musician sidekicks but as entertainers, they were serious about their profession.

Linda: Louis Prima's show was like a big jam session with wild trumpet, organ and drum solos. All the musicians had amazing talent and showmanship, each had an important part in the show, talking, jiving as well as playing. Louis was a fantastic trumpet player, masterful at delivering jokes and as a comic singer. His Italian novelty songs endeared him to the Italian Americans in the crowd.

During 'Just A Gigolo' the guys in the band joined him with a shout out, echoing, "Gigolo, Gigolo." Prima's 'I Ain't Got Nobody' was priceless. When he sang the part, "I'm so sad and lonley, sad and lonely, sad and lonely…," it was more of a tease, a reaching out to all the sad and lonely people in the audience to lighten up and they did.

He knew how to bring everyone into his party. He was insane, in constant motion, dancing and moving around the stage. Just when you thought the show was out of control, the band would prove themselves with some serious jazz or funk. Louis was the master of his music; he knew exactly what he was doing and precisely what he wanted. It was one of the most unusual musical acts anyone ever saw. The show gave the appearance of being loose when actually it was very tight.

Tony Horowitz, trumpet player for Louis Prima's band 1974-1975:
With every other band I was with we all traveled in airplanes. However, Louis would not fly. I told him that I had been over in Europe with Ray Charles, "You're a big star over there, you gotta go and cash in on this. You're an icon."

He said, "Oh no, Chief don't fly. If they build a bridge from New York to Europe, you know, Chief'll go."

I said, "You are nuts, you could have a half pint of scotch, knock

Photo: Louis Prima at the Nanuet Theater-Go-Round on 9/24/74.

yourself out on the airplane and go to sleep."

"Oh no, Chief don't do spirits anymore."

Louis always spoke of himself in the third person. Some people would call it ego, I called it an eccentricity. Frank Sinatra always spoke of himself in the first person; Elvis Presley, Ray Charles, every big star I worked with spoke of themselves in the first person except for Louis. A year or so later we were getting ready to open at the Playboy Club in L.A. and I'd called all my friends and contacted various jazz critics and said, "Hey, I'm going to comp you myself. You have to see Louis Prima." On the fifteenth of September, 1975 Louis' manager Carlton called me and said the Playboy gig was cancelled. I said, "You've got to be kidding. What the hell is happening short of The Chief going in the tank?" He said, "That's it. Louis just went into a coma."

Maria: After the tour we had a little time off so our dad and some of the family picked us up for a quick visit to our home in Pennsylvania. We visited Philadelphia composer Russ Faith to let him hear the songs we were writing. He encouraged us to keep writing while we were on the road, so that's what we did.

Linda: We were still thinking of our future, so we spent most of our time on the road writing songs. We even started carrying around this gigantic reel to reel tape recorder to record them, it must have weighed 50 pounds.

Maria: We had to carry it on board the plane, which almost made us late for our connecting flights. Here we were running through the airport with this monstrous thing. We had to stop every few feet because it was so heavy.... run, run, run.... clunk! We would barely catch our breath and then, run, run, run again—and we did this in high heels!

> **Stuart S. White, *Great Falls Tribune*, Aug. 4, 1974:** *The girls, though their personalities seep subtly through in their singing and dancing, are every bit a team, a matched set (curiously or perhaps by design, the vibrant sextet contains a brace each of blondes, redheads and black-haired beauties). Every move, from sexy strutting and furious twirling to mock chorus line, was choreographed and executed in perfect unison. Even the six voices were matched, almost interchangeable—a notable difference between theirs and the act that followed [Rich Little]. When the Golddiggers perform it is a show for both ear and eye. The girls are well in command of every singing mood.*

"If I have to lay an egg for my country, I'll do it." – Bob Hope

Linda: We went out on a college tour with Bob Hope in November of 1974. As part of his act he would always learn about the local sports teams and would base his routine on that. It went over very well, almost the same jokes every night, but he would just change the names of the teams. Every college we went to he used to say, "This is Bob 'Texas Tech' Hope" and change the name of the school. I think he did a TV special based on the tour.

Photo clockwise from bottom: Peggy, Wendy, Bob Hope, Maria.

Bob Mills, writer for *The Bob Hope Specials*: Bob knew how difficult it is writing material on a regular basis, you're just churning out stuff. He knew because when he first started doing topical material in vaudeville he had to find jokes. He told me he used to sit up in hotel rooms with a guy named Wilkie Mahoney and would actually cut jokes out of humor magazines that were popular at the time like *Captain Billy's Whizbang* and *College Humor*.

Maria: Bob Hope was the supreme stand-up comic, timely and quick witted but I wouldn't call his act strenuous. When I heard he traveled with a masseur, I thought, 'Oh to be a star and afford that luxury.' I guess the masseur came in handy when Bob traveled to his prestigious golf tournaments.
When I participated in the Miss USA World pageant I remember my father warning me to stay away from Bob Hope because he had a reputation of being a little frisky with the young ladies. So I kept my distance. During this run, Bob Hope's people asked us if we wanted to take pictures with him. Of course we did! They suggested we pose on top of a car and we were glad for the photo-op. Later our office learned that the pictures were being used as publicity for a car dealership. No compensation was given…. hmmm. Bob had a generous side too and arranged to give us a lift in his private plane for the tour.

Photo clockwise from bottom: Patti, Peggy (front), Linda, Wendy, Bob Hope, Maria.

Marge Crumbaker, *Houston Post*, November 1974: *You are not going to believe this, but so help me it happened, and just like a page out of* Airport '75. *Tuesday evening, when The Golddiggers and entertainment czar Louis Gavrel were winging here from Lubbock, the door of their private plane flew open. Golddigger Linda Alberici almost was drawn through the opening. She was saved by Louis, and his arm was nearly broken in the effort. There was absolute bedlam for a moment. The plane made an emergency landing at Bryan and they got the door closed. By Wednesday Linda and the other Diggers had calmed down, and they were happily lunching at Adam's Apple. They're starring in the Thursday Hofheinz Pavilion show with Bob Hope.*

Maria: Remember how somebody's eyes popped out in the movie *Airport '75*? When the door flew open Wendy hid her eyes, she was afraid they'd explode! It was an older plane with the passenger seats facing each other and I was sitting across from Linda; in a panic, I grabbed her so she wouldn't fall out. Bob had this big, gigantic road manager, he was really strong and he shut and locked the door while we were in flight. We weren't too far off the ground so the cabin wasn't highly pressurized. I asked him, "Are you sure that's not going to open again?!?"

***Daily Variety*, June 11, 1975:** *Golddiggers are shapely lookers, good dancers and vocalists each getting a chance to solo. They open with 'I Am Woman,' segue into a country medley, then toss in a generous supply of show tunes. Enthusiasm greets their "Chordettes" and "Andrews Sisters" theme carbons in the fast moving 30-minute package. Charles Sanford conducts the pretty party.*

Linda: The road, it's a rough life. Television's hard in itself but it's nothing like going out on tour. It was grueling, flying every week to a new place. At times I would be wandering around a mall and forget what town I was in. For another thing, it was really hard to stay healthy on the road because you had to eat whatever they had in the hotel, you couldn't get your exercise in the morning, your schedule was all thrown around. You're so tired with the time changes and everything. It was tough, often our days off from performing were spent traveling. I was a little disappointed when Colleen left the group in 1974. The original eight were slowly dwindling away. Now there were only three of us left. Colleen was very wholesome, she became uncomfortable with show business life. She also felt God had another calling for her. I thought she would eventually delve deeper into Christian ministry.

Patty Booth had been a Golddigger a few years before with a different group and now she was back again to replace Colleen. In my eyes, she was a woman of the world. I don't know if she was older than the rest of us or just had a lot of experience. She had been a singer in a big Vegas show and seemed to know a lot about the ins and outs of Vegas and the Greg Garrison organization. She had beautiful porcelain skin and platinum blonde hair with delicate features. She was nice but had a no nonsense way about her. I was a little wary of her at first; I thought she might be a spy for Greg's office.

There were a few comings and goings in the group during this time. We had one girl who joined our group but didn't even last a year because she did not have the physical strength and stamina to do two one-hour shows each night and travel. Sometimes personalities don't mix. There was another girl who didn't stay for too long; she, ah.... well.... thought she would like to date me. There, I said it.

Wendy Kimball, Golddigger 1974-1976: We used to see Kenny Rogers a lot, for some reason our paths crossed whenever we would tour the Fairmont hotels. They had nightclubs in San Francisco, New Orleans, Atlanta, Dallas; and Kenny Rogers was sometimes in town when we were so we'd have breakfast together.

Maria: We were on the same circuit with Kenny Rogers; a lot of the stars, like The Supremes, Waylon Jennings and Johnny Carson, worked the Fairmont chain. They offered patrons the opportunity to be wined and dined in their area and see the stars up close. Compared to the humongous showrooms in Vegas, the Fairmont showrooms gave us the chance to develop a rapport with the audience and connect on a more personal level. Communicating feelings through a song and reaching out to the public fulfilled a deep need inside of me. When you're living out of a suitcase the relationship with the audience becomes so important. However, sometimes our fans got too close. One night before the show we noticed some of our costumes were out of place. One of the girls became frantic when she couldn't find her hot pants outfit. Our names were written inside our costumes so we all began to check them until we were interrupted by a gasp. Someone had written on the crotch of one of the hot pants the words "I was here!"

Linda: That incident scared me a little and put me on my guard. While on the road Rich Little and Kenny Rogers both asked me out. I didn't date either of them, I was afraid to go out with these guys because I knew they were too slick for me. We knew in our hearts that we weren't really show biz people.

I met Johnny Bench, he was from Cincinnati and kind of knew Patti so I went out with him a couple of times. He asked me to marry him on the second date. I didn't think we had that much of a rapport so I thought it was a come-on line. Although probably not because he ended up getting married a few months later. He had that in his head, I guess.

Maria: We loved *The Wild Wild West* growing up and I thought Robert Conrad was so cute. I met him in person while he was drinking and I thought, "Oh, I'm sorry, that's not the idol I had in mind."

We were looking for somebody with the same values we had. I was very apprehensive about dating celebrities on the road. I thought they might just want to go out with one of The Golddiggers. But that was just an image I put on like a costume. Anyway, celebrities are so busy with their career and I was on the road most of the time. How could we have a relationship; what would we really have in common to start something? That said, it was interesting to meet the celebrities that Linda and I had crushes on when we were growing up. Some of them were a disappointment to see in person but not our heart throb, James Darren. We saw him backstage at a Jerry Lewis Telethon and I just had to go up to him and say, "I loved you when I was a little girl." He gave me a curious look, winked and said, "What about now?" I tried to answer him but I was just so flustered I couldn't talk, I just had to walk away!

Wendy Kimball, Golddigger 1974-1976: I was kind of innocent and very sheltered living in the suburbs of New York. I couldn't believe all the celebrities that wanted to meet The Golddiggers. We had a lot of male groupies after the show.

Linda: I once had a young man follow me around on the road for a few months. He wanted to break into show business and was under the delusion that I could help him. Automatically people would assume that since we were part of a big name group we had connections. Actually being on the road so much kept us from making the connections we needed to make it in the business. Somewhere along the way I was able to convince him of that and finally got rid of him. What a relief, even though he was mannerly the whole thing was very creepy.

Maria: Yes, there were quite a few men around attempting their various ploys on us. My father used to say, "You can't accept gifts from men. It's an old Mafia trick, they make you feel indebted to them and then they act like they own you."

Linda: I didn't understand what that really meant. In fact, I had a man offer me a mink coat. He bought it for his girlfriend and, in the meantime, they broke up. He promised, "This coat comes with no strings attached; if you don't want it, I'm just going to give it to the Salvation Army." In spite of what my dad taught me, I thought it would be okay and I accepted the luxurious mink. I had no idea that it's human nature for a person to feel they have some kind of claim on you if you accept their extravagant offering, no matter what they might tell you. Consequently, I learned you can't accept large gifts.

There's so much you have to be aware of when you're in that kind of situation. We were dumb and innocent in a lot of ways. I had some surprising offers from men, even a couple of big stars. Their come-on line was always, "I can set you up in a penthouse for the rest of your life," that kind of thing. That would be how they'd ask me out on a date. I supposed it worked for them in the past.

I thought, "In a penthouse? What do you do in a penthouse?" I tried to visualize what you might do when you're a 'kept woman'— you hang around the penthouse, then you work out and maybe go shopping? Afterwards, you have lunch with other 'kept women' and later that day get ready for the guy when he arrives home? What about when he got tired of you? Why would anybody want to do that? This was way outside my understanding or experience.

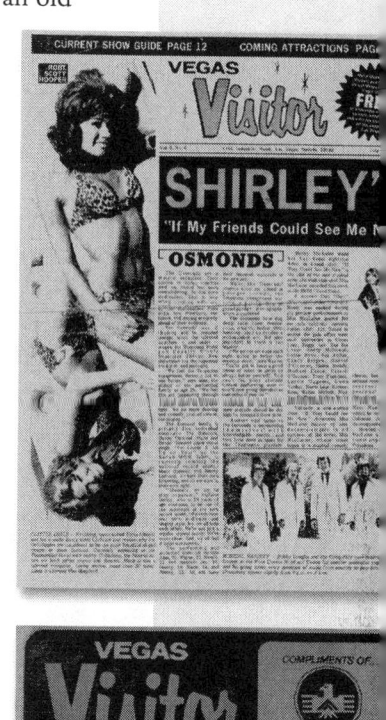

175

There were so many ways we could have gone. For example, at parties, people were always trying to shove cocaine under our noses. Thank God we never became drug addicts, it was there if we wanted, all kinds of drugs. We could easily have made that choice. There but for the grace of God....
I think our preservation also had to do with the strictness that we were raised with and, truly, we didn't want to hurt our parents. That was a strong incentive because we loved them and didn't want to disappoint them.

Maria: That's for sure! I always heard my dad in the back of my head telling me, "You're the oldest, you have to be an example to your younger brothers and sisters." What a responsibility—it was like 'Jewish guilt' but Italians get the same deal. Whatever the guilt trip was, it definitely kept Linda and I on the straight and narrow.

Earlier in our career, during our beauty contest days, Linda and I had offers to pose for *Playboy* magazine. We never considered it for a moment. We wanted to be respected as entertainers and we also wanted to find true love and get married some day.

I was living part of my dream, the life of an entertainer, but I wanted the whole dream. I wondered if I would ever meet someone of substance while traveling as a performer; probably not. Experience taught me that long distance relationships just don't work out.

After some time, I started dating our drummer, Barry. He was cool, he exercised, he had a motorcycle, he was into music, he was fun. I had a little bit of rebel in me, what can I say?

Everyone in the group knew about us but, of course, it was against Greg Garrison's rules so we kept it a secret. Barry and I were both into health foods and sometimes he traveled with a hot plate and I would cook greens or other fresh vegetables when I could. Naturally, I liked to cook with garlic and the staff would smell the food so that was a short-lived experiment.

From the back of Barry's motorcycle the lights of Sin City were more spectacular. The desert and the mountains seemed more majestic and beautiful. We rode through small towns outside the Vegas Strip that were rustic and quaint. I was seeing a different side of Vegas, where I felt the pulse of the city, outside the bondage of the casinos. Eventually, Barry and our conductor Charlie got into a tug-of-war about the music and Barry was fired. My heart was sad but my mind knew it was a natural end for us.

One thing my heart and mind could agree on was the anticipation of

Photo: The girls with Barry & Charlie.

opening for Dean and the sound of the orchestra warming up as I took a sip from Dean Martin's special drink, Martinelli's apple juice. A bottle of it was placed right outside the stage curtain alongside a few scotch glasses. When Dean made his entrance to the stage, he always carried a scotch glass filled with apple juice. Of course, he had a real drink planted in the audience!

Las Vegas Visitor, **December 5, 1975:** *Dean Martin is a tough act to compete with and who should know that better than The Golddiggers, six lovely and multi-talented ladies currently appearing with the MGM Grand's grandest star.*
The amazingly popular Dino and The Golddiggers are now in the midst of their third record setting Grand-stand together.
The problem of sharing a marquee and stage with Martin is simply the unbelievable popularity of the man. Dino is a legend, an institution, a superstar's superstar whose successes in the combined media of movies, recordings, nightclubs, and television have few, if any, equals.
While no one would be so bold to suggest that The Golddiggers will make the SRO audiences of the MGM's Celebrity Room forget "Ol' Red Eyes," the lively assemblage of beautiful ladies are a showstopping treat.

Wendy Kimball, Golddigger 1974-1976: Dean was the most beautiful man I'd ever seen. He was larger than life, he was exquisite to look at, and he seemed affable, a very nice man.
He also appeared to me to sometimes be uncomfortable with his celebrity, the way Frank wasn't and the way Sammy Davis, Jr. wasn't. There was something shy about Dean.
I can't say he didn't feel deserving of his celebrity. He got there because of his talent, his looks and his charm. But it almost seemed as if he would have been very happy just singing and going home and watching television or a football game. He didn't dig all that celebrity and glory.

Maria: Funny, I never heard Dean talk about going out on the town after our Vegas shows. Maybe he had "been there, done that" but the girls and

I were just beginning to taste the exotic flavors of Vegas nightlife. Sometimes, after we finished our opening bit for Dean, we would run offstage, hurry to our dressing room, rush out of our costumes, change into our evening outfits, sweep through the casino and into a waiting taxi to catch the headliner at another casino.

Wendy Kimball, Golddigger 1974-1976: We were like some of the girl or boy groups where you don't really know the individual names but the group itself is famous. We could get into clubs and places and dance the night away just by using the name The Golddiggers.

Maria: Dancing in the clubs was a nice outlet but I wouldn't miss the chance to see a dynamic performer work their talents on an audience. Tina Turner was an amazing live entertainer that was hot in Vegas. She was like the female Tom Jones, she just oozed animal energy.
Mitzi Gaynor was as glamorous and cute as ever. I met Mitzi backstage after her show, she's Hungarian like my mother and she looked fantastic; her figure and her high cheek bones are even more pronounced in person. I loved all the singing, dancing ladies.

Lola Falana was one of the hottest tickets on the strip and one of the most dynamic entertainers, she was Sammy Davis Jr.'s protégé.
When Elvis came to Vegas, his shows were always sold out months in advance so there was no way to sneak into the audience to see him perform after our act. Elvis' musicians were approachable though, some of us girls would socialize with them backstage after our performances. Patti was a big Elvis fan and loved his music; she even hired one of the musicians to arrange an Elvis song for her. 'The King' had amazing musical arrangements that have stood the test of time.
A couple of years later, Linda and I caught one of Elvis' last Vegas shows at the Hilton. He was the biggest thing on the strip.
I was looking forward to seeing Elvis perform live because I loved his movies. I was so disappointed, during his show he seemed like a caricature of himself. His movements seemed a little sloppy and he had a flippant attitude. For example, he told someone from the wings, "If I'm the king, hold the microphone for me while I sing." It wasn't funny. It seemed like he was mocking himself and his image. I felt really badly for Elvis that night. It was disheartening to see a legend like Elvis fall from his throne. I could see that he was on the road to his own un-doing and, not long after, he passed away.

> **Elvis Presley:** *The image is one thing and the human being is another. It's very hard to live up to an image, put it that way.*

Peggy Gohl, Golddigger 1974-1991: I saw Elvis in Atlanta at the Omni. We were in the sixth row and it was wonderful, very exciting. I wasn't an Elvis fan, Patti was into Elvis and she caught his scarf at one of his concerts. And Patti did a great Elvis, she looked like Elvis; she had black hair and she was gorgeous.
We had an Elvis Presley song in the act. We sang, "Since my baby left me...." and all the girls would smirk and our upper lips would turn up.

Maria: Vegas was losing some of its star power and glamour. The town was becoming more casual as bus loads of people were driven in to see the sights. Sometimes I would walk through the streets of Vegas just like one of the tourists. It was fun to see free shows at Circus Circus, to witness the wide-eyed children and their happy faces as they scurried around the casino clutching their little souvenirs, stopping to watch in amazement at the high-wire trapeze artists flipping and flying over their heads.

"Until we meet again, may God bless you as he has blessed me."—Elvis Presley

It seemed like every casino was advertising that their buffet was the biggest—and the cheapest. Most dining rooms offered an all-you-can-eat Prime Rib buffet dinner for less than four dollars; the Golden Gate Hotel on Freemont sold a giant Shrimp Cocktail for only a dollar.

Vegas was becoming more family friendly and that was all right with me. It was now up to the performers on the Strip to keep the ambience and allure of the early Vegas years alive, and that was my pleasure.

> ***Theater Arts* magazine:** *Everything is carefully and not so subtly engineered to keep the visitor gambling. Traffic patterns keep you in constant contact with slot machines and roulette tables. There is the endless Pavlovian jingle and bell ringing of mini-jackpots. The timeless casinos where clocks and windows are conspicuous by their absence. Or the dreary rooms in older hotel wings that keep you out in the lobby.*
>
> *But decadent it is not. That blue haired lady feeding the slot with a paper cup full of nickels in hand is with a group from a retirement village in California. Those folks whooping it up at the craps table are from an Elks Club in Ohio. Those women trying their luck at blackjack are attending a health food convention. That guy over there at the roulette wheel has a camper in the parking lot and kids over at Circus Circus. Where's the big money? The action that those* Godfather *folks went to all the trouble for? The guys out of Damon Runyon are playing in their rooms. The really high rolling Arabs and South Americans are in a private casino atop the MGM Grand.*

Maria: Montreal, Canada was beautiful but freezing in the winter. We appeared at the fabulous Queen Elizabeth Hotel for about a couple of months. We were intrigued to find out the hotel was where John Lennon and Yoko Ono conducted their Bed-In and recorded the song 'Give Peace a Chance' in 1969.

The QE had an entire city of stores with a transit system underground. Even though we did two shows a night Linda and I were bored so we took some dance lessons during the day for a diversion.

> ***The Gazette* (Montreal):** *It stands on 160 concrete pylons that cushion any vibrations from the trains that still rumble underneath. It was one of the first hotels in North America with escalators, centralized air conditioning and direct-dial telephones in each room. Its vast reception lobby is longer than a regulation football field.*

> ***Montreal's A-propos magazine/This Week SCENE:*** *The Queen E has always had it's share of 24 karat clients, Oscar Peterson, Al Marino Queen Juliana, but this month, Golden is their name and wide their fame (FOR OBVIOUS REASONS), catch this glittering girl's group at the La Salle Bonaventure Queen E Hotel.*

Linda: In Montreal they told us in a thick French accent, "You need sex shoes not those dance shoes!" "Sex shoes?!?"

We used to wear Capezio dance shoes which are very sturdy and good for your back, then we went to wearing stilettos because some people wanted us to look 'hotter.' Your whole body would ache after an hour of dancing in those extremely high heels. All things considered, after the Montreal gig, we went back to wearing our practical Capezios.

I discovered being in the same place for a couple of months was worse than hopping on a plane for a new city every week. Somebody save me, I was bored to death. No kidding, we were getting on each other's nerves. Fortunately the Phillies baseball team arrived in Montreal for some away games; they were staying in our hotel. We got to know some of them and a few of us met up in the coffee shop for a long lunch and some hometown stories. We couldn't believe the huge amount of food they ate to keep up their training weight.

When we were back in Philadelphia we contacted the guys and they comped us some tickets for our family. They were big Phillies fans. What a treat it was for them to be able to sit right up front with the Phillies families almost on the field.

Wendy Kimball, Golddigger 1974-1976: Peggy was like my best friend because we roomed together. We used to date two of the Montreal Expos ball players.

We decided we didn't want to go out with them anymore so we purchased these bathing caps that had attached hair. Talk about naivete, we walked around Montreal in them thinking the guys were not going to find us if we had different colored hair on. But we kept the chin straps on, so we just looked ridiculous. Stupid things that kids do.

Maria: I was delighted to find out that our tour would be taking us to *The Mike Douglas Show*, one of my favorite daytime television shows. It was being taped on location at the beach. What would we wear, I wondered? We couldn't wear our costumes on the beach so we were asked to send our measurements to Greg Garrison's office. They were going to make us denim short-shorts to wear for the taping, 'I hope they fit,' although that was the least of our concerns. We would be flying in from our gig, taping the TV show, and then flying out the same day to perform again that night in another city.

Ed Robertson, entertainment journalist, host of *TV Confidential*: *The Mike Douglas Show* was another touchstone for so many of us. It was an opportunity to see your favorite stars or your favorite actors relax or do things that they couldn't do on their own shows. Paul Newman did *The Mike Douglas Show* and he hardly did any television at all.

Mike Douglas, *My Story*: *Singing is my bag. Naturally, I like co-hosts who share my enthusiasm, people like Neil Sedaka, Paul Anka, Sergio Franchi, Petula Clark, Barbra Streisand, Olivia Newton-John, Liza Minnelli. That's where I'm at. The list is endless. Someday I hope it will include Frank Sinatra.*

Linda: We loved doing *The Mike Douglas Show*, it was shot in Philadelphia so it was like family, they were all down home people. Mike had such a peaceful vibe. Very smooth, like a nothing-would-ever-bother-him kind of guy. The previous couple of years the production started experimenting, going on various locations. We did a show live on an aircraft carrier for the troops with Mike and it was so windy it was hard to perform. I could barely keep my balance or hear the music track.

Maria: We did another show on the beach with Mike Douglas and Robert Goulet and they had a sand sculpture contest going on behind us. Robert Goulet was similar in personality to Dean, he was fun-loving but

Dean was more Casanova-ish. There was no denying that Mr. Goulet was a powerful performer, one of the best looking male stars of Broadway and a classically trained singer. His ex-wife, Carol Lawrence, was also very talented and one of my Broadway heros. She created the role of Maria in *West Side Story*.
I noticed that Mike's wife seemed like she ran a lot of what was going on, she was busy coordinating things and not just a pretty face on the sidelines.

Wendy Kimball, Golddigger 1974-1976: We were performing on a makeshift stage on the beach. I remember first seeing Mr. Goulet walk out, when he started singing I almost burst out crying! He had such depth and resonance in his baritone voice. Even though it was difficult competing with the wind, the waves, and the noise that comes with being next to the Atlantic Ocean, Bob wasn't fazed at all. He had one of the most exquisite and powerful voices I had ever heard.

I was lucky enough to be considered a friend and toured with Robert Goulet for several years, after The Golddiggers. I was even invited to his wedding in Las Vegas, when he tied the knot with Vera. He is one of the most misunderstood stars, and even though he had his moments with the press, he remains, to me, one of the most human of human beings. Very real, very down to earth, very emotional, very fragile, and yet very solid. A great boss, and I miss him *very* much!

I can tell a very funny Robert Goulet story. He was a great cook and used to bring a crock pot with him on tour. He put everything but the kitchen sink in the pot and would leave it on slow simmer in his dressing room, while he went on stage. I believe that his dressing room must have had a portable stove somewhere, I don't recall, but.... during one performance, Bob must have eaten too much of his "Bob Goulet Gumbo" and had to leave the stage immediately to attend to matters in the bathroom. He just left the stage and the orchestra had to play for 10 minutes until Bob returned. I was on stage, sitting on a stool, with the other backup singers, wondering where he was going. When he returned, he simply told the audience that he had to go to the bathroom. It brought the house down and that's what I meant about him—very real, very funny, very loved!

Linda: For many years to come, Maria and I continued our relationship with Mike Douglas and his show. Mike was one of the nicest good-hearted men I have met in the business. He continued to guide and support us as a sister act by having us perform on his show every now and then.

He was a good clean-living family man and he liked the idea of two sisters sticking together, attempting to make it in show business with his similar values. It was a tough road but we always kept in the back of our mind, if Mike can be successful in this business, we can too.

The More Things Change...

Frank Sinatra: *You can be the most artistically perfect performer in the world, but an audience is like a broad—if you're indifferent, Endsville.*

Maria: Every once in a while we would start to think about leaving the group. I was getting itchy to unleash my dramatic talent and expand my vocal repertoire. Linda and I even hired a musical arranger to write a duet and solo number for us. Once in a while, we were thrown a bone and allowed to do our stuff in The Golddigger show but not often enough to nourish our growth as artists. We knew the only way to get stardom and respect was to go out on our own. Also, we didn't know how long the group would last or if Dean would want to keep us around much longer.

Linda: Even though we were considered to be part of the 'In Crowd' we never really felt like that. We were still young girls but we were stuck doing the same show every night. Maria and I wanted to go into modeling and commercials and we wanted to pursue more of our artistic goals.

Maria: It was confining being in The Golddiggers, it was like playing the same role over and over again. You have to take a break and ask yourself, "Who am I? Why did I go into this business in the first place?" So we made the decision to leave the group and said our goodbyes. We wanted to expand our horizons and maybe do some acting. Immediately, we enrolled in acting lessons with different teachers, one of them being Estelle Harmon.

I was happy to hear that Susie and Deborah were getting work as actresses. Like Linda and I, they were different in personality and looks. Susie was spirited, an all-American beauty and Deborah was more serious, an exotic beauty. They encouraged us to get theatrical agents. My agent thought my name, Maria Elena Alberici, was too hard to pronounce so I dropped Alberici and went by Maria Elena for a while. That didn't work out because I was only called to try-out for Spanish speaking roles and I didn't speak Spanish. I tried Marie Alena but newspapers misspelled it and my agent didn't like that either. He said,

"You have an up-scale look; you need a non-ethnic, popular sounding name if you want to get called for leading roles." I remembered what Shakespeare said, "A rose by any other name would smell as sweet," so I changed my name to Maria Lauren.

Linda: It was kind of scary, letting go of the connections that came with being a Golddigger, very scary and sad. These ladies were our best friends, our support system. We kept our departure upbeat, vowing to keep in touch and see each other soon.

Maria and I were intent on taking acting lessons and learning more about the craft. We jumped right into the experience trying a variety of classes. We relished interacting, rehearsing and growing with our fellow actors.

Then, my bubble was burst–when I was harshly criticized for not letting my acting partner touch my breasts in a scene we presented from *Tea and Sympathy*. After my lines, "Years from now when you talk about this–and you will–be kind," my partner was directed to touch my breasts. When I refused to let him I was scolded. "How do you expect to be an actress if you won't allow your breasts to be touched?" That was a sharp jolt of reality, it got me thinking more about the acting profession and what might be required of us. Maria and I decided

Maria on the Vegas Visitor cover - March 26, 1976.

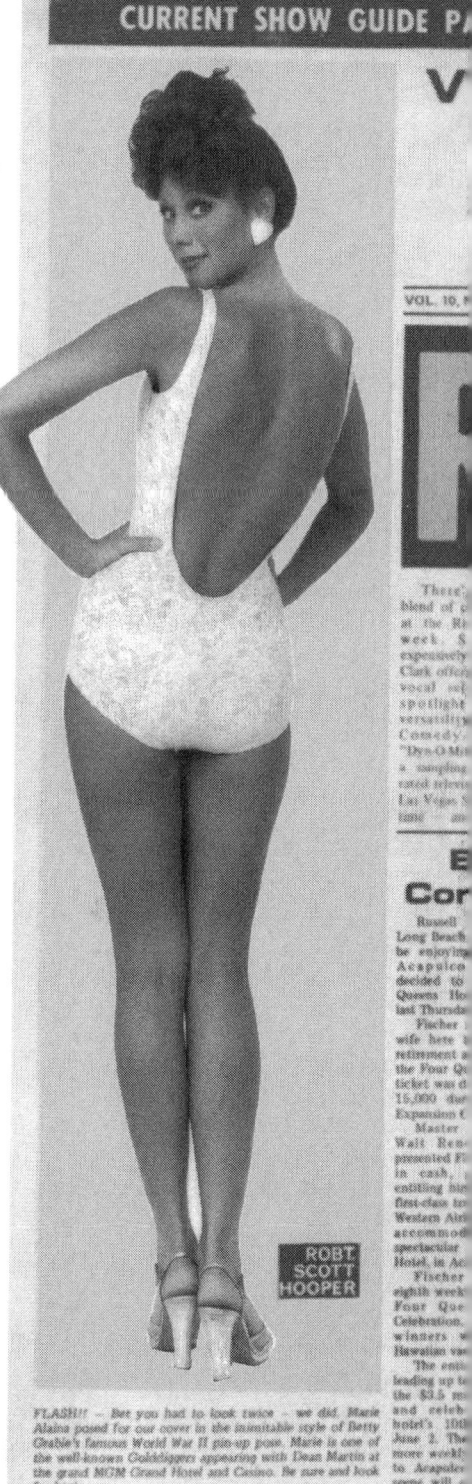

it would be better to spend our time developing our singing act. We put a show together for ourselves and rehearsed new 'live' material. In between, we would often get away and spend time at the beach getting back in touch with ourselves, God and nature. I have to say, I think that's what we needed the most, some time to just be still after the intense few years we had experienced.

Maria: We heard a lot of buzz about the hits coming out of the Record Plant in Hollywood so we decided to record one of our original songs there. It was an impressive studio with gold albums covering the walls with labels from the hottest albums of the last decade. In walked Linda and I, we must have seemed so green to the staff. When our time was up we asked if we could continue recording but the sound engineer said, "Sorry, we have Barbra Streisand booked."
I thought he was kidding but when I walked through the back sound doors, I almost smacked right into Barbra herself. There was maybe an inch between us so I had to focus to recognize her. At once I sensed her charismatic confidence and then I saw her luminous skin. She was radiant. I was told that she was finishing up tracks for her album, 'Lazy Afternoon,' one of my favorites.
Linda and I gained confidence in our new sound and focused on learning vocal recording techniques. With this confidence came liberation from The Golddigger image so I permed my hair for a more earthy look and Linda cut her hair.

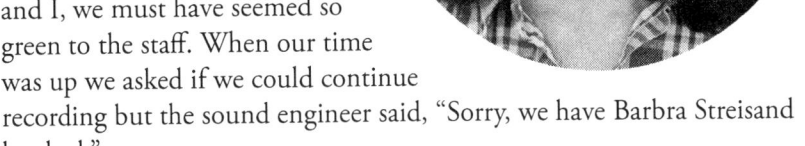

Linda: Shortly after that, out of the blue, Greg's office called to see what we were doing. Janet confided that the girls who replaced us didn't work out. You see, Greg didn't hand pick those girls. He had definite ideas about who should surround Dean, especially for television, and a lavish musical special and a possible weekly series was coming up. They would start taping next week, we had to decide right away!

Maria: Greg asked us back, he always had good things happening, so why not? Let's face it, it's not bad doing television and playing the big rooms in Vegas. Now, we were able to bring what we learned back into the group, the break refreshed us.

Linda: Theresa Bishop was new in the group. She was a knockout in the looks and talent department. Her look was reminiscent of Raquel Welch and Rita Hayworth. Happily, when I got to know her, I discovered underneath her fabulous face and figure was a sweet and compassionate girl next door.

Peggy Gohl, Golddigger 1974-1991: We were doing a big run up in Montreal for fourteen weeks when Linda and Maria re-joined us, we lived there basically. Afterwards they flew us down to do *Dean's Place*, they were trying to start a new series for Dean.

Lee Hale, Musical Director, *The Dean Martin Show*: We did two of them. If the interest had been good then, sure, we would have done a series. We

Photo: Theresa Bishop and Dean.

took over a nightclub on La Cienega Boulevard in West Hollywood, it had closed so we had full reign of all four walls inside so our decorator could make the most of it. And it looked pretty good I thought.

Linda: I couldn't believe they wanted me for the *Dean's Place* special. I had cut my hair really, really short. Surprisingly, Greg and Lee liked it short, they thought I looked like Kim Novak. Greg tried to bring back the old Dean and the sexy material with *Dean's Place* and later on another pilot for a series starring Dom DeLuise but the public wasn't buying too much of that sexual innuendo stuff anymore. They had toned it down a bit when Maria and I first got into the Golddiggers group because of women's lib. Still, Greg decided to gave it another try with these new shows.

He revived some old comedy skits, I did one where Dom DeLuise was a dentist and I was his nurse. Greg actually said to me, "I want you to laugh now and I want you to make your breasts jiggle."
In another classic skit, I wore a bikini and played a menu with the entrees written on my stomach. "Oh, they're serving rump roast today!" Those things were very sexist and embarrassing but you did things like that back then.

There were two *Dean's Place* pilots that were broadcast as specials in an attempt to get the public interested in watching Dean in that familiar variety setting again but it didn't get picked up as a series.

These were Greg Garrison's last gasps at the old formula. Greg had fallen from grace. He was the end-all for years at NBC and then his formulas weren't working anymore. Women's lib came along and blew that all apart for him.

Maria: The first *Dean's Place* special kicked off NBC's fall season in 1975, it was loaded with big stars. It was a variety show with a twist, all the action took place in Dean's supposed nightclub.
The Maitre D' was the great Broadway actor Jack Cassidy, probably the biggest ham in the business and the father of David Cassidy. Foster Brooks was there to do his drunk routine with Guy Marks as the

bartender. Guy Marks would do these incredible impressions of famous people like Humphrey Bogart, Robert Mitchum and Gary Cooper that kept Dean in stitches.

Patty Booth, Golddigger 1970-71, 1975-1976: Nancy Reagan was in the makeup chair next to me and she just started chit chatting, "You girls are so beautiful and so sweet." She was such a lady, so dignified. Very proper but very sweet. And Ronald Reagan had a big smile on his face. In Vegas I met John Wayne, Cary Grant and all of those people and Reagan had that demeanor, he had that personality. He walked tall, as they say.

Maria: Our first couple of years on tour was such a whirlwind, getting used to our traveling schedule, airplanes, hotels, restaurants etcetera. It was all so new to us.

After taking acting lessons, I realized that I played one role on stage, that of a Golddigger, and the rest of the time I walked around with blinders on. This time, I went out on the road with the intention of paying more attention. I learned more about the different towns where we performed. I found out about southern hospitality and how southern people took pride in being down to earth. They didn't put on airs and that reminded me of life back home with my family. The accent was infectious and by the end of our tour, I would be speaking with a southern drawl without even realizing it.

One night while we were performing, a snake slithered up toward the stage, it looked like a Giant Boa Constrictor. We screamed and ran to the back of the stage. We were in a frenzy!

One of the girls said, "Excuse me, ladies and gentlemen but I don't want to continue the show. I don't want a snake crawling up my leg!"

Two big men came up to clobber the snake with something, I looked away but I could hear the commotion. After that, we had to continue the show. How do you top that?

Linda: We always had 'snakes' approaching the stage and approaching us, what else is new?

Another time we had a couple making out in the front row and they were almost to second base! We thought that maybe the woman didn't want her boyfriend paying attention to us. If that was the case it worked.

We had a couple of odd audiences but usually they were wonderful. We met all kinds of people from all different backgrounds.

Once when we were sitting in a coffee shop, I overheard someone say something about one of the girls in our group being Jewish. It made me very uncomfortable. I couldn't wait to get out of there.

There were other people who were a blessing to us. After being on the road for a long stretch, we were all starving for good family values and home cooking and the Maislins invited us into their amazing family, for the week we performed in the area. Maislin Trucking was one of the most important trucking companies in North America but their family came from humble beginnings just like we did. They knew just who we were and what we needed at the time. They were like angels, the way they served us with wisdom, humility and love. Their down to earth demeanor taught me a lot about how to handle success.

We had the same experience with the Fenton family, just your regular all American folks. When show business was exposing us to many of 'the snakes' in life, they came to the rescue with their goodness. They invited us into their home and Ann Fenton made us the most delicious dinner with a cheesecake for dessert. It was heavenly. She was gracious enough to share her yummy cheesecake recipe with me and later I enjoyed it with my friends and family.

Then it was back to the grind of the road. Week after week a new city, our schedule was insane. Performing the same two shows, almost every single night, the new material was already feeling stale. I felt like a work horse. We were all going stir crazy.

Someone dared Maria and I to smoke some grass and do the show high. I thought why not, that would be a challenge. It turned out it was a very bizarre challenge. What a weird feeling. I didn't like it. No one found out but we didn't ever want to do that again. We didn't take drugs but the monotony finally got to us.

Later on in our tour I was approached by an amazingly good looking young man after a show. His eyes would light up when he laughed and he had wavy blond hair. He bubbled over with personality. I wanted to know more about him.

I was very surprised when he told me he was an evangelist and he was in town to speak at a big Christian event. He would be talking about his past and how he conquered a drug habit and helped others to do the same.

I was very impressed. I could see how charismatic he was and imagined how he could get a crowd going. It was very unusual to meet someone from that kind of background on the road so we kept in touch. It happened that, when we were performing in another state, he was speaking nearby so he came out to see me.

We started dating; it was a long distance

relationship but it was more of a relationship than I had experienced in years. He even flew out to visit my parents. Things were starting to get serious between us.

Maria: Linda's friend looked more like a movie star than a minister. I didn't hang around them much. I'm not sure why, maybe because of his Hollywood air and strong selling personality. He wasn't like any preacher I'd ever met.
I almost gasped inside when I heard that he was going to meet our dad. I never told my parents my apprehensions because I knew Linda liked him. I was curious. What would our dad think of him? Well, mom was always a sucker for a handsome face, so she was sold. My dad seemed to enjoy the meeting but was thoughtful too. I was waiting for him to say, "There's something I don't trust about that guy," but he didn't. Dad only mentioned that he didn't like the idea that the preacher was a past drug addict. He said, "You know drugs stay in your genes and could affect your children." As for me, the verdict was still pending.

Linda: As I got to know him, he told me how he prepared for a sermon. He would pray and fast for three days and he would also tan his face under a sun lamp he traveled with. I thought that was a little strange. Another odd thing was how often our touring schedules brought us into close proximity.

Fortunately, on one trip, I had the opportunity to meet some of his friends. We had dinner and afterwards we played card games in their suite until very late. The group seemed very classy and well educated. I said I was getting tired and one of the men completely bewildered me when he offered me amphetamines, which I declined. I had an awful feeling in the pit of my stomach. I wondered, how could my anti-drug preaching boyfriend allow this? It was the same night one of the women took me aside with a very concerned look on her face, "I can see you're a nice girl, I'm so sorry I have to tell you this..." She went on to tell me that this man I had been dating—and was falling in love with—was married. I was destroyed.

After that, it was hard for me to trust my judgement. I felt so foolish. How could I be duped like that? I entered a very dark period where I thought God didn't care about me and I was a loser. I got depressed and I even started dating 'bad boys.' At least they were honest about who they were. It took a while to get back into the light but I did when I discovered I had been looking for something from men that only God could offer me.

I may have given up on God but He never gave up on me. Eventually, through God's love and faithfulness and the love of my family, I healed.

Theresa Bishop Miller, Golddigger 1975 -1976: Maria and Linda had such inner strength and power. I remember them telling me when they were young their dad whispered in their ears at night, saying that they were good and kind and could be anything they wanted to be. It was so amazing. I vowed to do that for my children, enable them to be powerful. Their dad was a great example of parenting.

Darlene (Alberici) Cianci, our younger sister: Our family would visit Linda and Maria whenever we could, wherever they were performing. Due to the expense, we couldn't fly with such a big family so we'd take the van and drive all across the country.

Our whole family had unbelievable stamina. We would all take turns driving all through the nights. Everybody had their own particular quirks. I would put on my Christian music, Broadway tunes or Mario

Lanza and I could drive from Pennsylvania to Florida without sleep. When my brothers drove they would put on baseball games and I would hate that.

We tried not to let our dad drive because he would put his religious tapes on. That would kill us because it was always, "Wah, wah, wah." I mean, we were all very good Christians but this was not real refreshing stuff. Things like, "Honor your father and mother.... Wives submit to your husband...."

One of my other sisters got pulled over in the middle of Idaho for speeding. We were all like, "How can you possibly drive a loaded down Maxi Van like this, with suitcases on the roof, so fast that you would get pulled over?" My sister was crying and my father was apologizing to the officer saying, "I must have fallen asleep!"

My father was strict in some ways but exceeding the speed limit was okay since we had places to get to. We all burst out laughing when my father said to the policeman, "You sound like Andy Griffith" and the officer said, "That's my favorite show!" My father knew the right thing to say to bond with this nice police officer. He probably sympathized with my dad for having so many children because we didn't get a ticket that day.

If my father cut somebody off on the road and they beeped at him he'd say something like, "Ah, go sell bananas" and just keep going. If he cut someone off he would just drive on never considering or noticing the chaos he might have left behind him. My mom never learned to drive since her nerves were bad. She hated these trips, especially due to my father's driving being pretty wild. He sometimes would eat or shave while he was driving and often would pick up hitchhikers. Here we were, all jammed into this hot car, hearing on the news about escaped prisoners from the local penitentiary and then here's this strange guy we just picked up on the side of the road. It would make us crazy but my father liked to talk to the hitchhikers about their life and Christianity.

Maria: When the Santa Ana winds blew Christmastime around, Greg and Lee came up with the concept of *Dean's Christmas in California*. We taped this special on location near Malibu and at Greg's ranch in Hidden Valley, it was beautiful. It looked like Pennsylvania with enormous trees and rolling hills; they could have filmed *Bonanza* there. The streets were like country roads, zoned for horses and it was not that far outside the city.

Some of the guest stars were Dionne Warwick, Michael Learned from *The Waltons,* and Freddie Fender who had the number one hit 'Before the Next Teardrop Falls' in 1975, the year the show aired. For this Holiday treat The Golddiggers actually got to dress like normal human beings—no costumes.

I was assigned to wear a very trendy summer outfit that I absolutely loved. Yes, it spoke to me and I made sure my name was attached to it before it was put back on the costumer's rack. Later, when it came time to wear it, I couldn't find it anywhere. I was told that Ms. Warwick wanted to wear it and I was given another outfit. That figures! Oh well.

Luckily, we were at the beach so I took a deep breath of that wonderful ocean air and joined in the fun.

Linda: I had mixed feelings when I heard about doing a special on the beach. Naturally I was interested in doing something new in an outdoor location but I had this fear that Greg would want to put us all in bikinis and have us frolic on the beach. He didn't go there, to my relief; we got to wear some nice contemporary clothes. We also had a scene where we all wore matching jumpsuits and played softball and other games on the beach. It was pretty cold and overcast for California that morning so I was especially glad to be wearing long sleeves. The music we were given was straight forward, easy to pick up. The biggest challenge during that shoot was at the crack of dawn. Early one morning we were ready

Middle photo: Greg Garrison & Lee Hale.   Bottom: Freddy Fender meets The Golddiggers.

to roll tape and were told Dean couldn't make it. He had the flu. Dean was never sick so I was shocked when I heard the news. I wondered if something serious had happened him and they gave us the flu story to cover it up. The crew was flying around at first, deciding how they should re-block the scenes without Dean. It ended up Lee Hale had to stand in for some of Dean's parts while they focused the camera on the guest stars. It was a tedious day of 'hurry up and wait' because of all the takes they had to get from different angles. The camera crew set and re-set their cameras, shooting enough footage for the editor to be able to piece the whole thing together and I spent a lot of that time trying to keep my hair from frizzing up in the humidity.

The next day we moved from the beach to the ranch and Dean showed up looking a little pale but ready to go. He even hopped on a bicycle and rode it down the street for one scene. Dean and crew eventually went back to the beach to finish taping his part in the show. The special ended up coming together pretty well and received warm reviews.

Peggy Gohl, Golddigger 1974-1991: We were all in our costumes on a lunch break and I was talking with the associate producer Janet Tighe.

I said, "Janet, how come Greg never highlights us anymore? We're standing behind the horses. Why doesn't Greg come out on the road and see what we're doing? We're sending him back our reviews and they're all ovations, they're rave reviews.

Unbeknownst to me Greg was standing behind me.

"Why don't you ask the man yourself, he's right behind you."

So Greg looks at me and says, "Get your ass up the hill, I don't want to hear any more bullsh*t out of anybody." So in all the next shots he cut me out of all the closeups. He demanded to be respected on one level but how he treated us.... we thought that maybe he hated women.

Maria: Greg took his time producing *Dean Martin's Christmas in California,* it was done like a movie with breathtaking panoramic views. 'We Need A Little Christmas' was our big group song, naturally it was

Photo: Dean and Peggy Gohl.

seventy-five degrees and sunny when we were filming.
After all the fun, games and jokes, Dean brought the spirit of Christmas home with a sentimental holiday carol to end the show. In the most casual but endearing way he could interpret lyrics like he was intimately talking directly to you. That was his trademark and Greg was smart enough to let Dean do what he did best.

Patty Booth, Golddigger 1970-71, 1975-1976: At the ranch, Dean said to Greg, "This is really beautiful," and Greg said, "I'm glad you like it, you paid for it." Dean missed a day of shooting because he had the flu so we taped around him while Greg or Lee sat in for him. Dean knew me and felt comfortable with me because I was with him a few years earlier in a previous Golddigger group. So when he came back to work to record a song I was requested to go in the booth and sing with him, just the two of us.
He was like a little kid, "I was so sick the other day." He was a sweet, down to earth guy; his eyes smiled before his teeth showed up. When he's about to crack up, especially with one of his buddies on the TV set, take a look at his eyes, he's already laughing out loud.

Linda: During a performance in Vegas with Dean, some time before we filmed the Christmas special, someone from Greg Garrison's office called one of the girls and started asking her

Top photo: Dean with Patty Booth.　　　Greg Garrison.

questions about Wendy. By the end of the conversation she got the feeling that Wendy might be let go.

The look of the group as far as uniformity in height was not appealing to some people because Wendy was shorter than the rest of us. When Lee Hale chose her, he was hoping that people would overlook her height and see her exceptional talent. As far as Lee and the rest of the girls were concerned, she was our little dynamo and she kicked the talent level of the group up a notch. We all loved Wendy.

Maria: Wendy had a fun loving personality but was a top-notch professional too. Having her in the group was a reminder to me that there is more to performing than being sexy and cute and fitting into the Golddigger mold. We all got along with her so well. It was a disappointment when she was let go but I guess 'image' carried more weight than I thought.

Wendy Kimball, Golddigger 1974-1976: This was the end of the line for me with The Golddiggers but not the end of my friendship with the girls. I was in awe of the sisters' unwavering discipline and their resolve to exercise daily and make healthy food choices.

They seemed to thrive on discipline and the ritual of those disciplines. I remember thinking how incredibly glamorous they were when I first met them in the dressing room right before they were going on stage. When they were not performing, the sisters were so down to earth and really fun. I wish that I had spent more "down" time with them.

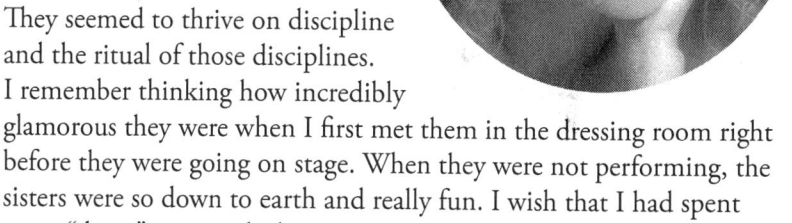

I once shared a room with Linda in Vegas, she was a very gentle, peaceful person, she made a great roomie. I remember soy milk, facial creams, stretching, sunning, vocalizing, and the sisters talking about their Mom and Dad. They always talked about their parents with so much respect and love.

Greg Garrison and I, on the other hand, were not exactly the best of friends. He didn't like me at all, from day one, because I did not fit the mold. I'm really small and I'm with these tall, gorgeous beauties and I guess he felt I didn't measure up. So Greg was never impressed with me.

I did not like Greg Garrison in the slightest. I don't like to say bad things about people but I have nothing nice to say about him other than he was an astute business person. And he liked horses.

Peggy Gohl, Golddigger 1974-1991: I never ran into anybody who liked Greg Garrison. He wanted to tell a joke one day and told me, "I want you to bump and grind up for me against the wall" and I wouldn't do it. He literally pinned me up against a wall to do this joke and I just wouldn't do it.

Linda: It was difficult to replace Wendy. We tried several girls but they didn't last long, maybe a few months. Shortly after we finished taping the special, Theresa Bishop decided to leave. She stayed in the group about a year but she fell in love with our new drummer, who replaced Barry, and they got engaged. I remember Greg being pretty upset about that.

Theresa Bishop Miller, Golddigger 1975 -1976: We were in Montreal from June through mid-August, 1975, two and a half months headlining at the Queen Elizabeth. That's where I met our tour drummer, Glen Miller. We were friends, strictly platonic. We were not allowed to date. We didn't— until August when he said, "If you weren't in the Golddiggers, I'd go for you." I said, "I'd let you!" At the end of the Montreal gig, I was devastated as our plane took off. We had forgotten to exchange phone numbers and addresses. I didn't know when we would be back on the road together again. I already missed him. We eventually started dating and, because of that, he was no longer allowed to drum for the group.

Linda: Around the same time Patty Booth also decided to leave the group. Joyce and Robyn were chosen to step in and they were a perfect fit. Teaching the same act that we performed over and over again every night was not something we enjoyed doing; it was tedious. Thank goodness Robyn Whatley and Joyce Garro were not only beautiful but also seasoned professionals. Robyn was statuesque with vibrant red hair, a lyrical soprano. Joyce, a petite brunette, had a sultry alto voice which added a

Drummer for The Golddiggers - your ticket to romance!

rich bottom to our group sound.

We set out for familiar territory familiar territory, John Ascuaga's Nugget near Reno. Whenever we played the Nugget, all us girls would stay together in a gorgeous penthouse in town. It was fun, like having a week long pajama party.

Joyce Garro, Golddigger 1976-1978: I was originally from Chicago. I had moved to California and I had been singing with a couple of bands here. I had a roommate at the time who said, "Oh, there's an audition for The Golddiggers at NBC." I said, "Oh please. I'm not blond, I'm not tall, I don't even have any go-go boots anymore." I didn't want to go, I just didn't think it would be right for me. I went with her because she did not want to go alone. Sure enough I got the job. She wasn't too happy that she didn't get the call. My first show was in Acapulco which was very exciting, we then went to Guadalajara and then to Mexico City. In Guadalajara we worked the Hotel El Tapatio.

Robyn Whatley, Golddigger 1976-1987: For the first day at NBC studios I was the first one there because, of course, I'm new and I'm nervous so I arrive fifteen minutes ahead of time. The door opens up and in walks the first girl, Patti Pivaar, who was the captain. Unbelievably gorgeous, like a young Elizabeth Taylor. My mouth just dropped. Then the door opened and this five foot eight girl—she looked taller than that—with black, bouncy, curly, long thick, thick hair; incredible motion in the body, loose as a goose, just a complete dancer walks in with full energy. That was Maria Elena. And then the sister Linda comes in and she's strawberry blonde with green eyes and she looked like a baby Zsa Zsa Gabor. I started to wonder if they knew what they were doing when they hired me and in walks Peggy talking a mile a minute making an entrance à la Carol Burnett. Then, I could see how each girl's personality fit into the big picture.

Joyce Garro, Golddigger 1976-1978: After our Mexico tour we were in Vegas opening for Dean and that's when I got to meet him. When I was fourteen years old I was a go-go girl at the Navy Pier World Teen Show. The dancing school that I went to provided the dancers for the show and I danced with Dino, Desi and Billy. I got to work with Deano Jr. then, ten years later, I went to work with his father.

Linda: Dean and Joyce immediately hit it off. He loved having another female "paisano" around.
Extraordinarily, during this period, Dean finally made peace with Jerry Lewis. Frank Sinatra brought them together on Jerry Lewis' 1976 Labor Day MDA Telethon at the Sahara in Vegas; it was almost exactly twenty years to the day since their split in 1956. The event made headlines all over the world but it was not news to us.

Maria: Before the Telethon reunion, Dean let us in on the private messages and jokes written with our lipstick that he had been leaving for Jerry Lewis via his dressing room mirror. Jerry played the MGM Grand and had left Dean some razzing but good humored remarks on the mirror prior to our engagement. Dean was like a little boy bragging about it to us, "Look at what I wrote to Jerry; look what 'Crazy' wrote to me. I answered him real good…." He was so cute!

Linda: When I congratulated Dean on making up with Jerry he blushed and said, "Aw, Frank's idea, he wouldn't leave me alone about it." I asked him, "Are you going to stay in touch?" He only shrugged his shoulders as if to say, "Who knows?" In any case, the world had been waiting for this moment for two decades and the press had a field day. And the Telethon took in boat loads of money because of Dean's surprise visit.

That's why they called Frank Sinatra The Chairman of the Board.

Vaudeville babies

Wilder Penfield III, *Toronto Sun*: People who have been living in holes may have missed the phenomenon but the Golddiggers are the final word in media finishing schools. They are twelve lovely legs, and six splendid smiles, healthy, happy, fun loving, and ornamental. At the end of their whirlwind guided tour of fantasy lands old and new, I was left with a rare desire to get to know each of them individually.

Maria: Life is full of changes, ups and downs, and at this point we'd had the experience of performing in Las Vegas, Acapulco, Guadalajara, Hollywood, and New York— not to mention a hundred or so other beautiful venues all across the country and Canada, all the while sharing the stage with many of the stars we idolized. So when we saw a six week block of bookings in the fall of 1976 for something called The Roy Radin Vaudeville Review we had to wonder what was in store for us.

Linda: They told us this would be a bus tour mostly of the northeast, we'd play some historic music halls but also high school auditoriums and small town VFW halls.

Maria: I was not too happy about going out on a bus tour because I would get motion sickness and it did not sound that glamorous despite the fact we'd be working with Donald O'Connor.
At least we didn't have to travel with J. Fred Muggs, the chimp from the *Today* show who was on board for one of the earlier trips. Yikes, I can't imagine how crazy that must have been.
The tour's music conductor, Tim Fowlar, was a regular guy with a sense of humor that helped us to feel comfortable right away. Trust me, a sense of humor was needed to survive this kind of a bus trip.

Tim Fowlar, Musical Conductor, Roy Radin Vaudeville Revue, 1973-1978: On the Roy Radin Revue we had everybody from rock and roll acts all the way up to Milton Berle. These were police and fire benefits, we played everything from Symphony Hall to Elks lodges, wherever they could put on a show they did.

Producer Roy Radin kept the ticket prices down to three to five dollars per person so it was affordable, that way they brought in two or three thousand people per engagement. Roy didn't make any money off of the tickets, he made it selling advertising in the programs. He was a very shrewd businessman.

For our 1976 tour we had Donald O'Connor, Georgie Jessel, The Golddiggers, the Harmonica Rascals, Joe Boatner's Ink Spots, and the headliner was Milton Berle.

We had a rule on the bus that each person could have only one suitcase because there were so many people on board. And here come The Golddiggers. They were a large group, there were six of them, so they would have two or three suitcases apiece because they had to have all their normal clothes plus all of their wardrobe and makeup for the shows.

The back three rows on both sides of the bus were stacked from floor to ceiling with suitcases and every once in a while, if the bus driver hit the brakes and made a quick stop, all of this stuff would come raining down on the musicians sitting in the back.

The girls were a lot of fun to work with, they would sing on the bus, sing on the plane. They were in a class by themselves, they were experienced road people and we were all just young kids. I mean, they were the same age as us but they had been out doing TV and nightclubs for years, they were in a higher strata than we were at that point.

I had been out on the road for several years but for a lot of the musicians this was their first professional job. They were all brilliant, I pulled them all from the Berklee School of Music, they were some of the best musicians in the world but they were very young.

The Golddiggers were polished professionals. When they came out it was solid music. They hit the stage and it was medley after medley, rapid fire from the time they started until the time they stopped.

We really didn't get to associate with them that much because Roy Radin and the stars would monopolize their time. Roy would have them to dinner or the bodyguards would be chasing them around.

Maria: The musicians seemed like they were loving this gypsy caravan but I must admit, it was not my cup of tea. Actually, there was no tea to be found on this tour!

The newer girls, Robyn and Joyce, took everything in stride. Joyce was quiet but had a good repartee with the musicians and Robyn seemed to be enjoying the whole experience.

Linda: Joyce was very cool. We had an instant connection because of the Italian heritage and love of jazz we both shared. We became close very quickly. She was an honest, no-nonsense kind of person who spoke her mind. She had a unique style on stage. Her gift for jazz was highlighted in the show with her solo number.

Maria: Robyn was a former beauty contest winner with a Southern charm. Her blue eyes sparkled with a zest for life. She had a knock-out figure and if she didn't get her way, her lips would pucker in a pout. It tickled me how it made the guys melt.

Linda: Robyn helped me see everything that was happening around us through her rose colored glasses. She was

Top photo: Linda and Donald O'Connor.   Bottom: Robyn Whatley.

full of enthusiasm while I was growing jaded of the amazing journey we were on. Robyn's free spirit was refreshing and intriguing, it gave me a new perspective on things.

Tim Fowlar, musical conductor, Roy Radin Revue 1973-1979: Donald O'Connor lived to be on stage, when he was offstage he was kind of like, "What do I do now?" That's all he knew, his family was one of the biggest names in vaudeville; in fact, the O'Connor family was billed as the 'Royal Family of Vaudeville.'

He actually went out on stage for the first time when he was five days old. His mother had him wrapped up in a blanket and placed him on the bench beside her while she played piano for the act because she knew he'd be safe there. When he was old enough to start walking they would leave him offstage.

As a toddler one day he came wandering out on to the stage and lost his balance and fell down. The drummer caught him and the whole audience roared.

After that they started working him into the routine because that's what you did in vaudeville families, as soon as the kids were old enough to walk you put them into the act.

Donald was the sweetest guy in the world. I was with Donald for thirty years as his conductor. Most conductors are with an act five, six years at the most and then you can't stand each other. And I was with Donald for thirty.

We would be walking through an airport and somebody'd go, "Oh my God, that's Donald O'Connor!" and he would stop and talk with them. Donald would never, ever push any of his fans away. Every place we worked everybody revered him and the musicians loved him more because he was such a musical person.

The only sad part was, because of his drinking, he pretty much killed his career and then had to fight to get it back once he stopped. The only good aspect about the whole Roy Radin ordeal for Donald was it brought his whole alcoholism thing to a head and finally got him into treatment where he eventually found his sobriety.

Linda: I could tell Donald was having a problem with alcohol but I never saw him get mean. He was sweet, soft spoken and had a humility about him that I liked. Perhaps this was because he'd been up and down so many times in his life. Donald had an undying passion for performing. He loved his audience and they loved him back.

Jack Salley, trumpet player, Roy Radin Vaudeville Revue, 1973—1979: Donald was the kindest, nicest and most gentle man that I ever worked with. A great entertainer but by the time we met and were working with him, he had a monkey on his back. He was an absolute stone cold alcoholic.

Audiences remembered him in his younger years performing all of those incredible acrobatic dance scenes where he was bouncing up and off the walls. Years of drinking and extremely poor health habits had taken its toll. Those kinds of stunts, at this time in his life, just weren't possible. It's one thing to be a singer and performing screwed up, it's totally another being a dancer well into your fifties and in poor physical shape. He always was though, in any condition, a consummate professional, never missing a show.

His portion of the program wasn't really all that long but, with all of us holding our breath, somehow he always managed to deliver to the fans, every night. His smile and the songs that made him famous

Donald O'Connor on the bus.

ended with standing ovations.
He was the "Pro of Pros." There's a saying in the business that, "The only ones that ever come on as 'stars' are the ones who aren't and the ones who really are truly never do." Put Donald O'Connor at the top of the "never do" list.

> **Donald O'Connor:** *It's so wonderful....*
> *if your whole day is rotten, once they start the music, it seems to melt away.*

Maria: Donald O'Connor still had that little smile and twinkle in his eyes that he had in the old movies. He had a distinct way of wrinkling his nose when he smiled. I would see it when he performed and sometimes I would see that same expression offstage too, when he'd talk about the good old days.
He was a gentle spirit. Sometimes he was a little intoxicated when he performed but the audiences didn't know it. He had his shtick down and knew how to engage the crowds, they loved him.
I guess it's the love, the approval from the audience and the paycheck

that kept us all traveling on that bus. I usually sat by the window and watched as the world whizzed by. The monotony of the movement made me drowsy. In between resting my eyes, I would read for a few minutes from my pocket-sized, paperback Bible. It was pretty worn by that point but it was a peaceful and faithful companion while I traveled. There was a lot of noise in the back with the musicians and they smoked. Once in a while, I would join them and listen to their funny stories. There were some laughs but the smell of smoke made me feel nauseous, so I sat in the front of the bus. Donald O'Connor always sat in the front too. He was very sweet, we talked, mostly about his family and growing up in vaudeville. I would tell him how Linda and I started singing with our mother when we were growing up. He could relate to that sort of thing. That's the way he grew up—but usually he would sleep in the seat in front of me because he was hung over most mornings.

Tim Fowlar, musical conductor, Roy Radin Revue 1973-1979:
Believe it or not everybody rode on the bus. Everybody loved it, we were a big family traveling around. Even some of the stars that had a limo available to them would ride the bus. You'd think it would be tedious, and at times, yeah. We were out doing forty one-nighters in forty days. It could be brutal but once we hit that stage you'd never know everybody was as tired as we were.

Maria: This was no fancy, upgraded tour bus, it was your standard Greyhound variety. There were some travel annoyances that we had to contend with like packing and unpacking but no real harassments. I don't remember having any trouble with the musicians or bodyguards. We got along great. They were mannerly and helpful.
The musicians took their lead from Tim Fowlar, not only on stage but on the bus too. I think they respected us or our connection with Dean Martin and we did have a road manager who kept a pretty close eye on us. However, it troubled me to see these stars of once-upon-a-time now faded and worn. I could hear my father's voice in my head, "Show business is no kind of life. If you can't do it first class, come home and sing in church." I wondered was my father right? Is this where show biz leads?
Georgie Jessel had an aura of bitterness and a 'devil-may-care' air about him and Donald O'Connor broke my heart as I watched him struggle with his alcohol addiction. Once off the bus, all of that was forgotten when we heard the cheers of thousands of people from the audience. This was the heart of America, to everyone this was a once in a lifetime event. Knowing that kept my spirits high.

The Ink Spots were inducted into the Vocal Group Hall of Fame in 1999.

Donald O'Connor, *Fresh Weekly*, 1979: *You have a feeling that everybody wants to be entertained. They don't go in as critics. They have an open mind, a willingness to accept. They generate enthusiasm; it permeates the place. Once you get those vibes you put out so much more. Remember, if you do the same act for 20, 30 years it gets a little boring unless you've got something else going for you.*

And the orchestra really kept you going. They'd laugh at all your jokes, even if they'd been hearing them for the last 30 years. They'd get in there and work right with you: you'd show them your music, they'd sniff it and they could play it. They used to make you come alive. Even if you fell down they'd bring you up. And if you had a good audience, they'd bring you up more. And if your act was any good, and you worked hard, everything was working then.

Linda: Traveling by bus was pretty rough with the long distances, a new place every day and never being able to fully unpack. I was tired a lot of the time. I just wanted to close my eyes and block it all out of my mind. I would have liked to have been able to bury my head in a book but reading made my stomach feel queasy. That left me time to pray and meditate.

The first couple of days of the tour, I made a vain attempt to maintain some Golddigger glamour and wear a little makeup but that didn't last long. One thing about being in such close quarters, pretty soon everyone lets their hair down and you all become a family of sorts. I was still kind of shy so I didn't jump in right away to get to know everybody but eventually I loosened up a bit and came down off my cloud to make the best of it. Tim and the rest of the gang started growing on me. Tim was as nice as can be and I could tell it came from his heart.

Tim Fowlar, musical conductor, Roy Radin Revue 1973-1979: Milton Berle, Georgie Jessel, The Ink Spots, and Donald O'Connor, these guys came out every night and did the same numbers but the act was different every time. They had a rapport with the audience and the spontaneity of a live band that could do something off the cuff if somebody yelled out a request. All of a sudden they'd pop into a tune and we'd be off and running.

A lot of inside jokes would happen between the entertainers and the musicians, they'd make some smart remark about something that happened at the hotel or on the bus and the audience would be in on the joke. It was a family show and it was a clean show, it was one of the last of the clean shows, none of the comics used foul language on stage and there were very few double entendre jokes.

It was a hell of a lot of fun but at times it was a train wreck too. Most of the stars were heavy drinkers. After the show everybody'd head straight for the bar and we'd all hang out and drink until the place closed. God forbid we'd be in New York because that meant we'd stay until four or six in the morning then have to be on the bus at eight to move on to the next town. Everybody was hung over every morning. Georgie Jessel used to get on the bus in the morning with a little glass of milk and he'd pour scotch in the milk and drink that.

Jack Salley, trumpet player, Roy Radin Vaudeville Revue, 1973—1979: A lot of the acts at that time, be it the Four Tops, Gladys Knight or The Temptations, would travel with their own musicians and rhythm section then hire local contract players to complete the orchestra when they got to each city. We had a completely intact show, a totally self-contained traveling unit, the smallest orchestra we ran with was twelve musicians.

Maria: Mostly the guys all hung out together. Believe me, we would look forward to some girl time or quiet time, away from the bus commotion. It seemed as if we would drag our suitcases into our hotel rooms and then turn around and drag them out again. Somewhere in between we would clean ourselves up, find some decent food, do our show and try to get some rest.

A welcome pleasure was doing some exercises in my room. I always traveled with light weights in my suitcase; the kind that wrapped around the ankles or wrists. My routine of resistance training, calisthenics and stretches gave me a sense of control, something the road didn't offer, especially this bus tour. Boy, were we a mish-mash of distinctive personalities and habits but we readily accepted each other's differences.

Our group didn't join the performers and musicians who met for drinks after the shows. A girl needs her beauty sleep, not to mention her space, especially when she had to face a long bus ride and a tomorrow filled with God only knows what!

Milton Berle, *Milton Berle an Autobiography*, 1974: *I'm still searching for an answer, still running to the next show, still* *coming alive under the lights, still making love to the audience that I know will go home to make love to another and leave me alone again. When I am on the road I think of [my son and wife] Billy and Ruth, and I want to be with them so badly that I hurt inside. Yet, when I am home for more than a week, I pace the room like a trapped animal, worrying about when I go to work again.*

I realize now that I spent my whole life working for the jackpot, only to find out when I won that there was no payoff for me. I had paid too much along the way for the prize to have any meaning to me. I guess I've made all the dreams Mama and I had come true, but I spent so many years chasing those dreams that I don't know how to stop running.

Tim Fowlar, musical conductor, Roy Radin Revue 1973-1979:
Milton was the emcee throughout the show, he tied the whole thing together and then did his own stand up spot. Milton came up in burlesque and vaudeville, he was actually great. Everybody always said he was very difficult to work with but the only thing he expected was for everybody to do their job and to do it well. We never had a problem with him at all.

Milton Berle, myself and two musicians would go hours ahead to set up the stage for the show that night. Milton always had to be there, he knew how he wanted the stage to look. That's how particular he was about how things went.

He would stand out in front of the stage and I'd have to hold the lead alto music stand and walk around until he told me, "Okay put it right there" and then we'd build the band around that.

To do the sound check Milton would take the mic and he invariably sang the Ethel Merman tune, 'Everything's Coming Up Roses' which was the song Peggy Gohl did in the Golddigger's act. We figured the reason he was doing that was because he had the hots for Peggy. He did it every single rehearsal. He could pick anything from the show to sing for the soundcheck but he always picked that tune.

"If opportunity doesn't knock, build a door."—Milton Berle

Billy Berle, *My Father, Uncle Miltie*: Dad would do his hair with that spray paint—I'm certain it's classified as some toxic hazard by now—that covered the top and back of his head with a thick coat of the black stuff. He had a bald spot that was somewhat lighter than his hair color, graying by then from its former black-ish brown.

The sight up close was almost frightening. Various coats of thick makeup, blackish gray spray paint over bare skin and old hair alike, crusty wax pencil streaks in front of a faded and thin hairline, all sort of poured and arranged over a wrinkled, sagging head. He didn't look any younger, just a painted version of the same elderly man, like a rubber Halloween mask.

He looked at himself in the mirror and grinned, checking out how he would look to the audience with a different facial expression. Staring directly into the blinding light bulbs that surrounded his face, he tightened the facial muscles that pulled his expression back from the depths of age and experience. He smiled at himself.

It was stunning. From within this old head, a jolt of energy turned on and shot out through his eyes and mouth, seeming to envelope him. There was more light coming from inside him than there were lights shining on him. A second later, it was gone. In that brief moment, he'd found Milton Berle.

Maria: One night early in the tour Milton Berle came out and started clowning around in the middle of our opening number and he ruined it. Each girl had a couple of solos here and there in our medleys and Milton grabbed my microphone and started clowning around with it right before my solo. By the time he finished my spot had ended. Thank you very much!

Linda: I liked the way Maria told him off backstage after that and I thought, "Wow, she's got guts. Doesn't she know that's Milton Berle?"

Maria: I meant no disrespect, I always thought Milton Berle was a consumate entertainer but backstage I took a deep breath and confronted him. I wanted him to know that we were professionals too and not chorus girls that stayed in the background and didn't speak up.

I just said, "You know, I wouldn't come on stage in the middle of your act and start talking in the microphone, so I would expect the same courtesy." After that, he treated us with more respect for the remainder of the tour.

Robyn Whatley, Golddigger 1976-1987: A few days later Milton wrote a note to the girls and asked us to come to breakfast where he apologized and told us we were the greatest thing since sliced bread, so professional and always on time. It changed the tone for the rest of that tour.

Peggy Gohl, Golddigger 1974-1990: Milton thought he was the whole act. He had thousands of jokes stored at home, Milton stole every joke that ever was. He and Charlie Sanford knew each other from back in the vaudeville days. Charlie used to conduct one hundred piece orchestras for silent films in New York City when he was fourteen.

Joyce Garro, Golddigger 1976-1978: We were the only women on the bus and the guys were very respectful. Milton Berle used to save me a seat every day on the bus. He took to me, he was married to a woman named Joyce. He was good friends with a friend of mine, Bea Wain, so I would see Milton often at the Friar's Club when Bea and I would have lunch there.

Maria: I saw Milton Berle with other famous comedians performing at a fundraiser at the Friars Club in Beverly Hills. The way it worked was that each comedian would sit at a table with their guests. When it was their turn, the comedian would come up from the audience and do their bit. It was fun when some of the comedians would heckle from the audience but Milton Berle would overdo it. That man never had an 'off switch.' He was always 'on.' He liked the limelight so much that he couldn't control himself.

Top photo: Uncle Miltie with Joyce Garro.

Jack Salley, trumpet player, Roy Radin Vaudeville Revue, 1973—1979: Milton was the spokesperson for the Lum's restaurant chain at that time so in every location there was a life size cutout of Uncle Miltie welcoming you as you walked in the door. Countless times, Milton would turn around on the bus—he rode with us too, but up front—and ask, "We haven't eaten yet, have we? Let's go to a Lum's."
We'd be in some obscure area and the bus would pull up, then Milton would walk into the Lum's and go right back into the kitchen and start barking out orders – taking over total command of the operation. "Are you cooking this right? What are you doing over there?" and he'd go into an act.
Everyone in the restaurant from the manager to the busboys, not to mention the patrons, could do nothing but drop their jaws in shock, look at each other and say, "Where did this guy come from, is that really him?"
Then he would play waiter, "C'mon, c'mon, this guy likes his hamburger medium rare—put this down over here, c'mon, c'mon." It was hilarious; it was like General George Patton walking in. Or he'd just stand next to the cardboard cutout of himself in the front lobby and

Top photo: Maria and Peggy Gohl.

watch the people enter and freak out. Afterwards he'd walk around and pick up everyone's tab.

Tim Fowlar, musical conductor, Roy Radin Revue 1973-1979: Joe Boatner's Ink Spots consisted of brothers Ralph and Buster Brown along with Billy Hudson. Ralph and Buster were both old vaudeville tap dancers, they were great performers, really nice guys.
George Jessel was known as the 'Toastmaster General of the United States.' His was not the most exciting act but he was funny. He was an icon so the fact that he could actually walk out on the stage at his age was just incredible. Being in his eighties and doing a show like this with all that travelling all day was just unheard of.
We were going from a Howard Johnson's in one town to another Howard Johnson's three hundred miles away. The bus driver Wally pulled into a totally different Howard Johnson's restaurant to eat along the way.
Georgie Jessel asked me, "Hey Tim, why don't you have a couple of the guys come and have lunch with me and I'll pay for it?" I said, "That'll be nice" so I got a couple of the guys and the three of us sat down with Georgie and we ate. When it was over he told us, "Ah, go on out to the bus and I'll take care of it." He signed his name to the check and gave them the room number from the last hotel a hundred miles away. The waitress caught up to me and said, "Hey, look what happened, look what he did."
I said, "Oh, he's old, he just got confused" so I grabbed the other guys and we ended up paying for the meal including Georgie's.
That was Georgie, he was famous for stiffing hotels. When we got to the Boston Sheraton they wouldn't let Georgie check in until Roy paid his bill from the time before.

> **Eddie Fisher, *Been There, Done That*:** *Jessel had become a caricature of himself, wearing a military uniform and medals. He would wake me at seven-thirty in the morning to complain if I'd failed to mention when introducing him that he'd been named Toastmaster General of the United States by five presidents.*

Robyn Whatley, Golddigger 1976-1987: Milton Berle and Georgie Jessel were telling jokes and arguing about who wrote what joke because they actually knew the people. They would argue and argue and argue and it was hysterical. Georgie Jessel finally said, "I'm not staying on this bus anymore" and rode in the limousine after that because he and Milton just had too many arguments.

Patti (Pivarnik) Gribow, Golddigger 1973-1985: We often played cards with Milton Berle in the front of the bus while touring from town to town. He would keep us entertained with his slapstick humor sharing stories of his days on the *Texaco Theater*. This was great fun!

Georgie Jessel, on the other hand, would chase us around making lewd remarks, which was not fun. We may have been touring the world but we were not worldly girls. He probably thought he was going to 'get lucky,' if you will, with one of us. That's a bit disgusting if you ask me. But, bless his heart, he was a very talented man.

Tim Fowlar, musical conductor, Roy Radin Revue 1973-1979:
Georgie was a character. He was a bit of a pervert. What he used to do was, when he got to a hotel, he'd leave his door open a crack and get on his bed with no clothes on, just his USO cap, and lay there and wait for the maids to come in.

One day Donald O'Connor saw the door open and stuck his head in and said, "Georgie, what are you doing? You left your door open." He says, "Yeah, that's how I get lucky every once in a while."

We were in Poughkeepsie, New York at a Holiday Inn and I was walking down the hall with Donald O'Connor and George Gobel from *The Hollywood Squares* and all of a sudden we hear a scream and this maid comes running out of his room. She goes, "Oh my God, oh my God, George Jessel's in there and he's got no clothes on!"

She looks up and realizes the person she's hanging on to was Donald O'Connor. She screams, "Oh my God, you're Donald O'Connor!" And she turns around and there's George Gobel and she screams again and goes running off down the hallway. It flipped her out but that was Georgie.

Linda: Georgie Jessel looked like he needed some help with his grooming. He usually had bits of old makeup flaking off his face. His toupee never fit quite right; I felt a little sorry for him.

Once I was talking to him and he said, "Oh, could you give an old man a kiss on the cheek?" I went to kiss his cheek and he turned his face around and he tried to French kiss me! Who would think someone that old would do that? He must have been eighty.

I was told that he was very handsome in his prime and dated all the best looking women in the 1930s, Broadway stars and silent movie queens like Pola Negri, Helen Morgan, Lupe Vélez and Norma Talmadge. I guess he was still there in his mind.

Robyn Whatley, Golddigger 1976-1987: They rehearsed *The Carol Burnett Show* next door to where we rehearsed at NBC and I used to stick my head in and observe because I loved that show.

I watched once when they were rehearsing Tim Conway's little old man routine. As soon as I started working with Georgie Jessel I realized that Tim Conway must have seen Georgie Jessel and that's where he got his character from because that was exactly the speed that Georgie Jessel would chase us around. He'd say, "I'm going to get you" and he was walking like Tim Conway's little old man.

George Jessel, *The World I Lived In*: *I am as unashamed of my life as a poodle with a pillow.*

Linda: Georgie was incorrigible. I was a little relieved when the whole Roy Radin experience was over. It was somewhat depressing to see famous stars lose their luster but, in spite of that, this tour allowed some legendary talent to be seen in places they wouldn't ordinarily be. A whole new generation was introduced to Vaudeville entertainment and that was a wonderful gift to all.

We had some fun but now the challenge was to rest up and prepare ourselves for taping two Dean Martin specials that would take us back in time to the roaring twenties. This time the shows would be shot not in a studio at NBC but in art deco locations all around Los Angeles.

Photo: Georgie Jessel's lovers—Helen Morgan, Lupe Vélez and Norma Talmadge.

L.A. Times, November 6, 1976: *The music, fashions, and humor of the mid-1920s will all be featured on Dean Martin's first special of the season,* Dean Martin's Red Hot Scandals of 1926, *Monday, Nov. 8 from 10 to 11p.m. Appearing with Dean are Jonathan Winters, Dom DeLuise, Abe Vigoda, Hermione Bedeley, Georgia Engel, Charlene Ryan and the Golddiggers.*

Linda: The special opened with a row of antique cars pulling up to a beautiful theater as we sang 'Red Hot Scandals of 1926.' We purposely sang in the jazzy style of the 1920s using high, thin voices. We sounded just like the ladies in the *Gold Diggers* movies from the 1930s. The scene shifted to 'Dimwitty University' with Abe Vigoda as the professor. We sang, danced and cheered to a song made popular in the twenties called 'Collegiate' wearing old fashioned cheerleader outfits alongside our male dance partners. We then threw on raccoon fur coats for 'Do The Raccoon.' Dean attempted to follow the movement and added comic relief by mugging for the camera while wearing a beanie on his head. All that was missing was the little propeller for the top.

Lee Hale, Musical Director, *The Dean Martin Show*: We were all over the place shooting that one. We were at Warner Bros., we were at the Music Hall in Santa Monica, we did some at NBC. A lot of wonderful locations for those shows.

Robyn Whatley, Golddigger 1976-1987: We were in front of the Burbank studios made up to look like a university campus. We did some kind of cheerleading song with racoon coats on; true blue, full-length raccoon coats, it was like wearing a polar bear skin, unbelievably hot. And Dean was there in his letter sweater like he's a college football player, always cracking cute little jokes, going wherever we pushed him. One of our jobs as The Golddiggers was to, without anyone seeing it or noticing it, very graciously get Dean to wherever his mark was. He had no idea where to go, that's why he always looked so cute and befuddled—he was! It was the longest day but everyone had so much fun.

We did a cute takeoff on Rudolph Valentino where everybody was dressed in Arabian garb and Dean was in a safari outfit with the riding crop in his hand.

All of us were lucky to be involved in this, you knew it at the time, that entertainment was not going to be like this any more, with this level of talent. All of the people that they got to surround Dean were the best of the best. We just got to soak it up and learn from everybody.

Lee Hale was his stand-in so Lee would sing all the songs and do all the dance moves while Dean would be in his nice, cool dressing room watching what he, Dean, was supposed to do. Like he would say onstage in Las Vegas, "It's in my contract. One bead of sweat and I get to walk."

Maria: It took my breath away when we arrived at the Los Angeles Biltmore Hotel to film one of our musical numbers. As I entered the impressive lobby, it resembled a palace with its gold carved ceilings, rich wood paneling, beautiful marble with elaborate embroidered tapestries and rugs. The hotel was built in the 1920s so it was the perfect setting. I heard it even had a Prohibition era secret liquor compartment somewhere in the back. We wore gorgeous clothing to represent the era, some were cute and some were more sophisticated with exquisite antique beading. I wore an authentic vintage hand painted velvet cape over my cocktail dress that instantly transformed me into the twenties time period. One of our song and dance numbers was 'Puttin' on the Ritz.' Well, I was definitely feeling ritzy.

In one scene, Dean Martin joked individually with each of us and we all did a little singing solo spot too. We had a blast doing 'Happy Days Are Here Again' with Dean. During the song, I was right next to him and at the end of each musical phrase, we would bump hips. Greg Garrison loved to get candid reactions from Dean so all the girls caught on and started doing the same hip action all together. We were knocking Dean all over the place. The look on his face was amusing, to say the least.

Linda: We sang 'Old Broadway' with Dean Martin as Rudy Wiffen Poof, the leader of our All Girl Orchestra. Maria was featured with Dean in a little skit where he introduced her as the gorgeous Fanny Frisbee—"former pom pom girl who had the best poms on campus." Shortly after that, we all joined Dean for 'Ain't We Got Fun.'

Joyce Garro, Golddigger 1976-1978: I have a tattoo on my back behind my left shoulder and the costume people were freaking out trying to cover it because our gorgeous costumes were mostly backless.

Maria: Georgia Engel and Charlene Ryan knocked out a show stopping 'I Wanna Be Bad' in flapper outfits. I was surprised at how well Georgia could dance. She was rather sexy baring her slim legs; who knew? She always played the wide eyed, soft spoken innocent.
We jazzed things up a bit too in our 'Chicago' number, it was busy with choreography, highlighting our dancing skills. The special was directed by Bob Sidney, the choreographer for Dean's weekly series, he was famous for creating the dance numbers for *The Singing Nun, Where the Boys Are, Valley of the Dolls* and one of Mitzi Gaynor's specials.
There were lots of jokes about mobsters and, of course, drinking. Abe Vigoda played the gangster Big Louie while Dean was Elliot Mess, hot on his trail. Since it was the

prohibition era and Dean was the law, he naturally checked to see if liquor was being served. He pointed to a glass and said accusingly, "I can tell it's bathtub gin... it's got a ring around the cup!"

Linda: You had to see the look on Dean's face as he delivered his lines, he was able to get away with those corny jokes. Dean went on to preach about the evils of liquor when Abe comments, "It's easy for you to say." Dean answered with a smirk, "That's what you think."
We rode into the next scene in antique cars singing, 'California Here

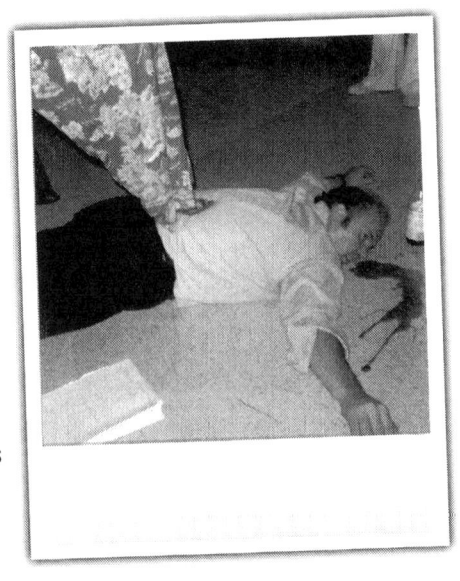

Photo: Dean Martin with Dom DeLuise and the Cast.

230

I Come.' All of the songs in the show had special lyrics added to make them unique and funny.

Peggy Gohl, Golddigger 1974-1991: We were rehearsing once and a bottle of grape juice had spilled so Dom DeLuise did a pratfall and pretended he was lying dead in this pool of grape juice. He was that sort, he was so real and unaffected and very different from a lot of the show bizzie people.

Robyn Whatley, Golddigger 1976-1987: Dom DeLuise was on the two *Red Hot Scandals of 1926* specials and he would do things that were so outrageous, just his natural character was so hilarious. He kept the camera crew and Dean in tears. He would come running in to a scene just saying the most outrageous things that weren't in the script at all and the crew would get so torn up that the cameras would shake and we'd have to do it over.

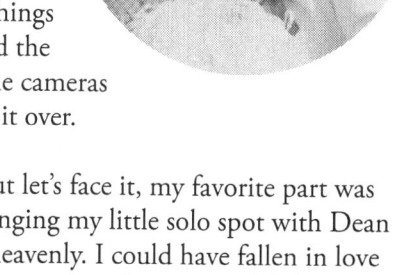

Linda: That was all well and good but let's face it, my favorite part was 'Now's The Time To Fall In Love.' Singing my little solo spot with Dean and being wrapped in his arms was heavenly. I could have fallen in love right there and then. Before the filming wrapped we were told there would be a sequel—*Red Hot Scandals Part 2*. Oh joy!

Dom DeLuise: *There was one time when he sang a song and it was just great and I said to him, I said, 'Dean that was great.' And then I saw this little boy in Dean Martin, a little tiny boy who was getting complimented by me! And he said, 'was it?' He had no protection at that moment and he was as in need of a compliment as I was, as you were, as we all were.*

Linda: After an exhausting fall touring and filming TV specials we were thrilled to be headed back to The Latin Casino to perform with our dear friend Jerry Vale and once again be close to our family. We also made a stop in Smithville, New Jersey appearing with the star of the hottest show in the nation, *Welcome Back Kotter's* Gabe Kaplan, where a reviewer called The Golddiggers an "entertainment package that makes one forget everything but pleasure for awhile."

Courier Post, Cherry Hill, N.J. Aug 11, 1976: *Six gorgeous girls; five—that's right, five beautiful costumes, an hour of songs and dances. You want more? Then a comic who is so funny that you're laughing before he says one word? They don't make shows like that anymore, right? Wrong!*
Take a ride down to Smithville Theater any night from now through Saturday, Aug. 15th and you'll see everything the marquee claims. First the girls. Yes there are six and only five costumes, but that's five costumes for each girl. Besides, they don't need that kind of gimmick. What they do in an hour's worth of stage time is well worth the price of admission. They're the Golddiggers of TV fame, and if it ever can be said that the tube

doesn't do a group justice, this must be the case!
Their finale, a stirring 'Aquarius' and 'I Don't Know How to Love Him,' was whipped cream on this sweet dessert of an act. Each was featured in a solo pointing out the difference in style and range while underscoring the effectiveness of their harmonies. They left to a well-deserved standing ovation.

Joyce Garro, Golddigger 1976-1978: Before every show we joined hands in prayer and asked God to bless our performance and bless the audience and Dean. Minutes before we could be arguing about something—like who sprayed hairspray in someone's face without looking to see if they were behind them—we could be so mad at each other over something but we didn't hold grudges. We said our prayers, did the show, and it was like nothing happened.

I think it was the way Greg Garrison and Lee Hale chose us. They wanted us to be sexy, to have sex appeal, but Greg always wanted us to be the kind of girls you could bring home to mama.

All men make mistakes, but married men find out about them sooner. - Red Skelton

Maria: Following our run with Jerry Vale we opened for Red Skelton. We appeared with him a couple of times but this time we traveled to Lake Charles, Louisiana.

Red was very handsome and tall in person. I was quite surprised because I thought he would be more like a clown but he had a lot of stature.

He had class and sophistication too. His performance showed the many aspects of his talent, he could bring forth laughter and sympathy from the audience and they loved him.

Linda: It was an eye opener, there was so much more to him than I ever saw when he appeared on television. He was a serious artist and that's what he projected when we met him.

Arthur Marx, *Red Skelton an Unauthorized Biography*: Of course, Red had never completely retired, not even after his Las Vegas announcement. He had continued to pick up easy money at places like the Indiana State Fair; he also appeared once a year in a place called Sparks, Nevada—a small mining town that paid big money—where he was a tremendous favorite with the local dice-throwers. And he had even emceed part of the annual movie Oscar show in the spring of 1976.

New York Times, March 14, 1977: *He is verging on sixty-four years of age—the third of Mr. Skelton's three ages of man, which are youth, middle-age, and, gee, you look good—but he needs no rejuvenation. He is as hilariously rubbery as ever, nimble legs, facile hands, plastic-putty face, and expressive eyes.*
Those who came to see him knew what they wanted, and Mr. Skelton delivered to taste, backed by a seventeen-piece band. He has a warm stage presence, one that envelops and disarms you, more than perhaps it does on screen or television, and he is a consummate clown.
Mr. Skelton gave a clean family show. He lapses touchingly and unflinchingly into sentimentality. But most of the time he makes you forget whatever intellectual pretensions you may be harboring, and he makes you laugh. Laugh hard. Anyone that can do that these days (as they've been saying for the last century or so) should be invited to town more often.

Robyn Whatley, Golddigger 1976-1987: Red Skelton used to take photographs of us. He said, "I have a scrapbook, I take pictures of everybody I worked with." He was like the kid who was star struck.

Red Skelton: *If by chance some day you're not feeling well and you should remember some silly thing I've said or done and it brings back a smile to your face or a chuckle to your heart, then my purpose as your clown has been fulfilled.*

Linda: Our next stop was the Beverly Hills Supper Club in Kentucky. We were jazzed to be returning to one of the nicer showrooms. The club was across the river from Cincinnati where Patti's parents lived. They were two of the sweetest people; it was going to be delightful to see them again. I fondly recalled the last time we performed at the Supper Club, Moms Mabley was our co-star. Wendy was in the group then and she and Moms had formed a special bond. Moms was an interesting character on and off the stage.

Wendy Kimball, Golddigger 1974-1976: Moms was a hoot. We were all in the kitchen, she was in a wheelchair by that point, and we were all getting ready to go on and I was really nervous. How can you not be nervous doing one of these shows, you always want to be perfect. And she was giving me advice, "Honey, listen, when you get to my age...." She was just darling.

Wayne Dammert, employee of the Beverly Hills Supper Club: I dealt cards at The Beverly Hills for four years for the Mafia, after I got out of the Navy. Back in the mid-thirties it was burned down by the mob because they wanted to take over from the guy that owned it, a little girl got killed in that fire. They took it over and I went to work for the mafia in '57.

The Cincinnati suburb of Newport was called Sin City then, it was a wide open town. Most of the gambling places you went in you didn't have a chance, there were pyramid games and everything you could imagine. It was all illegal. The main guy down there was Moe Dalitz, the mafia guy from up in Cleveland; there was Sam Tucker and John Croft, all these mobster guys. The Flamingo Club, the 4-11 Club, all kinds of clubs were down there.

The Beverly Hills Supper Club was tied in with the Desert Inn in Las Vegas, the same people owned it, and it was a square place. We had four roulette tables, eight or nine blackjack tables, and four crap tables.

I used to go on the stage every night after the show and call Bingo, I got to play golf with Tony Bennett, all the big stars were in there then. Frank Sinatra came in and Dean Martin and Shirley McLaine, I got all of their autographs on a baseball. I saw Errol Flynn there before he died.

After all the gambling clubs were closed in 1961 the Shilling family bought the place and it became a banquet facility and a nightclub. Everybody but me moved on to Vegas, I was the only one who stayed here.

Above: Postcard for The Beverly Hills Supper Club.

235

That place was my life, it sat up on a hill and it was fantastic. The main showroom held close to a thousand and we had the old showroom that held nine hundred. We had banquet rooms all over the grounds. They had a gigantic garden, its own chapel, chandeliers; it was immaculate, beautiful.

The Golddiggers were there two different times, I actually made friends with a couple of the girls. In late 1976 they were there for about a week, at the same time Franki Valli and the Four Seasons were there. I actually had to hold the front door closed and the line went out a couple of blocks down the drive.

Maria: We had a short break from touring after our run at the Beverly Hills so we flew back home. It was always amazing to see how much our brothers and sisters had grown, especially the younger ones. During this trip, we went to SIGMA Sound, a big recording studio in Philadelphia, home of Gamble & Huff. We recorded with producer Vince Montana, Jr. of the Salsoul Orchestra, who wrote some sensational hits in the seventies. Working with him in the studio was an uplifting learning experience. He produced Freda Payne's 'Band of Gold' and was also working with Frank Stallone, Sylvester's brother. We ran into Frank at the studio, this was after the *Rocky* days. He was trying to make a name for himself, away from the shadow of his brother.

We saw Frank again on Christmas Eve, I asked him, "What are you doing for Christmas?"

He said, "Well, I don't have any plans."

I couldn't believe that he didn't have any place to go for the Holidays so I invited him to spend Christmas Eve at my parents' house. We drove him to our home and, on the way, Frank sang along with our car radio and we did harmonies. I was very impressed with his voice and vocal riffs.

He slept on our couch and on Christmas morning he stayed for a while and watched us open presents. We wrapped up some cologne to give to him after we all ate breakfast together. It was enjoyable but puzzling and sad too. I thought, "Why aren't you with your family?"

In December of 1976 Elvis played his 837th and final show in Las Vegas.

I couldn't imagine being away from my family on Christmas.

Linda: I was joking around when we came downstairs on Christmas morning, "Look what Santa Claus brought you for Christmas, Frank." Frank was a good looking guy and all my sisters giggled. All of us made him feel welcome. That day he wasn't a superstar's brother but a human being, part of our family.
The Alberici Christmas chaos must have been entertaining for him. That day he told me he was going to fight in his first boxing match soon. I thought of him possibly getting beaten to a pulp like his brother was in *Rocky*, and I became concerned. He was a little worried about his face getting scarred too. We saw him again when we performed on a Donny & Marie Osmond telethon years later, he was doing exciting things with his band Valentine and moving in a good direction.

Maria: It was always wonderful to spend family time at Christmas. Of course, that meant rolling up our sleeves and getting down to work. Forget about keeping a manicure! There were chores to be done, big meals to prepare and then the clean up afterwards.

Linda: The house was filled with a flurry of activity. There was a lot to do. Buying and wrapping Christmas presents for so many relatives was overwhelming, especially when you're on a budget. In the same way, the opening of the gifts was exhilarating but also exhausting. It was a long process.
Dad insisted on having his picture taken with each person after he opened their gift. That took an extra hour right there. He loved Christmas and wanted to savor the moment. He also loved the attention. My dad would milk the time he got at Christmas like our conductor Charlie would milk the audience for an encore at the end of our show.
After another successful run in Vegas with Dean we had a nice diversion from our usual circuit with an unbelievable extravaganza that was put on at the Cal Neva Lodge in Lake Tahoe. It was a special Gala. We were given the royal treatment, making us feel like guests even though we were there as Dean's opening act.

There were dozens of superstars there that night. I remember staring into Cary Grant's eyes from the stage as we performed our opener, 'I Am Woman.' His eyes were magnetic; I just wanted to melt. I couldn't believe he was in the audience. He was the ultimate movie star to me.

Maria: Lake Tahoe captured the rustic beauty that I had only seen in paintings. I couldn't wait to find the beach and go for a swim. The lake was really cold but refreshing and absolutely crystal clear. I remember floating in it and feeling such a sense of peace, nature always made me feel more alive and balanced.

Lake Tahoe was also a setting for great sadness when we discovered one evening that our conductor, Charlie Sanford, had suffered an aneurysm in his room and died. All of us were speechless. How could we do our show without Charlie? Well, you know the saying, 'The show must go on.' Our drummer knew the tempos and we could do the routine in our sleep. Performing the show without Charlie felt weird. I missed his encouraging smile and joyful energy on stage. It wasn't until our encore that I felt Charlie's presence, as we sang 'Jesus Christ Superstar' and 'Let The Sunshine In.' With the utmost respect, we sang like angels and I sensed Charlie's spirit lovingly conducting us from above.

Tim Fowlar, musical conductor, Roy Radin Revue 1973-1979:

Charlie was a great guy, I was horrified to hear he'd passed away. At least he went the way he wanted to go, to be in the midst of a tour, doing what he loved to do.

They were ready for the show and Charlie hadn't come down, somebody went up and found him dead and they still did their show. That's what we all learned from these vaudeville people we were on the road with, that no matter what happened you did the show.

Robyn Whatley, Golddigger 1976-1987:

Charlie had different speeds he would conduct in. He would read the audience. Some nights the show would be really fast and perky and on other nights it would be a much slower tempo and we'd look at each other and go, "Oh, okay, we can actually sing all the lyrics."

Charlie was having the time of his life. How many seventy-six-year olds get to travel with six vivacious young women all over the world? We all would carry

Frank Sinatra was an owner of the Cal-Neva Lodge from 1960 to 1963.

nitro-glycerin in our purses because he could have had a heart attack at any time. He told us, "That's fine, that's how I want to go, doing a show." He almost made his wish come true, he was getting ready for the show when he died.

Joyce Garro, Golddigger 1976-1978: He was so much fun, a hard worker. He smoked a lot, back when everybody was smoking cigarettes. We called ourselves Charlie's Angels, Charlie Sanford's angels.

Peggy Gohl, Golddigger 1974-1990: We were in Chicago once staying at the Palmer House. Charlie Sanford was in the hallway at the cigarette machine getting some Camels. I jokingly told Charlie, "You better get out of town because here comes Al Alberici." And he took off like a shot into his room because he thought the father was coming around the corner!

Linda: Charlie usually tried to avoid my dad because he knew my father would say something about his smoking. He had experienced his lectures in the past. Charlie was always meaning to cut down on the cigarettes but he didn't have much success with that.
It was strange and sad continuing on without Charlie. I missed him and his impish smile; he could light up a room. I felt the loss of his amazing energy behind me as he conducted and we performed. Without a doubt,

he lifted us up during our shows. Charlie was as much a part of the group as my Golddigger girlfriends.

Anticipating our upcoming gig in Chicago, Joyce's home town, helped ease my grief. Her family was always so warm toward us. Our repeat performances there were an occasion we all looked forward to. Along the way we also made some friends at the beautiful Blue Max Room. The crew there was the best. The Golddiggers would be following singer/actor, James Darren into the showroom.

> **Jackie Savaiano, *Chicago Tribune*, April, 1977:** *The Golddiggers performing at the Hyatt Regency Blue Max Room offer a good hour of sparkling old fashioned entertainment. And they do sparkle. From the moment the six pretty women file onstage, they flash smiles that challenge Farrah Fawcett's and gyrate so energetically that even the light that dances off their sequined chiffon gowns sparkles. The technically competent performers change rhythms, sing, dance, and include the audience in their revue of old and new country tunes, torch songs, show themes, love ballads and light rock numbers.*

Joyce Garro, Golddigger 1976-1978: The Blue Max was in the Hyatt in Chicago, it was a top showroom. It really was a classy place. They had a great band, the conductors were either Joe Vito or Joe Gatone. The room was intimate because it wasn't really big, we could reach out and touch the people. We would get guys out of the audience to come dance the Hustle with us onstage.

Irv Kupcinet was a Chicago newspaper columnist, he put on a Purple Heart cruise every year where he would rent a boat and take out a group of veterans for the entire day. We performed on one of the cruises when we played The Blue Max, it brought so much happiness to those veterans to have all of us girls there.

> **Margaret Carroll, *Chicago Tribune*:** *On Sunday Joyce Garro won't have to sing for her supper and neither will five fellow Golddiggers who will observe their one day of rest by partaking of an Italian feast at the Cicero home of her parents George and Delores Garro.*

Suburban Week, May 4 & 5, 1977 'As Good as Gold' by Lorelei Czarnecki:
If you like pretty girls, good harmonizing and a fast-moving show, you'll strike it rich with The Golddiggers. The six members of the showy song-and-dance group flash their gams in the Blue Max night club at the Hyatt Regency O'Hare through this Saturday. But each Golddigger works hard to prove that she's not just another pretty face. Each attractive member has talent.
They demonstrate a professional onstage attitude of respect for one another. Though their image is sexy, The Golddiggers have a clean wholesome appearance.

Maria: Chicago was a familiar stomping ground for our group during the 1970s so we felt more comfortable socializing and venturing outside the hotel. During one of our engagements, Don Cornelius, the host of the TV series *Soul Train*, picked us up in a limo and escorted us to one of his star studded events. Quite often, I would watch *Soul Train* to copy some funky and trendy dance moves while the R&B recording artists performed their hit songs. The program originated in Chicago starting in 1971, it was the hottest dance show in the nation by 1977. We loved working in Chicago. The manager of the Blue Max, Arnie Fleishman, was very cordial and after our show he took some of us girls on a tour of the Windy City. As I strolled the boulevards I couldn't help hearing Frank Sinatra singing the

city's theme song in my head.
We visited some very high-end jazz clubs that had a gangster feel to them. Arnie made sure that we were all treated like 'stars'. His job gave him the opportunity to see many performers entertain and he encouraged Linda and I to branch out from The Golddiggers to perform our own act. His confidence in our talent meant a lot to us.
Chicago had a vibe and a rhythm all its own; it's like the song says, "Bet your bottom dollar, you'll lose the blues in Chicago, Chicago..." The glittering lights, the pulse of the clubs and the earthy sophistication of the people were just a dazzling prelude for what was to come.

Frank Sinatra, Latin Casino, Cherry Hill, N.J., May 5, 1977: *Here we are in our love-in. Every night's a love-in. And on Friday, Saturday, and Sunday—twice a night. Delighted to be with you again. I like coming down here, the people who own this great place are fabulous human beings, sweet and gentle with us and the audiences have been well, indescribable actually. And that's appreciated very much because without that there would be nothing to look forward to.*

And I'd like to make an announcement. It's already leaked out but I'd like to tell you officially that we'll be back here in June.... with Dean Martin and myself. And it's going to be loads of laughs here with Drunky. If he can find the joint he'll be here every night. He's marvelous to work with. He's a lovely man, he's a hell of a guy.

Ol' Blue Eyes

& Ol' Red Eyes

243

Anthony Bruno, crime writer, author of *The Iceman*: The old joke is, you walk into a first generation Italian-American's home and there's three pictures on the wall—Jesus Christ, John Kennedy and Frank Sinatra. Somehow Frank became the premier Italian-American entertainer. Dean, I guess for a couple of reasons, wasn't as revered. Certainly he was respected. Dean was from the midwest for one thing and I think the drinking image that he cultivated might have turned a few people off.

> **Dean Martin, *Dean Martin Roast of Frank Sinatra*, 1977:**
> *I'm truly fortunate to be counted as one of Frank's friends. I'm pretty lucky. Every night I get on my knees and pray. I pray that I can get* off *my knees!*
> *This man's success should serve as an inspiration to every American boy. Frank Sinatra was born in Hoboken, New Jersey as an unwanted child. And now he's wanted in five states. Especially in the state of New York. As you know, New York City has been having its financial troubles. Nobody knew Frank had lent money to New York until they found the Statue of Liberty with her arms broken.*

Linda: We were booked for what was being nicknamed the Rat Pack Tour in early summer 1977 with Dean and Frank Sinatra. Frank was already on the road with Pat Henry as his warm up so Dean brought us along for his opening act. Dean would have his conductor Ken Lane whereas Frank brought along Bill Miller to lead the orchestra while he sang.
We'd worked with so many legendary Italian crooners and now to share the stage with both Dean and Frank Sinatra—it was a thrill of a lifetime.

Jody Gerson, daughter of the Latin Casino owners: My father booked Sinatra in 1976 and they had such a

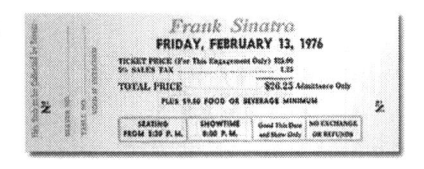

good time together and it was so tremendous that Sinatra said to my father, "What can I do for you? I'm going to come back, what can I do for you?" My father said, "Bring Dean Martin with you." And Sinatra said, "Okay, as long as you play golf with him every day."
I remember it very well, I was sixteen at the time. And my father did play golf with him every day.
They were amazing performers, there was an element of class. There was a certain decorum in dealing with fans and dealing with people. They were gentlemen, whatever they were behind the scenes as soon as the curtain came up they were gentlemen. I remember all kinds of people calling our house when they were playing, looking for my dad, trying to get tickets.

Maria: We were scheduled to do two shows a night, Pat Henry would go on first, then The Golddiggers, then Dean and finally Frank. After Frank's set, Dean would join him on stage for some comedy and a long medley of their hits. For the two hour concert they would be on stage about an hour and fifteen minutes.

Nancy Sinatra, Frank's daughter, *USA Weekend*: Dad and Dean Martin were very close. Neither one of them had a real brother, so they thought of each other as brothers—blood brothers. They actually pierced their fingers one day and mixed their blood.

Shawn Levy, author of *Rat Pack Confidential*: It's funny with Dean. He went from a partnership with this short-tempered, talented, in many ways kindred, only child from New Jersey—Jerry Lewis.
Then he had an unofficial partnership with a short-tempered, volatile, gifted and in many ways kindred only child from New Jersey in Frank Sinatra. It makes you wonder what was going on with Dean that he was drawn to two personalities that were so similar.
In Dean and Jerry, Dean was famously the straight man and Jerry was the comic. Next to Sinatra, Dean was the comic and Frank was the straight man.

Laurence Leamer, author of *King of the Night*: *Johnny [Carson] was sitting at the bar at Jilly's with Joanne and Ed McMahon. The door swung open and Frank Sinatra walked in with more bodyguards and hangers-on than an Arab Potentate. An aura of uncertainty surrounded Sinatra. The room grew so quiet that you could hear the flattery drop. Johnny waited until the singer reached his table. He looked at Sinatra, then at his watch, and back at the singer. "Frank," Johnny said, "I told you twelve-thirty."*

Maria: Before we left for the first date Greg's office instructed us in no uncertain terms not to go up and talk to Frank, he had recently added a clause to his contract that stated no one, no matter how famous, was to be allowed backstage or to approach him for any reason. They told us, "Just be polite, don't go out of your way to speak to Frank or his family or his entourage of bodyguards." We were "Dean's girls," that was the speech given to us before embarking on our journey.

We were scheduled to kick off the tour on May 16, 1977 with two weeks at the Westchester Premier Theatre in Tarrytown, New York to be followed by a week at The Latin Casino, where we'd appeared so many times before. That meant home sweet home for us. After that we'd travel with Dean and Frank to Chicago's famed Sabre Room for four nights. We would do two shows a night, our first started at 6:30 but our second performance didn't begin until 11:00 so there was plenty of time to rest up and maybe get something to eat. That meant Dean and Frank would take the stage at around 11:30 for their last hour or so on the stage.

We had worked with Dean many times in Vegas and on television but this was far different. For one thing Dean rarely traveled outside of Las Vegas or Lake Tahoe to perform. It was practically unheard of.

It was an honor to be opening for Dean and Frank together, they were bigger than rock stars, they were the top. When the first day of rehearsal at the Westchester Premier Theatre arrived there was an air of respectful anticipation backstage as everyone hurriedly prepared for the headliners as if history was in the making. We began to feel the weight of their celebrity. Was Frank in the building yet? Would Dean arrive first to break the mounting tension? I lingered around with the rest of the backstage workers to get a first peek, I had never seen Frank Sinatra in person.

They both showed up for rehearsal in tuxes. Frank was a little more casual, he was wearing a black top coat instead of his tux jacket. They faced off onstage like two matadors in search of a bull.

> The Sinatra era Rat Pack, also referred to as "the summit" or "the clan," consisted of Frank Sinatra, Dean Martin, Sammy Davis, Jr., Joey Bishop, and Peter Lawford. The original Holmbly Hills Rat Pack included Humphrey Bogart, Frank Sinatra, Judy Garland, Sid Luft, Katharine Hepburn, Spencer Tracy, Lauren Bacall, David Niven, George Cukor, Cary Grant, Rex Harrison, Swifty Lazar, Nathaniel Benchley, and Jimmy Van Heusen.

Our first rehearsal with the orchestra ended up like a private audition for Frank Sinatra. When we assembled on stage we were told Frank wanted to see our act—so we gave it our best shot. Would he like us?

Well, he loved us. I never remember Dean or any other star asking to see our performance before the audience arrived so this revealed a lot about Frank Sinatra.

Opening night, some of us Golddiggers were backstage sitting on the stairs having a little chit-chat. We were waiting for the stage manager to give us the cue to take our places in the wings before the show. All of a sudden we gazed up to the top of the stairs—standing in the archway was Frank Sinatra. He had a powerful aura, he wasn't a big man but he was bigger than life. Of course, we were speechless. He broke the silence by wishing us a good show and told us to "get that audience all worked up for us."

Wow, it felt like the king had arrived and was addressing his court.

Shawn Levy, author of *Rat Pack Confidential*: Frank was an Italian-American boy from Hoboken, New Jersey born in 1915 with no siblings. How is that remotely possible? We're talking about a generation where people had nine kids.

In those years Frank was lonely and he was better to do than his neighbors. He was like a Little Lord Fauntleroy, he always had new clothes. The kids on the street called him 'slacksie'

because he always had new pants.

There's a wonderful description that Kitty Kelley got from one of his childhood neighbors of him standing on the stoop of his house in Hoboken and watching the other kids playing, being too hesitant to be a part of that. Whether it was because he didn't want to put a hole in his new pants or he was afraid because he was a little guy with big ears, whatever it was.

That guy? I can understand how that guy grew up to always want to be in the middle of a party. And when he was rich and famous the party came to him, he could throw the party whenever he wanted. Dean had a more typical family upbringing. Little Italy of Stubenville was really little and he could walk to all his aunts' and uncles' and grandparents' houses. Growing up in that environment you wouldn't have the same thirst from the womb for companionship that Frank always had.

Joyce Garro, Golddigger 1976-1978:
I'm one hundred percent Italian-American, all of my grandparents were born in Italy, so this was a thrill for me because of the Italian connection. My mother always had Dean Martin, Jerry Vale, Al Martino and Frank Sinatra records playing in the house.

At the rehearsal on the first day of the tour Dean came up to me to say hello and asked, "Have you met Frank?" I said, "You know, actually Dean, I've never met Frank." So he brought me over to Frank and he said, "Hey Frank, I want you to meet little Dago."

He's the only person who could ever get away with calling me that. It was actually endearing, it didn't even bother me, it was sweet the way he said it. I was really touched by that. Again, it's that very important Italian connection that we have with each other.

Maria: There was definitely a thick Italian atmosphere backstage. Dean introduced us to Frank as, "the Italian Sisters." Frank smirked, "Sisters?" Everyone was always surprised that we were related because our coloring was so different. "We're really half breeds because our mom is Hungarian." Dean joked that, "We won't hold that against you!" Frank really gave us the once over, looking back and forth at our faces and

"You only live once, and the way I live, once is enough."—Frank Sinatra

then up and down. He seemed to like the combination but there was no telling what he was thinking.

Then, Linda broke in, "Our Italian grandfather had light hair and blue eyes just like you." Frank asked, "What part of Italy does your family come from?" That was pretty much the vibe before the show, light and fun; except for the bodyguards hanging around the edges with their steely gazes.

Helen Costa, wife of Sinatra's musical arranger Don Costa:
The reason they called him Ol' Blue Eyes—a lot of people have blue eyes but he had a tremendous energy coming from his eyes, when he

walked into a room it was electrifying. His eyes were it, I think that's what really endeared him to the audience because they connected through that energy and he made every person feel he was singing to them. It was more his talent for phrasing than having the greatest voice ever; it was enough that he had the phrasing and the energy to simulate that intimacy on stage. He had that power, he was very intense all the time.

Sinatra's success stemmed from musicianship. If you were good he hired you, that was it. He had three or four or five top musicians that used to do his arrangements. He was very generous in his appreciation for musicianship, he always gave them credit. He was particular, had perfect pitch and great ears for any kind of mistakes.

Marty Walsh, studio guitarist: I was doing demos for Don Costa with my buddy Bob Walden, we used to do all the guitar work for him. Don had a publishing company and had these writers so they were hiring me and a bunch of inexperienced guys to play on their song demos. All of a sudden Don started calling us his rhythm section because we were getting pretty good, you know?

Don was a brilliant musician, he started out as a guitar player. He was a very personable guy, real likeable. We would go to his house to record and it was kinda like "My house is your house. Go hang out in the kitchen, have food, talk to the wife."

One day my phone rings and it was Don's brother Leo calling to book me for a Sinatra session. I couldn't believe it. I was like, "You're kidding me." I thought Don Costa was pretty cool to call the young cats to play. We were pretty green, man. He was starting to use us on his albums but nothing of this magnitude. Frank was really cool. The guitarists' chairs were in front, pretty close to his vocal mic. He walked in, came right over and said hello, shook our hands and was really sweet. It was crazy, man.

His back was facing the glass for the control room. They had a couple of baffles set up in front of his mic and stand. He had his guys that were like taking care of him, right? He would put his hand on the other side of this baffle so you could just see his hand and he snapped his fingers and this dude came flying out of the control room, "What can I do for you Frank, what can I do?"

The conductor on the date, Vincent Falcone, was wearing a blue, long-sleeve shirt and about a half hour in he was soaked head to toe he was so nervous. He was literally dripping.

> **Dom DeLuise:** *Frank was a good friend of mine, I worked with him on* The Dean Martin Show. *I asked him one time, "What did your father think of your singing?" He said, "My father said get a regular job already, what are you doing? What is this with the singing? Get a job!"*

Robyn Whatley, Golddigger 1976-1987: I was talking to Frank Sinatra, this was during a rehearsal day and we're just hanging out while the lighting guys were doing their thing. Frank was going on and on saying, "This girls' group, you guys are fantastic." Then Dean walked up on stage and Frank Sinatra said, "I want these girls Dean, they're just the best. I want 'em as my girls."

Dean said very slowly, "My marquee says 'Dean Martin and The Golddiggers.' That's how it's gonna stay. You can look at them, listen to them but I get neck massages, jokes and kisses, noooo waaaay you're getting them."

Maria: In their own right, Sinatra and Martin were brilliant performers, more than pros, they were living legends. Frank and Dean had charisma, no doubt about that, but Dean had a cool swagger and a naughty boy gleam in his eyes while Frank had that purposeful strut and a devilish way of teasing.

Dean had a natural way of making people feel comfortable. He didn't go out of his way to make an impression or try to be charming, he just was.

May 23, 1977 Frank & Dean appeared in New York City for the State Lottery drawing.

Time magazine cover story, May 16, 1977: *Why does the Mafia attract so much attention? Many Italian Americans complain that the notoriety is excessive, and damaging to millions of law-abiding citizens; to assuage their sensibilities, the Justice Department has stopped referring to the Mafia by name. No matter what the organization is called, it dominates much of American crime. Many nonmember gangsters are allied to it, usually kicking back a share of their take to the dons; some criminologists estimate that at least 50,000 hoods can be considered confederates of the Mafia. The Mafia is by far the best organized criminal group in the U.S. and the only one with a national structure: 26 families—five of them in New York City—of from 20 to 1,000 "button men," or soldiers.*

With Frank you had to know he was in command but, even though he had a take charge air about him, he displayed a wider range of emotional colors when he performed. Frank was all about getting inside the music, it was the art of seduction for him.

They were both known as swingers, not only in their music but in real life. They lived a lavish lifestyle by any measure but they never bragged or flaunted their legendary status as the nucleus of The Rat Pack. They just were who they were. No explanations. No apologies.

Helen Costa, wife of Sinatra's musical arranger Don Costa: There were times Sinatra was verbally abusive but then that was his outlet. He had a piano player in the 1960s, Bill Miller, and he was very nasty to him, he was like somebody to take it out on. He had an extreme conflict in his personality of being a great artist, generous of heart and then being as mean as possible. God knows you can't throw stones because you can't get inside of him, you don't know what it was like to have that pressure on him.

Linda: The Westchester Premier Theatre, where we opened on May 16, 1977, was the place where Frank was photographed backstage with the area's most notorious mafia figures just a year earlier. That picture would haunt him for the rest of his life after the FBI got a hold of it.

Anthony Bruno, crime writer, author of *The Iceman*: The Westchester Premier Theatre was a money making scam for the mob. The idea was that they were going to exploit their contacts in entertainment and get more out of this place and sell out at big ticket prices. They did

"Ya wanna know the truth?" – our mom

except that their instincts got the better of them. Usually when the mob takes over a business they do what's called a "bust out"—use it as collateral for loans they have no intention of ever paying back, sell off the assets. They'll do anything to make money. In 1976 they were really strapped and cooler heads decided, "Let's try to keep this thing going" because it was a money maker, they made a big profit the first year. They turned to Frank Sinatra and asked "Frank, will you come back and do some more dates and get your pals to come and work here?" As a result, it became the premier theatre on the East Coast for Vegas style acts.

> **J. D. Chandler, 'Frank Sinatra and the Mob', Crimemagazine.com:** *The [Westchester Premier] theater was huge and very well appointed. The biggest acts in show business were booked there and the gross for the first year was estimated at $5.3 million. But by December 1976 the theater was near bankruptcy.*
> *Only a run of performances by Sinatra and Dean Martin in May 1977 delayed the closing of the theater. Federal agents, investigating another matter, tapped the phone of Tom Marson, a friend and Palm Springs neighbor of Sinatra. They recorded a conversation between Marson and De Palma in which they discussed skimming cash from the upcoming Sinatra appearance at the Westchester Premier Theatre. The result of this conversation was 10 indictments handed down by a New York Grand Jury in June 1978. During the investigation it came out that Sinatra was paid $50,000 "under the table" for his first appearance there. Sinatra was never indicted.*

Linda: Whenever a group of guys in suits came to visit Frank, Maria and I would give each other this knowing sideways glance. Okay, we pretty much assumed that these people were connected. We heard stories and our imaginations would churn but our naive and somewhat innocent minds could never begin to conceive whatever might have been the real truth.

Gay Talese, 'Frank Sinatra Has a Cold', *Esquire*: *On the one hand he is the swinger—as he is when talking and joking with Sammy Davis, Jr., Richard Conte, Liza Minnelli, Bernie Massi, or any of the other show-business people who get to sit at the table; on the other, as when he is nodding or waving to his* paisanos *who are close to him (Al Silvani, a boxing manager who works with Sinatra's film company; Dominic Di Bona, his wardrobe man; Ed Pucci, a 300-pound former football lineman who is his aide-de-camp), Frank Sinatra is* Il Padrone. *Or better still, he is what in traditional Sicily have long been called* uomini rispettati—*men of respect: men who are both majestic and humble, men who are loved by all and are very generous by nature, men whose hands are kissed as they walk from village to village, men who would personally go out of their way to redress a wrong.*

Peggy Gohl, Golddigger 1974-1991: I have a photo of Jilly Rizzo, who was Sinatra's bodyguard, with a little tiny gun sticking out of the back of his sweater while Frank and Dean were on stage with thousands of hands reaching up from the audience.

Frank Sinatra about Dean, Westchester Premier Theatre May 22, 1977: *You realize Dean's the best friend I ever had in my life? And he once said this about me—that I had an affair with a deaf and dumb girl and then broke her fingers so she couldn't tell anybody. That's the best friend I have that said that.*

Anthony Bruno, crime writer, author of *The Iceman*: Frank was kind of a mob groupie. He benefited from Willie Moretti who was a New Jersey boss back in the thirties and forties. Moretti was really the Godfather character that helped Sinatra, got him out of trouble and helped him with his career and got him out of contracts he'd had with band leaders so that he could further himself.

Not that he actively sought out these people. Because his mother operated a bar he probably just knew these guys. It was natural that they would reach out to him and he would accept their help. If you grew up in Hoboken, New Jersey in those days, you know, the local mob guy was the butcher, the baker and the candlestick maker. He was just like another guy in town.

It wasn't that unusual to know them. I come from a similar town, Orange in New Jersey, and I grew up in the sixties and, you know, we knew who the mob guys were. You didn't have to deal with them but they were just a reality of life, they were there.

Frank had that one guy, Jilly Rizzo, who was his constant companion everywhere. I imagine that Frank liked to act like a Don. He admired that lifestyle, he wanted to surround himself with protectors. He liked the fact that people feared him.

I think a lot of it is exaggerated. I don't think he was a criminal himself, I don't think he was ever involved in any crimes but I think he knew these guys, I think he respected them. Maybe looked the other way in some cases but he was a complex guy.

Photo: Jilly Rizzo with Frank and Barbara Sinatra, June 29, 1977.

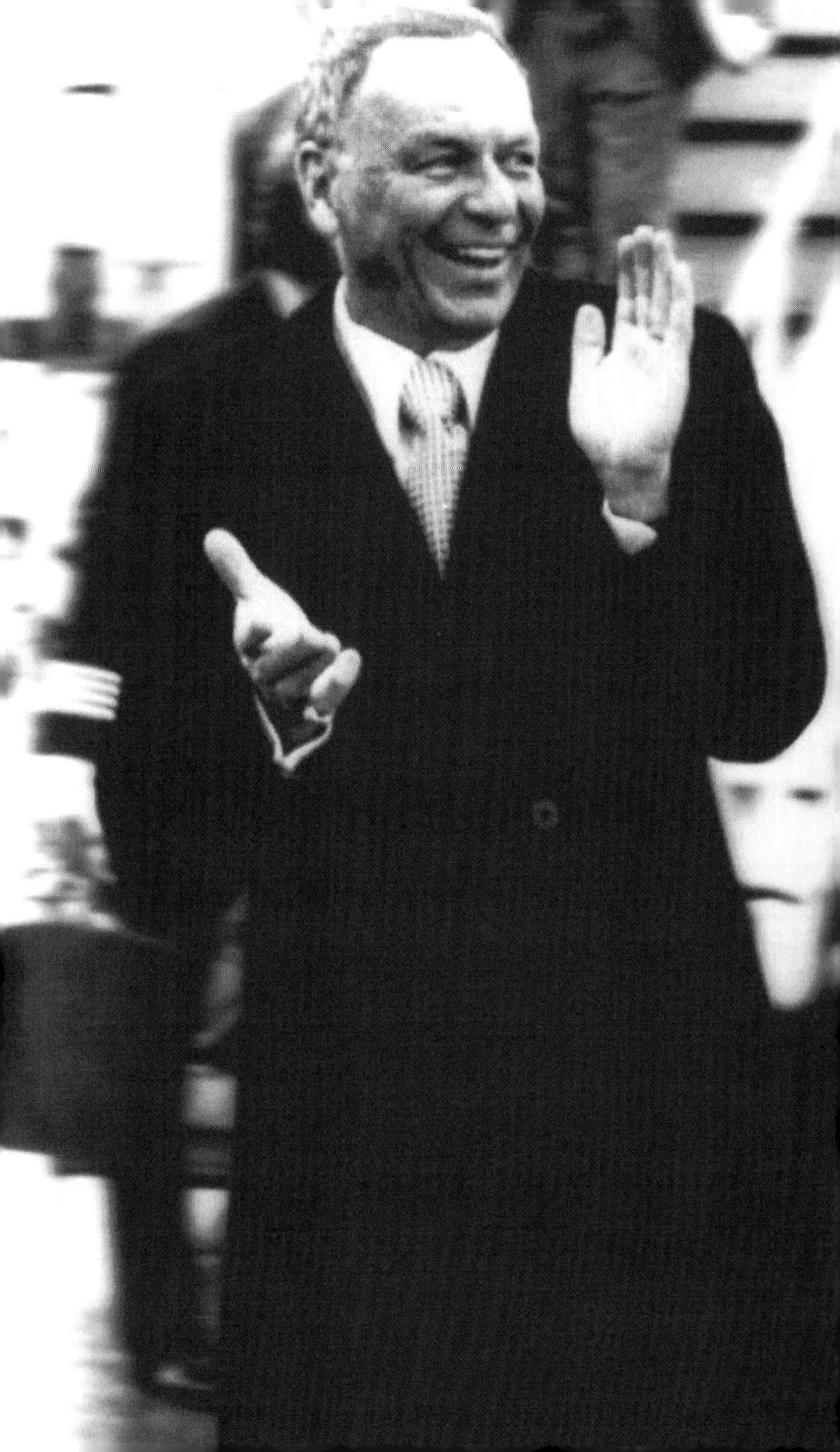

Here's a guy who starts his life as a liberal, pro-civil rights and so on, and he ends up his life arch-conservative, hanging out with Reagan. And yet it all seems to fit with him.

How much power did he actually have? I have no idea. Could he ruin a career? I don't know. Could he make a career? Probably could. It's very hard to say. But he liked acting like a Don, going into a restaurant and taking over, that kind of stuff.

Chuck Anderson, guitarist: One night I asked a guy I worked with, "Who do you work for?"
He said, "I work for the mob."
I said, "You're a conductor and work for the mob?"
He says, "Yes."
And I said, "Well, how do you find working for the mafia?"
He says, "They leave me alone, they're very nice, they're very polite, they expect me to be on time, they expect me to be sober, do my job, and they pay me very well."
So it gave me a very different view of our television and film idea of the mafia guys. South Philly was the Angelo Bruno family and all the different crime families were in Philadelphia and in New York. But it never affected the music. It's not really that much of a surprise, Vegas was founded by Bugsy Siegel. The mafia was kind of a big, organized corporation. It wasn't the St. Valentine's Day massacre.

Helen Costa, wife of Sinatra's musical arranger Don Costa:
Don did a few things for the mob so they liked him; he wasn't really involved too much with them, just on the fringe.
I don't know how much influence the mafia had, they just needed something done so that if you ever needed them to do you a favor there was an exchange of favors there. You just don't say no, that's all.

Linda: At the start of our run newspapers all over the country ran photos of Dean and Frank performing together on stage again, The Rat Pack was back and we were right in the thick of it.
Frank was the Chairman of the Board and he traveled with his kingdom wherever he performed. And the court jesters were these shady

"Cock your hat—angles are attitudes." - Frank Sinatra

wise-guys that followed him around everywhere. It was really something. Every once in a while they would quickly assemble and look like they had something important to attend to but mostly they would just hang out. Frank's wife Barbara was around a lot to watch rehearsals, she was very elegant and regal. Barbara even instructed one of the girls on how to apply her makeup in a more glamorous fashion. Barbara gave her some marvelous tips. We learned a lot about presence, Frank had a regal bearing and so did Barbara. They knew who they were, who was in their kingdom and who wasn't. They projected a feeling of being very secure in themselves.

Maria: Frank added the song 'I Love My Wife' from a show of the same name that opened in New York that summer. I never heard anyone sing it but Sinatra, the song had beautiful lyrics that meshed perfectly with Frank's musical arrangement, artfully penned by Nelson Riddle. The sweeping violins from that lush, full orchestra Sinatra had at his fingertips filled my heart with emotion. The song took on a life all its own since Barbara was present for some of the tour. They were newlyweds after all. I'm sure she appreciated Frank's sentimental nod to her, a tribute to their love for each other.

Helen Costa, wife of Sinatra's musical arranger Don Costa: In later years Frank was singing and he had a seizure or something and he fell off the stool in the middle of the performance and the audience just froze, there was dead silence and nobody knew what to do. His wife Barbara went up and said, "Oh, it's nothing, this happens to him all the time." Nancy, his first wife, was there and she's the one that called the ambulance and was concerned about it because he was always very generous with her and they remained friends after the divorce. Barbara was as cold as steel.

Maria: Frank was the master chess player, the manipulator of the chess board. One night he invited us all to dinner in a lovely private room backstage. The beautifully appointed tables were situated outside the receiving area where we spoke with his wife Barbara before we were seated. She looked stunning with her hair pulled back, accentuating her perfect features. When it was time for dinner the bodyguards were close by and escorted us to our tables.

Linda: Patti was bold, she grabbed the first open seat closest to Frank. I sat about four or five places away from him. I felt a little awkward, in the way someone would if they were having dinner with royalty for the first time. I didn't know what to talk about so I mostly listened. Frank talked a while about Italian cooking and visiting friends who lived in the area, he liked to cook linguine for his guests.

Peggy Gohl, Golddigger 1974-1991: There were two big round tables, Dean and Frank were at one table and I sat at the table with Jilly where he proceeded to tell us his personal anecdotes, like they were old war stories. He almost reminded me of a kid talking about Cowboys and Indians. He said that he and Frank had dinner in some restaurant in New York where they had words with the owner, I don't know what this disagreement was about but Jilly said he exploded a bomb in the toilet. I was kicking the girls under the table like, "Oh my God." He also talked about being on the run in Monte Carlo, jumping over bridges while a hoard of angry people were chasing him down the streets.

Pat Cooper, comedian: Sinatra had an entourage of people who thought he was Jesus Christ. I'm talkin' about tough guys who bent down for this guy. I mean, this guy had an army of people that adored him, "Hey, Frank, I love you Frank. Mention me to Frank. Tell Frank I'm outside. Tell him I loves him." Not one of them were men, not one of them were men if you know what I'm talkin' about.

Robyn Whatley, Golddigger 1976-1987: Frank had lots of bodyguards. That just went along with the image that Frank created. There was Big Mike, one guy was Hammer and another was Lefty, another guy was Whitey. Jilly had one eye, he was the main bodyguard. It's like that old joke, "Is that a gun in your pocket or are you just glad to see me?" Except it really was a gun in this instance. Our group had to be fully dressed, ready to go on stage about a half hour before show time. Frank Sinatra admired that so he started saying to some of his entourage, "You go over there and watch those girls, take care of them." So we ended up sort of having our own bodyguards for a while, that was fun.

Linda: Dean had the "broads," Frank had the "goons." When the two of them were together they fell right into their old Rat Pack personas, even offstage, entertaining anyone who was within range. It was rare but once in a while we got to witness how they liked to rib each other in private.
Sometimes Frank got pushy and too intense but one thing about Dean, he could stand his ground with him. Dean would have none of that. After all he didn't need the adulation or the money. If it wasn't fun, forget it. Frank was a little guarded with us but also very gracious.

Robyn Whatley, Golddigger 1976-1987: Dean was naturally very funny so he had Frank laughing all the time. They had such a routine and fell right back into it even though they had not been together in concert for a decade or so.

Dean never rehearsed but Frank Sinatra was very professional, into details, let's put it that way. Our dressing room was right next to his and the walls were paper thin. He would literally do vocal rehearsals for at least thirty minutes before every show. And Dean would come in and kinda go, "Ah, is the stage still where we left it?"

Maria: As the concerts got underway, the music from the stage drew Linda and I like a magnet. It was suggested that we shouldn't hang out with Frank and his people but one night my sister and I slipped into the backstage area and towards the outskirts of the stage. When one of 'Frank's people' came over to us my heart stopped but we were cordially invited to come closer to the stage area. We were even offered some high stools to sit on. I began to breathe again as Linda and I sat demurely, trying not to be too conspicuous.

Dean was introduced as he always was in Vegas, with a drum roll and a guy backstage announcing, "....straight from the bar, Dean Martin!" The orchestra played his theme song as he strolled out on stage, grooved to the music and expertly stumbled as if he had been drinking. The audience laughed hysterically and egged him on.

Dean would lazily croon most of his tunes but he could get down and grind out a song too. During 'That's Amore' he would prance and dance around the stage while he sang. When he ran out of breath in the middle, he stopped singing and hung on the piano to run through some jokes with orchestra leader Ken Lane. After the interlude Dean would jump

Photo: Dean and Frank at the Westchester Premier Theater.

back into the song with a tempo change which led to the big ending. Dean had a signature riff, a series of high notes that cued the audience into a rowdy applause. The pacing was genius but Dean would turn to Ken and say, "No more fast ones, it can get you hot. The last time I was this hot I had a kid!"

Linda: I loved listening to the show after we performed our spot. Dean's opening 'When You're Drinking/Bourbon From Heaven' seamlessly led into his monologue. He would ad-lib a lot so each night was different, women inevitably went wild and randomly shouted out vows of love to Dean. He was always so clever and quick with the comebacks. While singing 'Everybody Loves Somebody Sometime' Dean shamelessly flirted leaving the ladies speechless. Then, to prime the audience, Dean brought them into the Rat Pack mystique by adding Frank and Sammy jokes to his patter.

Dean Martin, from the tour: *Remember the great words of Sammy Davis, Jr. who said to his Rabbi, "You're gonna cut off my what!?!"*

Maria: From our more intimate perspective offstage I could see that Frank was attempting to portray a hipper image. He had changed some of his standard arrangements to be like the trendy music played in New York's Studio 54 where the 'Jet Set' partied. Frank opened with 'All or Nothing at All' set to a driving disco beat. Of course, this arrangement still had the big band sound that had become part of the Sinatra experience. Frank also performed 'Night and Day' with that percussive big brass beat. Sinatra was so smart to get on the disco bandwagon, he was always adapting to new musical styles and the top forty in 1977 was crowded with disco remakes of familiar songs. I liked the flavor of the music but Frank seemed a little out of his comfort zone, especially with the rhythm. Frank's style fit better with his standard swing arrangement of 'Night and Day' but I would have jumped at the opportunity to sing to this new hip version.

Linda: Dean liked to make wisecracks about Frank's womanizing and reveled in making sport of Sinatra's mob connections. He brought up an incident when Frank phoned him saying, "Hey Deg, why don't you come to Vegas." Dean said he didn't dare ask him "why" because he was afraid Frank might "make a phone call."
Dean brought out Frank's playful side on stage. They had a sizzling chemistry together and fed off of each other's energy, they were able to get away with a lot of gangster humor and risqué one liners back and forth. It was 'politically incorrect' but the audience loved it and urged them on. Even celebrities weren't safe from the duo's roasting wit. I had to chuckle when Frank stepped out of character and did a ruthless Barbara Walters imitation. He hated Barbara Walters, he would also ridicule gossip columnist Rona Barrett or anyone else that irrated him at the moment.

Elaine Bissell, *Reporter Dispatch*, White Plains, N.Y., May 18, 1977: *The pre-curtain arrival of celebrities, including Gov. Carey, former New York City Mayor Robert Wagner and even the beautiful Barbara Marx Sinatra, caused a flurry of excitement in the crowded theater as they settled down in the first row center, but the real thunder of applause and shouts from the adoring fans came when first Mr. Martin appeared and swayed precariously through a number of songs and then Mr. Sinatra, who simply walked on stage as though strolling to the corner to mail a letter—and the roof seemed to fall in.*
For the next hour the flash of cameras and streaking ladies dashing down the darkened aisles to the stage to throw or hand flowers to the two singers in the spotlights was like half of an army choreographed in a ritual dance, while the other half sat with dazed faces and roaring with approval, with love, with worship, or moaning then shrieking with hysteria when either one walked anywhere near the edge of the stage.

Linda: Frank's act was superb. When people have their craft down like he did, you can't put your finger on one certain thing that makes it great but it was. He had a combination of attributes that were spellbinding in the same way his albums had an inherent quality with magnificent Don Costa arrangements on those immortal Sinatra classics like the swinging 'Night and Day,' or his signature tune in the seventies, 'My Way.' Before breaking into his traditional closer, Frank usually gave a shout out to Don Costa and Paul Anka, the song's author. 'My Way' could have come across as an arrogant declaration of will but Sinatra transformed it into a soul searching ballad that revealed his vulnerability and wisdom.

And then the comedy would start again. The most irreverent comments were made at the mobile bar Dean wheeled out after Sinatra finished 'My Way,' that's where they fired off silly toasts and told jokes. I'm not sure if there was real alcohol in their glasses but the more they drank, the nuttier they got. After that, Dean and Frank launched into a lighthearted medley of songs including some of their hits—'I Can't Give You Anything but Love,' 'Embraceable You,' 'The Lady Is a Tramp' and 'When you're Smiling.' The audience cheered as the two pros harmonized together, Dean taking the lower baritone notes with Frank taking the higher tenor notes. All of it was sheer magic.

Frank and Dean purposely wrecked the medley, of course, forgetting what came next or stopping mid-song to carouse. Ken Lane casually vamped behind them to let them have their kicks. Truth was, Dean had a new bounce in his step since his recent divorce from Cathy Hawn. Their troubled marriage only lasted three years, now he was dating a woman named Rocky. She was an athletic gal who shared Dean's passion for golf. I was caught off guard when I met Rocky because she was different from the glamorous women he usually went out with but they seemed very content. During the show Dean changed some of the words to 'Bad, Bad, Leroy Brown' and inserted Rocky's name into the song. Frank and Dean

Photo: Dean and Frank at the 'bar'—sure looks like booze to me!

changed the words to songs quite often but I don't think it was always on purpose.

> **Dialogue from the 1977 Rat Pack tour:**
> **Frank:** I want to ask you a question. What the hell were you doing drinking 7-Up? How dare you, you're out of the club.
> **Dean:** I wasn't drinking 7-Up.
> **Frank:** What were you cleaning with it? Your lighter?
> **Dean:** No, I was pouring it for Rocky.
> **Frank:** Oh, Rocky. I didn't know he drank 7-Up either. You go out with him now?
> **Dean:** Yeah, what the hell.... I'm gettin' tired of them girls.

Linda: Months later, Dean told us they had broken up. He said the reason was that he was too laid back for her, Rocky was a lot younger than Dean. He had a few girlfriends that were short-lived but Rocky was very distinctive.

Maria: The audience also enjoyed Frank's opening act Pat Henry but he pretty much stayed to himself. We didn't get to know him too well. We'd see him coming offstage when we were going on, that kind of thing. Sometimes when you perform that's all you ever see of your co-star. Later in the tour, I gathered up my courage and made a point of lingering backstage before Pat did his act. I was curious to know how he felt about working with Frank Sinatra. We made some small talk and I came away with the feeling that Pat treated this like any other gig. Bottom line, it was a good job.

Linda: One evening I asked Dean about our being told before the tour began to "stay away from Mr. Sinatra." His reply was, "I'm keepin' away from him too!"
I wasn't sure if he was serious or joking. Dean explained that Frank was bugging him to stay out late and party with him. I wanted to know more but wouldn't dare probe into their relationship. Dean, being a man of few words, didn't go into much detail except to say that Frank's nocturnal lifestyle was not for him anymore.
Dean didn't take himself quite as seriously as Frank did. He was a simpler

guy. He talked to us about his golf game, working out, TV—especially his favorite westerns— and his family. That was enough for him. He didn't go around with a 'kingdom' surrounding him like Frank did. For the most part, The Golddiggers were his entourage now. Dean was never like the boss, he was like a part of our family. He never gave off a vibe of pressure; he was the most gracious, cool guy, really.

He had this little act that would pump him up before the show. He wanted to see each girl before he went on. Oh, and if you were late or you missed him, you would hear about it, in a funny way. He used to kid around with us, "Where were you? I missed you."

Maria: While we were backstage waiting to go on, Dean also used to let us play with his makeup, or rather lack of it. "I think I need some rouge," he would say and we would all kiss him on the cheeks, then rub it in for him. All our lipstick shades together gave him the perfect blush.

At a certain point I think he didn't want younger girls to replace us, I guess he thought that would look a little ridiculous as he got older. Or maybe he had a soft spot for us, I don't really know.

Patti (Pivarnik) Gribow, Golddigger 1973-1985: We were completely protected. Dean told us at the start of the tour, "Now if anything goes wrong you just let Frank or me know and we'll take care of everything." Frank got upset once when we didn't have Kleenex in our dressing room. He'd gone into our dressing room and saw we didn't have Kleenex boxes and he got all over the stage manager's case.

Robyn Whatley, Golddigger 1976-1987:
I've been a photographer since I got my first camera, a Brownie, when I was nine years old. The girls used to say they didn't recognize me without a camera in my face.

I obtained permission to take photos of this history making reunion of Sinatra and Martin. Two days later, I had the proofs and wanted to show them. By then we only had to go through Jilly, Sinatra had gained respect for us.

The difference in the style of the two men, Sinatra and Martin, showed itself once again that night. Even though I was ushered in and announced, Sinatra wouldn't look up so his lovely wife Barbara got to see the first photos taken of that rare performance.

By contrast Dean put his arm around me and, in his smooth warm baritone, said,"Oh good, let me see those," and proceeded to look at all of them and asked for two enlargements. Such a dear.

Maria: One night during the Westchester run my ears perked up—instead of hearing 'Night and Day' wafting into the dressing room backstage as Frank took the stage, the orchestra struck up 'The Lady Is a Tramp,' a song that caused me to rush to a spot to get a good listen. When the tour began Frank's next to last number was 'See The Show Again.' After a week or so he replaced it with what he called his "saloon song," maybe because he was feeling more expansive as the performances progressed. Most evenings I would listen eagerly for that spot when he would sing a different ballad from his songbook. I would inch myself closer to the stage to catch his pensive interpretation of 'Send in the Clowns' or 'One for My Baby.' Most nights it was 'Here's That Rainy Day,' a heart-breaking ballad that Sinatra called "maybe the best saloon song ever written."

> **Frank Sinatra, interview with Bill Boggs, WNEW, September 22, 1975:** *I will turn around and say to [conductor] Bill Miller, "Skip the next two tunes and go to the third one," because there's something about the audience—I'm not getting the vibes from anybody, so we go to something that might grab them a little bit more. And that not only amuses them but it mystifies them a little. They don't quite understand why you're switching around like that.*

Linda: Audience members would literally gasp with delight when Frank began to sing one of their favorites like, for instance, 'It Was a Very Good Year'. As soon as the first notes were struck everyone was rapt in anticipation.
It was a reminder that Frank had been a teen idol that sent young girls into a screaming fit when he sang back in the 1940s, when many of the ladies in our audience were in high school. He still had that power, an innate ability to transform grown women into giggling children.
Just outside the stage door Frank had a big limo waiting with the motor running. As soon as he got offstage he was escorted directly to the limo by a bunch of guys in suits. They were trying to escape before the audience was let out of the theater. It was very much like a scene out of a mafia

"I'm a performer. I'm better in the first take."—Frank Sinatra

movie with the bank robbers making their getaway.

> **Vincent Falcone, Sinatra's former conductor,** *Frankly, Just Between Us*: I can recall many nights when, at the end of the show, I would start the bow music and then run out of the orchestra pit to join Sinatra in his limo to return to the hotel. We would be halfway back to the hotel and the crowd would still be applauding and yelling, "Encore!"
> He never did an encore. He gave his all at every performance but when it was over, it was over. Sometimes I remember thinking, I'm just glad to be around Frank Sinatra. When he finally "left the building," I was glad to have had the chance to be a part of all the excitement.

Maria: Greg Garrison filmed our performances at the Westchester Premier for a television special he was producing. They had several cameras set up around the stage for close-ups, one for long shots, but I heard something mysterious happened to the tapes before the program could be edited together.

> **Lee Hale, producer,** *Dean Martin Specials*: We had five cameras going. When I came back to put it all together for an NBC special it was the oddest thing. Every time I'd put up a reel, let's say 101, it was the same as 102, 103; they had the same thing on every reel instead of having every different angle the cameras should have captured. So we abandoned the idea of making an NBC special out of it.
> Thirty years go by and I see all these tapes in the archives so I went in and looked at everything again and discovered that we taped four different performances, two nights and two shows on each night. So that one particular camera was in a different position on each night. I put together an hour show of Dean and Frank using that one camera covering the different shows and it worked well because the orchestra was always the same tempo. I thought it was remarkable but, by then, nobody wanted the show.

Linda: It wasn't all laughs and inside jokes on the tour. Frank fired his long time friend and opening act Pat Henry over a bad bet or something. I heard Pat never got over that. After that the atmosphere of the tour got a little more tense. I must say, I was tip-toeing around. We always stayed out of those kinds of conflicts but with the amount of ego on that tour, you couldn't help but wonder what really went down.

Peggy Gohl, Golddigger 1974-1991: Sinatra also fired a flutist one night because he was off pitch.

Maria: May 29th was our last performance at the Westchester Premier; we woke up on our day off to devastating news that the Beverly Hills Supper Club outside of Cincinnati had caught fire the night before, killing one hundred and sixty-five people. Newspaper headlines called it one of the deadliest fires in American history. That club was one of our favorite stops along the way.

> **Rob Kaiser, *The Cincinnati Enquirer*:** *Karen Lee Prugh came to the Beverly tonight to see John Davidson. The singer never took the stage. Instead, it was a fire that made the grand entrance, blowing open the double doors of the Cabaret Room with a theatrical bang as it burst upon the crowd in a dark cloud of smoke. The lights went out. Some of the people panicked. A man in front of Karen leaped up and began running across tabletops like a squirrel traveling from tree to tree. Martinis and ash trays tumbled to the floor. "Stop pushing," a woman shouted. Now, as the stars come out over Southgate, black smoke billows from the doors of the supper club and rises to blot out the heavens. Many will be dead by sunrise, some still clustered around their tables as if waiting for the next act.*

Wayne Dammert, employee of the Beverly Hills Supper Club: The night The Beverly Hills Supper Club burned down there were approximately twenty-seven hundred people in there. Gangsters wanted to take over, it was very lucrative. The owners were making money faster than they could count it. They had already expanded like crazy, if you wanted a banquet you had to book three years in advance.
They were getting all these threats and finally, on the busiest night we had, May 28th 1977, some mob guys torched it. We could see exactly where it started. There were these two guys working in this room all day long, they had been there during the week because my friend, the busboy, kept seeing them running in and out.
And a waitress got threatened, she had a party to get ready for and

they told her, "Get out of here we're working!" "Well, what are you working on?" "The air conditioning." There was no air conditioning. This girl also saw three people wiping the walls all the way back to the showroom, which is a real long hallway; we found out later they were wiping the walls with liquid graphite. We figured they put a timing device in there with a balloon of accelerant and, at a certain time, that went off—and it blew like crazy because within five minutes the whole place was engulfed in fire.

They threatened Shirley's life and her children's lives if she told what she knew. We know how it was set and who did it but no one wants to hear about it.

Patti (Pivarnik) Gribow, Golddigger 1973-1985: I'm from Cincinnati so I would frequent the Beverly Hills nightclub often. We were just really, really lucky not to be there when that fire broke out because the dressing room was so small, and it was upstairs. I know John Davidson lost his conductor because he went back in to get his music. It was an impressive place and the Shillings were a nice family. My heart was broken for them and for those who lost their lives.

> **Jack Lloyd, *Philadelphia Enquirer*, June 1, 1977:**
> *Frank Sinatra hasn't become the Latin Casino's "house vocalist." It just seems that way when you consider that he opened at the Cherry Hill, NJ spot one month ago and returned last night for still another engagement. The catch this time, of course, is that Ol' Blue Eyes brought along one of his old pals to share in the festivities, Dean Martin. Not to mention six beautiful females known collectively as the Golddiggers. It was almost like the old days, when the notorious Rat Pack was riding high out in Hollywood and assorted other glamour spots of the world. And Frank Sinatra was Chairman of the Board. Sinatra continues to amaze.*
> *While his voice was an inconsistent instrument when he decided to retire from "retirement" some four years ago (downright woeful on given nights), of late that voice seems to be getting better with each fresh appearance.*

Linda: After our two weeks at the Westchester Premier we had a day off before we ventured on to Cherry Hill, New Jersey and the Latin Casino for five nights. I was looking forward to staying with my family, close to home, spending some time resting and eating good healthy home cooking. We were nutritionally starved after living out of hotel rooms for

Echoes of 'Rat Pack': Sinatra at his best with Dino at the Latin

so many months. Once again we were reminded that preparing meals for a family of eleven and cleaning up afterwards took us all day. Everyone pitched in, either cooking or cleaning.

Maria: It was wonderful for us to have the rest of the Golddiggers join us at home with my parents, brothers and sisters. The country setting and taking turns jumping on the huge trampoline kept them entertained. Mom organized a buffet of healthy, no meat entrees and appetizers for everyone and they were all curious about how it was prepared... Sunflower seed burgers? How do you make them? They were intrigued about our eating habits and wanted to learn more about health. Dad was eager to oblige and was very long winded on the subject.

Our family always said a prayer before we ate and all our "Golddigger sisters" often prayed before our shows so naturally we said a prayer of thanksgiving on this occasion too. The girls loved looking at the pictures of our family around the house and were especially fascinated when they saw the photos of Mom from her singing and beauty contest days. They couldn't believe that she had opened the Latin Casino back in 1960 and now here we were.

Robyn Whatley, Golddigger 1976-1987: When I was a little girl I would hear about The Latin Casino, to finally be able to play a place with that kind of show business history was a thrill.

Chuck Anderson, Latin Casino guitarist 1969-1973: There was a tremendous feeling of romance in the room. It was a very formal place and people were dressed to the max; women came in gowns and men would arrive in suits or tuxedoes. Families were encouraged so the kids would be dressed up as well, nobody would dream of showing up there in jeans. It had the feeling of old time Hollywood or Vegas. They were basically trying to reproduce the vibe that was associated with the heyday of Las Vegas with all the famous performers and the neon lights flashing. This was a time when people really admired celebrities, with autographs galore and people excited to get backstage and meet the stars.

The only difference was that, even though it was called the Latin Casino, they had no gambling. I mean, I wouldn't be surprised if there were a few card games going on there but we never saw them.

Jody Gerson, daughter of the Latin Casino owners: I went to a private school in Philadelphia and one of my teachers, who probably had socialist leanings, said in class one day that there's no such thing as the American Dream, it didn't exist anymore. It was a fabrication, propaganda. I went to the club that night and my father said, "Tell Frank what your teacher said." And Frank said, "You're looking at the opportunities in America, you're looking at the American Dream. I'll happily go into your classroom tomorrow and tell your teacher she is wrong."

He told me privately, "If your boyfriend ever gets you in trouble have him call me, don't call your old man." Things like that. It was amazing to be around a man like that. Dean was much less personable, much more reclusive. He played golf, did his show, and that was that.

Frank Sinatra, Latin Casino, May 5, 1977: *I'd like to make a toast, if I may, to you lovely people. First of all again to thank you for coming to see the show. Secondly to wish you an abundance of good health and all good things for you and your children, your grandchildren, and all the way down the line. And I hope you live a thousand years and the last voice you hear is mine.*

Maria: When I told Dean that our family was going to be at the show on opening night at the Latin Casino he said, "Ohhh! Well then, I better do good."

I wondered what all my brothers and sisters would think when they witnessed the enormous adulation the fans had for Frank and Dean with

"The good Lord gave me talent and I'll use it until it runs out." - Dean Martin

us being a part of it.

My family, including my uncles, aunts and my grandmoms, dressed in their finest evening attire to see us at the Latin Casino. They never stopped talking about how they were treated like kings and queens at our show. Frank Sinatra insisted on taking care of the comps for this engagement, he had our family regally escorted to a long table right up in front, smack in the middle. I heard that Frank told the waiters and waitresses not to take any tips from their table or they would be fired. He would take care of the gratuity. At least that's what the servers told my relatives.

They never forgot that old school courtesy. It was the Italian way.... respect from great men. They could hardly believe it.

After the show, Frank and Dean were very gracious to meet our family backstage so they could say thank you. They even exchanged some words in Italian together. From then on, whenever Linda and I came into town to visit our family, our aunts and uncles would say, "The Golddiggers are in town." Even when we weren't in the group any more, they still called us The Golddiggers with a big grin on their face. I guess saying it brought back that wonderful memory to them.

Linda: To my relatives this was "the big time." And it was.
My grandmom Biro dusted off her mink stole and wore it to the show. More than anything I was proud that she could be part of this moment. She was beaming. For years my grandmother, in her own quiet way, encouraged our careers. I can't tell you how many times she told us, in her thick Hungarian accent, "You should be on *The Lawrence Welk Show*, you sing better than those girls." Now, finally at this moment, I could tell she was satisfied.

Darlene (Alberici) Cianci, Golddigger 1977: We were all excited to see my sisters perform in New Jersey with Frank Sinatra and Dean Martin. With my dad at the helm all nine of us packed into our van. We listened to some of Dean and Frank's greatest hits on our cassette player and sang practically the whole way there.

We arrived close to show time, the audience was already arriving and there was an enormous buzz. My head was spinning as I grasped the whole idea of my sisters rubbing shoulders with these superstars. Not only that, I was way up in front with the VIP's. In this huge setting, the show was spectacular! I was inspired.

After the show, my sisters asked me if I wanted to go backstage. I was feeling shy and maybe wondering if my dad would offer vitamins to the celebrities or something else embarrassing so I didn't want to go. Security was very tight but my mom was able to get backstage and she told me about standing near Frank Sinatra Jr. who was looking at his dad from across the room. She watched as his father talked to his adoring fans. My mom wanted to catch a glimpse of Sinatra's beautiful wife Barbara Marx but she never did.

My sisters told me that Sinatra and Martin got many gifts and a lot of homemade food. They would give the food away because Frank was afraid of the food being poisoned or a bomb being inside of a package.

Linda: Back on tour, we could hardly believe our good fortune when we were told that Frank was going to pose for pictures with us. This was not something he did ordinarily. It was a wonderful day, Frank was mellow and charming and we were on our best behavior.

Not wanting to waste any of Mr. Sinatra's time we had pre-arranged our pose so Joyce and Patti would be on either side of him, since they were more petite. Frank was not very tall. Dean stood by and watched with a twinkle in his eye. After all, he didn't want Frank stealing his ladies away from him.

Maria: We all wore medium heels; with my hair teased up I was taller than Sinatra so I tried to be unobtrusive. As the camera flashed I cherished the moment, I knew that the next stop would be our last on this merry tour and I was beginning to feel a flicker of melancholy. After the Latin Casino everyone had two nights off before our final four-night engagement in Chicago began on the seventh.

Joyce Garro, Golddigger 1976-1978: We finished our run at the Sabre Room in Chicago, that's my hometown. To be back home appearing with Frank and Dean was amazing. Frank got engaged to Barbara while onstage at the Sabre Room the year before.

Dean Martin on stage in Chicago, June 10, 1977: *Have I got time for another one? I just want to say it's a pleasure to be here in Chicago again and I know I'm going to come back because now I know the way. I don't usually play nightclubs, I play one night and go to Vegas and the only reason I'm here is because the other Dago brought me here. And I love it here, the audiences have been wonderful—up until now.*

Patti Gribow, Golddigger 1973-1985: During one of the performances Dean walked off stage almost in tears, he had received a standing ovation. He said, "Can you believe they stood up for me?" What a sweet, sweet man!

Ralph Lewis, *About Faces* magazine: *I wanted to insure that I could go on record in this magazine for all time to state that I have met a President, I have been in an audience with the Pope, but I have finally met the "King." My experience at the Sabre Room in Hickory Hills, Illinois at the Sinatra-Martin concert is my present story. I recognized the appropriate accolades attributed to Dean Martin, the mellow baritone, about his smoothness of style, and I agree his musical prowess was beautifully tempered with nonchalance. And I knew the plaudits directed to Frank Sinatra about his musical mastering of the legato, rubato, appoggiaturra,*
portamento, phrasing, and even the slur.
And I'm not even sure I know what those words mean. But I do know that after the beautifully orchestrated 1-2 punch of The Golddiggers and Dean Martin that Frank Sinatra appeared, waved his hand over the audience, beamed the precise smile of a benevolent ruler, and sang the songs that are so personally his.

Joyce Garro, Golddigger 1976-1978: My grandma made these delicious Italian cookies called pizzelles. She would make these cookies in a waffle iron, two at a time. She'd spend hours making these cookies. Sure enough she told me, "I made pizzelles for Dean, you gotta give them to Dean." I said, "Okay, Grandma." And I did bring Dean some pizzelle cookies. Backstage at the Sabre Room one night we were getting ready for the show and there was a knock on the dressing room door and they said, "Oh Joyce, there's a fellow here to see you." I thought, "Oh my goodness, what old friend or what guy from the neighborhood is trying to get into the dressing room." I went to the door and it was Dean thanking me for the pizzelle cookies that my Grandma made and he wanted her to know how touched he was. Dean's manager Mort Viner comped me about ten tickets for the show that night so I had my whole family at a front table.

My grandmother was there and she said to me afterward, "Oh Joyce, at the end of the show he came out and he was shaking everyone's hands and I wanted to say, "I'm Joycie's Grandma, I made the pizzelle cookies!"

Maria: On different nights, Frank would switch one or two of the songs in his set depending on his mood, whereas Dean never changed his song lineup.

Sinatra permanently replaced the disco 'All or Nothing at All' with a more traditionally arranged 'I Got You Under My Skin' as his opening number in Chicago. I thought to myself, "It's about time!" That was one of my favorites along with 'For Once in My Life' which followed Frank's opener.

Photo: Joyce Garro with Dean.

Dean on stage in Chicago, June 10, 1977: *Here's a song that maybe six or seven of you might remember. And I hope I'm one of 'em.*

Linda: Dean was high as a kite during one Sabre Room performance Maria and I had the opportunity to watch from backstage. It could have been that he was drinking but I don't know. That night his youngest daughter Gina came to see him. Could he have been nervous about Gina being there to see him work with her 'Uncle Frank'?

Dean was really loose during his monologue that evening, he started out stumbling over his words. Dean nicely reminded one heckler, "I don't need this at all, don't need this at all…. I love to work because I'm working with my good buddy, that's all." I realized, in that moment, that Dean didn't have to invite us on this tour either. He just wanted us to be there. My heart swelled and I appreciated how much he cared about us as a group.

Dean's singing was in rare form when he started, 'Welcome To My World' but the spell was quickly broken when Frank Sinatra wisecracked from a backstage mic, "Come on, it's my world, you're just livin' in it." It was a riot.

Of course Dean got back at him. After Sinatra started to sing, "When I was seventeen…." Dean quipped from backstage, "You were a pain in the ass!"

Maria: Frank continued his off mic comments during Dean's numbers and at one point succeeded in making him really forget the words. They got a kick out of messing each other up but it was the roar of the audience that kept them frisky.

Linda: Dean was on a roll that night. After he made fun of his poor memory and his Agita, he had a serious moment belting out, 'Brother Can You Spare a Dime.' Then he got silly again with 'That's Amore' featuring Ken Lane, or as Frank called him, "your friend at the piano with the helmet." Ken directed with these enormous headphones on. Towards the end, Dean leaned on the piano and, as if drunk, slipped off the side and said to Ken, "You move that piano one more time…!"

> **Robyn Whatley, Golddigger 1976-1987:** Dean's musical director Ken Lane was sweet. We couldn't get him to go out, we tried and tried but he would just go back to his room after the show. We knew his wife, she would go to luncheons with us, we used to invite her different places. She said Kenny had so many songs written that she thought were even better than the original hit he had, 'Everybody Loves Somebody Sometime,' but she was never successful at getting him to publish any more.

Maria: Ken Lane played the straight man and the target for Dean's jokes and foolery. It was cute how he constantly corrected Dean's slurred speech. Dean would make excuses like, "When you hit thirty-six, I'll tell you, man…." Ken would reply, "I think you hit it twice."
The kidding would continue throughout Dean's set but I noticed that the ribbing took on a harder edge when it was between Dean and Frank. When Frank entered the stage he lifted the mood with a jovial greeting, "Hiya, gang," and the audience went crazy. Sinatra skillfully and dynamically paced his set. He was the master of the dramatic pause. For instance, when he performed 'I Write the Songs' by Barry Manilow, Mr. Sinatra made the song his own after delivering the first line, "I've been around forever." He paused and the audience applauded in agreement.

Linda: The mood got eerily quiet when Sinatra went into 'Angel Eyes' for his saloon song. When he delivered the last line, "Excuse me while I disappear," I could actually feel the powerful man fading away before my eyes; he had me completely captivated.
What a final night! Our second shows didn't start until 11:00 p.m. so it was well after midnight when Frank and Dean joined together for their wild duets, living it up, razzing each other like two drinking buddies as they stood mixing cocktails at their onstage bar. At one point, Dean mocked 'My Way' and bragged to Frank about the birthday present Gina

"Alcohol may be man's worst enemy but the Bible says love your enemy."—Frank Sinatra

had just given him. Frank was almost incoherent, overcome by laughter, when Dean told his joke about being pulled over by a policeman, "I told that cop—I'm not walking that white line unless you put a net under it."

Maria: Their medley together had the usual goof ups but they were obviously having such a good time who could help but get caught up in it? A rousing version of 'The Oldest Established Permanent Floating Crap Game' from *Guys and Dolls* closed the show, and the tour, in Chicago on the fourteenth of June.

As we said our goodbyes Frank told us he was preparing to shoot a movie in a few days [*Contract on Cherry Street*] then would be heading to the Forest Hills Tennis Stadium for some dates with Milton Berle opening. I had to chuckle with the thought of Uncle Miltie interrupting Frank's show with some foolishness like he did ours. No, I don't think so. He wouldn't dare!

Dean Martin, *Dean Martin Roast*:
Milton Berle is an inspiration to every young person that wants to get into show business. Hard work, perseverance, and discipline.
All the things you need.... when you have no talent.

Summer of '77

Linda: After the Rat Pack tour The Golddiggers traveled on to Hershey Park, an amusement park and entertainment complex close to where we grew up. I developed vocal nodes from so much work so I had to stop singing during that engagement. When you work in parks and open areas you don't have the right kind of monitoring system, the acoustics are dead so you tend to over sing. Trying the rides at the park and screaming on the roller coaster a few days earlier probably added to my vocal strain. A doctor told me total rest of my voice was the only treatment and talking was as much of a problem as singing. For the remainder of the week I sat in the stadium, watched the show and took notes.

I was so relieved when my voice came back completely. This brought me a new appreciation for this gift and I was ready to go back on the road. It was perfect timing because we had a booking on *The Mike Douglas Show* where we performed a TV themes medley Lee created for us. The medley started with 'Happy Days', sung as a group, segueing into me singing a soulful 'Good Times'. Peggy was featured doing her Edith Bunker impersonation with 'Those Were the Days'. Robyn led the theme from *One Day at a Time* which blended into the theme from *Alice* sung by Joyce. Maria belted out 'And Then There's Maude' and Patti finished the medley with a reprise of 'Happy Days' then joined by all of us.... "Schlemiel, schlimazel, Hasenpfeffer Incorporated" from *Laverne & Shirley*.

Mike spent almost our entire interview segment asking about our diets, how we kept our weight down, what food we cheated on, who had weight struggles, etc. Here we were hot off an historic tour with Frank and Dean and he didn't ask us anything about it, he only mentioned it in passing. Apparently his viewers were more interested in diet tips than the Rat Pack.

Peggy Gohl, Golddigger 1974-1991: I was the comedian of the group. When I did my Edith Bunker impersonation, 'Those Were The Days,' on the big stage, I was very broad and very big, vocally. When we were on *The Mike Douglas Show* I had to tone it down for TV; I had a hard time pulling back.

Years later I ran into Mike Douglas one night on Sunset Boulevard, "I don't know if you remember me Mike but we did your show." And he said, "Of course Peggy, I remember you. You had the chops." He was so talented. I watched him in the afternoons, I would turn him on instead of the Watergate hearings.

In June 1977, The Supremes gave their final performance in London.

Linda: We headed back to the West Coast. Bobby Goldsboro and the Golddiggers were still an item at The Nugget in Sparks, Nevada. Once again, Bertha and Tina the elephants were our pre-opening act. Bertha and Tina were sweet and gentle animals that were used to lifting people up in the air with their strong trunks. It was sad when I saw that the animal handlers had an electric prod they used to shock the elephants before the show so they would defecate backstage and not onstage, in front of the audience.

> **Patti (Pivarnik) Gribow, Golddigger 1973-1985:** It's one thing to co-star with celebrities such as Bobby Goldsboro but an entirely other thing to be the second act following Bertha & Tina, the elephants. I remember Bertha's keeper holding her at the rear of the theater, backstage. When we hustled off stage for our costume change and had to pass Bertha, we hoped that we would not get groped by her trunk. However, the best story was Bertha's relieving herself on the audience prior to our going on stage. Pretty funny, but not if you were sitting in the first row of tables. That was one night a ring side seat was not the most desirable!

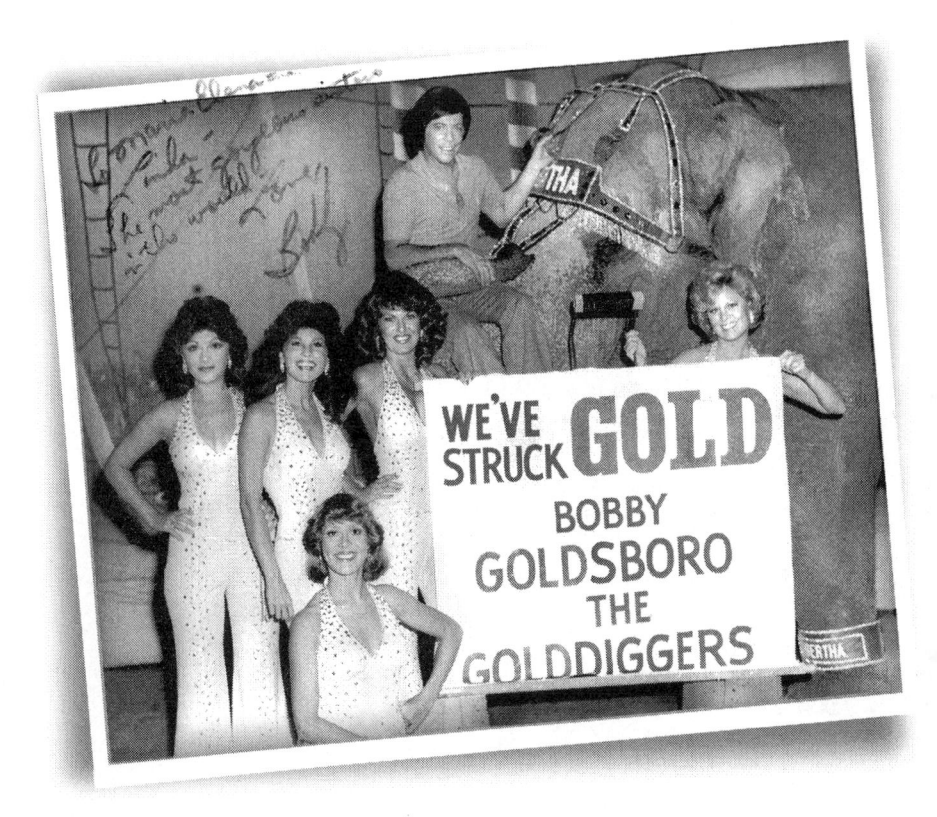

Linda: We always enjoyed the Sparks' gig but we were bursting with anticipation; soon we would be leaving for romantic Monte Carlo, the home of Grace Kelly and the apex of the international "Jet Set," playground to the rich and famous. I couldn't even imagine what that was going to be like—but I knew I was going to have to go shopping!

Maria: Riding in from the airport, peering out of the limousine windows, I could see the luxurious yachts with helicopters perched on top. They were so enormous they appeared to be floating hotels.
We stayed at the L'Hermitage where there was so much wealth and class surrounding us. Upon entering the lobby, I sat on a beautiful antique love seat while waiting for my reservation and suddenly felt a little more sophisticated.

Linda: We were all taken to our huge rooms, my balcony overlooked the lounge and every afternoon I had soft piano music playing right underneath my window. In the morning the waiter would come into your room and wake you with cafe' au lait and croissants with fresh homemade preserves. That's pretty much what we lived on since everything else was so incredibly expensive. You didn't have to go to the door and let the waiter in, he would just stroll in with the food and open the blinds, that's how you woke up.

We were given our own cabana on the beach which was just a couple of blocks away from the hotel. From there we could see the impressive form of The International Sporting Club where we would be performing for the next five weeks. It was suspended over the turquoise sea as if it were floating.

Our private cabana was perfect for taking in the scenery and people watching. All of the women on holiday in Monte Carlo would arrive on the beach in their bathing suits fully decked out in Louis Vuitton and Gucci, in high heels, wearing gold around their necks with jewelry draped around their waists. Oh my gosh, we felt so inadequate, we felt like farmers.

Robyn Whatley, Golddigger 1976-1987: The Sporting Club was a magnificent palace-like structure that offered a spectacular view of the twinkling lights of Monte Carlo. While singing onstage in the round showroom we had a perfect view of this Mediterranean panorama, there were no walls, just glass. We found out while there that even the illustrious Ella Fitzgerald performed for only two weeks at the Sporting Club, which made us feel even more fortunate and honored that we were here for five.

In the audience were the most beautiful women in the world,

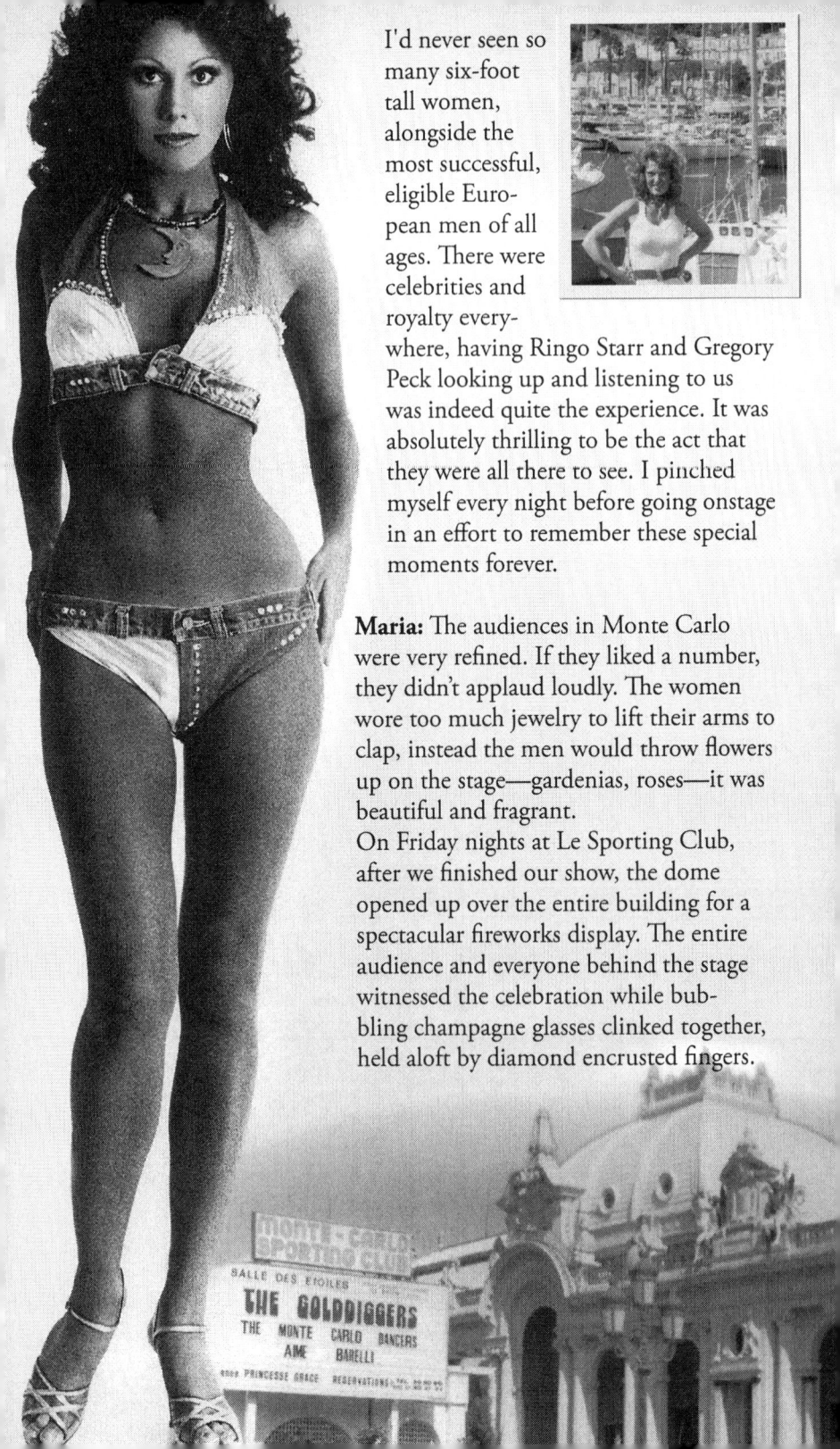

I'd never seen so many six-foot tall women, alongside the most successful, eligible European men of all ages. There were celebrities and royalty everywhere, having Ringo Starr and Gregory Peck looking up and listening to us was indeed quite the experience. It was absolutely thrilling to be the act that they were all there to see. I pinched myself every night before going onstage in an effort to remember these special moments forever.

Maria: The audiences in Monte Carlo were very refined. If they liked a number, they didn't applaud loudly. The women wore too much jewelry to lift their arms to clap, instead the men would throw flowers up on the stage—gardenias, roses—it was beautiful and fragrant.

On Friday nights at Le Sporting Club, after we finished our show, the dome opened up over the entire building for a spectacular fireworks display. The entire audience and everyone behind the stage witnessed the celebration while bubbling champagne glasses clinked together, held aloft by diamond encrusted fingers.

Amongst the revelry something even more spectacular in the distance captured my eyes; the lingering stars glistening atop the Mediterranean Sea.

In the mornings we would gather in a chic restaurant, all determined to order the least expensive thing on the menu while Patti glanced behind her in a makeup mirror at all the cute guys, wondering who they might be.

Luckily I brought some of my more fashionable outfits to Monte Carlo. Walking tall, I carried myself like I was wearing the real stuff, not rhinestones, as I joined the festivities. Monaco was like a set out of a movie, outside the restaurant were rows of designer shops even more decadent than the ones in Beverly Hills. Sometimes I would peer into the windows, imagining myself wearing one of those high fashion creations. Of course, I never went into the store, I wasn't really a part of the scene, just an onlooker.

Robyn Whatley, Golddigger 1976-1987:
In Monte Carlo we didn't have Charlie Sanford to watch over us, we just had our common sense because everybody wanted to meet us and wine and dine us.

As usual Linda, with her beauty and Hungarian blondness, would receive much of the attention. My friend organized an outing with a friend of his to show us around the various ancient towns and craft shops bordering Monte Carlo. Linda arrived "home," the L'Ermitage, with a lovely gold bracelet and I came back with a horse blanket poncho.... what's wrong with that picture?

Linda's quiet ways and soft voice would always attract attention and sometimes tokens of admiration. Many a time, in many a location, there would be a bottle of champagne waiting backstage after a show. We'd be eager to read the card—and usually it was for Linda. Thank goodness she was great about sharing!

Linda: Monte Carlo was a melting pot of all the richest people in the world. After our shows we all ventured out to a discothèque owned by Regine who opened the hippest and most exclusive nightclub in New York, Regines on Park Avenue.

Jimmy'z was the upper echelon place to dance and socialize—Princess Grace, Ringo Starr, David Niven, Gregory Peck and Roger Moore were there that summer. You couldn't even get near the elevator to go downstairs to the club unless you were a 'somebody.' I could hardly believe it when the maitre d' escorted us to a ringside table. Only the richest of the rich could afford to go to Jimmy'z, the prices of the drinks were ten times what you would pay anywhere else.

> **Peggy Gohl, Golddigger 1974-1991:** At Jimmy'z, if you were unescorted by a man, they would give you a free bottle of one hundred dollar Dom Perignon champagne. So we all trucked down there together in what we thought were our gorgeous gowns—but what were really discount store dresses or Lerners outfits from the mall. Of course, when you're young you can wear a rag and look great but all of the ladies in this club were adorned with original designer gowns and priceless jewels.

> **Robyn Whatley, Golddigger 1976-1987:** I was dancing across the dance floor and, being blind without my glasses, I landed within twelve inches of Gregory Peck before I recognized who he was. That was a surprise, even though I knew he had been in the audience that evening. Sitting with him at his table were none other than Princess Grace and Prince Rainier. Spinning around excitedly, I wanted to share with my "sisters" so I rushed back to our ringside table, plopped down next to Peg and pointed. She looked up and screamed, "Look, there's Gregory F**king Peck!"

> **Peggy Gohl, Golddigger 1974-1991:** By that time I was totally looped, all it took was a couple of sips of champagne to get me tipsy. I looked at one of the girls and said, "Look, there's Gregory F**king Peck!" and I fell over backward in my chair in the middle of the room in front of all of these sophisticated people. After that I never lived it down, if we ever saw a star like Cary Grant one of the girls would say, "Look Peggy, there's Cary F**king Grant" or "Look Peggy, there's Wayne F**king Newton."

Jimmy'z is the name of Regine's men's cologne. Jimmy'z Monte Carlo is still open.

Linda: Peggy was such a nut. She wore those vampire teeth in the club one night with all the most sophisticated people in the world. I don't know what they must have thought. She was always entertaining.

Robyn Whatley, Golddigger 1976-1987: I met a Prince at Jimmy'z. This tall, dark and handsome man walked up and asked me to join him at his table. I said, "not without my girlfriends," he replied, "perfectly fine, I have four gentlemen friends with me." So we all sat down and, when I asked his name, he snapped his finger and another gentleman handed me a card that read "Prince........"! We arranged for a rendezvous, that morning we were picked up in Ferraris and Maseratis and whisked off to an opulent seaside villa for a luncheon that could have fed thirty invited guests—but we were told this was a typical daily brunch. We're not in Kansas anymore, Toto.

Maria: In the middle of our engagement, Prince Ranier and Princess Grace created headlines across the globe when they announced that daughter Princess Caroline was going to marry the notorious European playboy Philippe Junot. Well, I think they called him an investment banker. You got the feeling that Monte Carlo was like a small neighborhood where everybody knew all about the Royal Family but didn't gossip about them.

J. Randy Taraborrelli, *Once Upon A Time*: *Indeed, it was difficult for Princess Grace to accept Philippe Junot as husband to her daughter, it seemed even more heartbreaking for Prince Rainier. Caroline, as his firstborn, obviously held a special place in his heart. Though he had for years been training his son, in terms of education and example, to one day take over the sovereignty, his daughters were also important to the Prince. In some ways the manner in which Caroline was handling her whirlwind romance with Philippe Junot was not surprising to him, even if it was disappointing.*

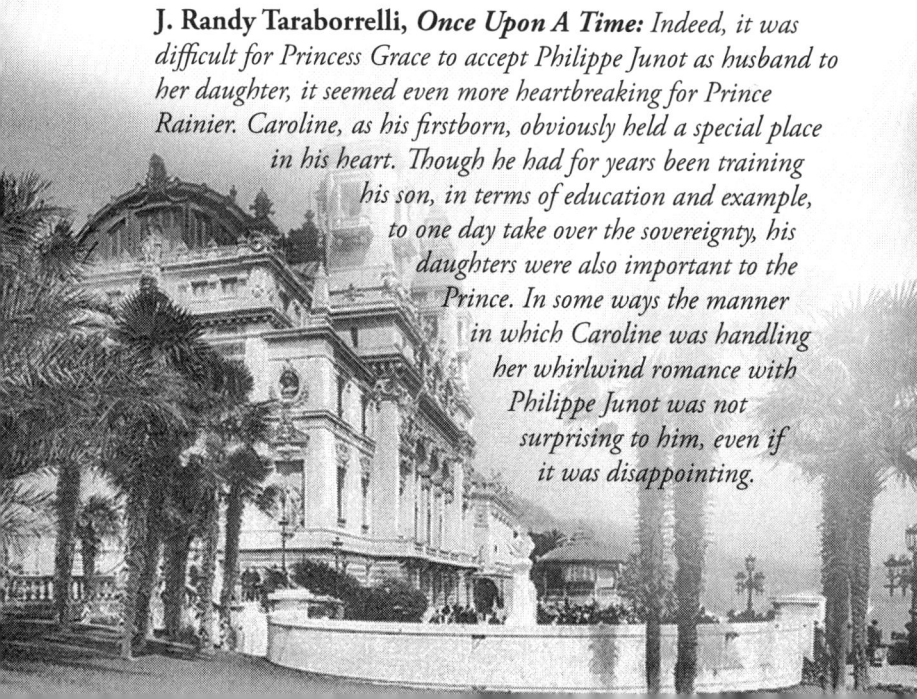

Robyn Whatley, Golddigger 1976-1987:
We were loving our introduction to high society. A few times we enjoyed afternoon tea or cocktails at the Hotel de Paris, located next to the Casino Royale. It was laughable to us that the lavishly attired people looked so stoic, judgmental and apparently soooo into appearances. I mean really, doesn't *your* yacht have a helicopter on it?
We had another laugh at Jimmy'z watching the seriousness of these stunningly beautiful women while they were preoccupied with trying to capture one of Europe's most eligible bachelors. Literally, with glittering diamonds coiled around their arms, they didn't smile or talk. Quite a contrast with the six of us having a blast on the dance floor, pulling people up and including them for the majority of the dances, there was laughter and joy that I know was appreciated.
Monte Carlo is *not* a hard place to be, on top of that to be paid for something one loves to do! It was truly a magical vacation, we were free to tour, have lunch together as friends, and shop for fresh produce in the open air markets.
Since we were the "belles of the ball" that summer of course we had many social invitations. Our days were filled waterskiing behind classic mahogany motor crafts with young millionaires, brunching at the famed seaside Cap d' Estel on the Cote d'Azur—the Blue Coast of the French Riviera—lying around our private beach cabana, or taking side trips to nearby Saint Tropez and Nice.

Peggy Gohl, Golddigger 1974-1991:
We went to dinner one night and there was a gorgeous Italian man who didn't speak any English. All the girls were attracted to him, he was the most handsome guy there. For some reason he took to me, maybe he thought I was easy because I was so goofy. After dinner he took me to the top of a hill in his car where he kept trying to make out with me. But he kept saying, in his thick accent, "Oh, Piggy, Piggy, Piggy" and I was laughing so hard he had to take me back to the hotel. Being called "Piggy, Piggy, Piggy" is not exactly a turn on.

Maria: We were there for quite a long stay so we had many days off to travel. We went to Cannes in France and looked at all the shops. We traveled to Florence, Italy where the guys were very forward, always trying to pinch your butt. When I got off the train I was putting my bags behind me to protect myself.

We were always getting invited to this party or that event, Peggy and I were flown into Switzerland where the locals were so earthy and casual, so different from Monte Carlo. There were a lot of wide open spaces, I couldn't resist running up the rolling green hills and singing songs from *The Sound of Music*.

We met some friends in Monaco who took us out on their yacht for the day, the water was sparkling and still, surrounded by hillsides dotted with quaint little homes. I could get used to this but I was shying away from anyone with a Prince or Duke in front of his name. There seemed to be a lot of them around. What would they want with me anyway— a serious relationship? I didn't imagine so.

I did meet a handsome gentleman who was friends with the family who owned the prestigious Cap Estel, a secluded hotel nestled on a mountain peninsula right over the sea, between Nice and Monte Carlo. He asked me out on a date so we cruised down the Mediterranean in his Riva Aquarama speed boat for lunch at a port along the way. We would go speeding like a rocket through the water, and that was invigorating, but I favored the serenity of the milder ride. It was a heavenly way to spend the day so I was happy to repeat our date.

One late afternoon, we sailed into a summer storm and I started praying when the usual calm sea became rough and the sky, black and threatening. All of a sudden, our boat seemed way too small to sustain the frantic movement of the waves. At times my date would shut the motor off because any speed from the boat crashed us into the waves, like hitting a steel wall. I felt like a sitting duck! We were somewhere in the middle of the Mediterranean. But where? The radio was full of static. There was no land in sight and I was worried about being late for our show—and hoping my new friend knew what he was doing. He did, thank goodness. Was I ever glad to be on solid ground again and just in time to perform!

Linda: Monte Carlo attracted young modern Arab Princes dressed in trendy clothes. It wasn't long before one of them invited us to his vacation home for pool parties which were an everyday occurrence. Maria and I didn't know what they were going to be like so we stayed behind the first day, the other girls checked it out and told us the Prince was cool and they had a lovely time.

The next day I went by myself so I had to take a cab. What do you do when you're invited to the Prince's home and you arrive by taxi? When we pulled up the head of the household staff came out and talked to the driver so I thought it would be appropriate for them to pay the cab. I just walked away and let them talk amongst themselves. I didn't know, should I pay or shouldn't I pay? The women that were used to riding up to the house probably didn't pay for the cab. Right?

    Joyce Garro, Golddigger 1976-1978: Once I took my camera out to take a snapshot and the Prince got very upset, he did not want any pictures taken of himself.

Linda: The Prince was particular about pictures but he was a good humored guy. A young gentleman from England decided to make a clown of himself at an event at his villa and rode a bicycle straight into the pool. It was one of the funniest things we'd ever seen because once he was in the water he kept peddling away as he sank deeper and deeper.

    Dodi Al Fayed and Diana Princess of Wales were killed on August 31, 1997.

The Prince loved it. One of the friends of this Arab prince was Dodi Al Fayed. He had a penthouse at the hotel and invited me up to read a script he was investing in.

I was talking with him about the script, which had a big musical theme, and giving him the benefit of my whole four years in the business. He was wise for his young age and very astute in business.

Dodi seemed to really want to know what I thought about the idea but, at the same time, he was very hot. It could have gone either way, I started to think, "Oh, will we do something romantic or not?" I looked around the magnificently appointed room and saw a pair of false eyelashes lying in one of the ashtrays. "Oh, he's not all business. I better be in control of the situation." I was thinking, "I wonder if one of the Golddiggers was here?" Then again, pretty much everybody wore false eyelashes when you were into the fashion scene then.

Maria: Dodi loved American television especially the series *The Six Million Dollar Man*. I had to giggle when he dramatically recited the introduction that preceded each episode. He asked if I had any connections to people that made these kinds of television shows, like a kid who loved candy and wanted to open a chain of candy stores. I found out his movie script was about two male runners; oh well, no leading role for me in *Chariots of Fire*.

Joyce Garro, Golddigger 1976-1978: I stayed friends with Dodi after Monte Carlo, he would call me when he came to Beverly Hills and we would get together. He was a really great guy, I was blessed for the time that I was able to spend with him.

Robyn Whatley, Golddigger 1976-1987: On one of our invitations to the Prince's summer villa there were many other young people there for a pool party of sorts. It became abundantly clear that we had a different set of morals from many of the single women that were at the party that day.

One amazing gift that Greg Garrison had was choosing girls for the Golddiggers that had all the talent and pizzazz on stage and on television but possessed a strong sense of values, good judgment and a grounded sense of self. So, in a way, we changed Monte Carlo a bit that summer.

We were Regine's personal guests on the closing night of that summer and she told me how sad it was that the party had to come to an end, that we had so much "Joie de vivre" and made it so much fun for everyone that season.

Maria: Our group got along so well. I think the love we had for one another overflowed to whoever was around us.

As the invited guests of Sheiks and Princes, some of us went on a tour of the Royal Palace equipped with Palace guards more colorful than the pictures in my childhood storybook of *Cinderella*. As I walked through the interior of the Palace it seemed hard to believe that Princess Grace Kelly was brought up not far from where Linda and I grew up in Philadelphia. I began to reminisce back to my Miss Pennsylvania days when Grace Kelly's brother Jack took me on a tour of Philly's in-spots frequented by the Main-Line elite. As I looked around me, I began to ache for a little reality. I was missing my family back home, to be honest.

Linda: Maria approached Aime Barelli, the conductor for the Sporting Club and the club at the Casino de Paris, and told him about the sister act we were developing. She even showed him a photo of our younger sister Darlene, who was a singer back home and interested in following in our footsteps. Maria was a great promoter. Aime loved our part in the show and was very interested in having us return as a sister act.

After Maria was done with her sales pitch he promised to book us at one or both of his clubs if we ever left the Golddiggers. He gave us his contact information and Maria immediately sent a postcard to Darlene, "I hope you're getting ready, people are interested in booking us." The whole world seem to be opening up to us and we felt anything was possible.

DONALD O'CONNOR
ROY RADIN'S VAUDEVILLE '77

STARRING
(IN ALPHABETICAL ORDER)

BILLY BARTY
THE DRIFTERS
FRANK FONTAINE
ALIAS *Crazy Guggenheim*
STANLEY MYRON HANDELMAN
SHEILA MACRAE
JACKIE VERNON

SPECIAL GUESTS
THE GOLD DIGGERS

Produced and Directed by
ROY RADIN
THEATRICAL PRODUCTIONS

richard gersh associates, inc.
Public Relations
200 west 57th street
new york, n.y. 10019 pl 7-1101

Monday, November 7	Cleveland, Ohio	Friday, November 18	Portland, Maine
Tuesday, November 8	Erie, Pa.	Saturday, November 19	New Haven, Ct.
Thursday, November 10	Auburn, N.Y.	Sunday, November 20	Hartford, Ct.
Friday, November 11	Elmira, N.Y.	Monday, November 21	Danbury, Ct.
Saturday, November 12	Syracuse, N.Y.	Tuesday, November 22	Beacon, N.Y.
Sunday, November 13	Rome, N.Y.	Wednesday, November 23	Long Island, N.Y.
Monday, November 14	Montgomery, N.Y.	Friday, November 25	Southampton, N.Y.
Tuesday, November 15	Troy, N.Y.	Saturday, November 26	Poughkeepsie, N.Y.
Wednesday, November 16	Springfield, Ma.	Sunday, November 27	Middletown, Ct.
Thursday, November 17	Fall River, Ma.	Monday, November 28	Waterbury, Ct.
		Tuesday, November 29	Monticello, N.Y.

Wednesday, November 30	Wilkes-Barre, Pa.
Friday, December 2	Williamsport, Pa.
Saturday, December 3	Carlisle, Pa.
Sunday, December 4	York, Pa.
Monday, December 5	Washington, D.C.
Tuesday, December 6	Greenbelt, Md.
Friday, December 9	Miami, Fla.
Monday, December 12	Las Vegas, Nev.
Tuesday, December 13	Salt Lake City, Ut.
Thursday, December 15	Honolulu, HI.

For Booking Information:

Southampton, N.Y. 11968 • Box MMMM • (516) 283-9100 ROY RADIN ASSOCIATES Los Angeles, Calif. 90069 • 9255 Sunset Blvd. • Suite 405
(213) 550-8170

On The Road Again?!?

Linda: After our magical time in Monte Carlo and our exciting run with Dean and Frank we couldn't wait to find out what magnificent adventures were ahead for us. When Greg's secretary handed us the fall itinerary imagine our shock—we were scheduled for another Roy Radin Vaudeville Review in November.

Maria and I both said there was no way we're doing that again, if for no other reason than there was practically nothing we could eat the entire time we were on the road.

Donald O'Connor would be back on the tour again, that was nice. Jackie Vernon was replacing Milton Berle and Frank Fontaine, who played Crazy Guggenheim in those hilarious Joe the Bartender sketches on *The Jackie Gleason Show,* would be along too. We loved watching him on TV with our family along with Sheila MacRrae who played Alice Kramden in the color *Honeymooners* sketches, she was scheduled for the 1977 tour. Still, that wasn't enough to get us back on that bus. Besides, we were only scheduled to have two nights off in six weeks and one of those nights was Thanksgiving! Then we heard our drummer had insisted that his wife be put in the group to replace Patti, who was leaving to pursue another opportunity. Maria and I were thinking, "What?!?" She was a cute, pixie haired girl with a pleasant voice but she didn't have the dynamic energy needed for the Golddigger group.

We thought our sister Darlene, who had been starring in musical reviews back in Pennsylvania, was a better fit; she was dynamic, talented and beautiful. She had all the right ingredients so we took action.

Our family happened to be visiting us on the road so we convinced Darlene to try on our costumes so we could take pictures of her in them. The costumes fit and she looked great. The pictures got her an audition which went very well.

Without delay we went to Greg and basically said something very similar to what the drummer had told him, "We don't want to do the Radin tour unless you put our sister in the group." It really wasn't worthwhile to us. We wanted to work on our own thing. It only made sense if we could practice with Darlene and possibly work her into our sister act while we were doing the tour. Greg took to the idea without too much convincing but he called us "barracudas" for our tenacity. Immediately after hearing about the change in the group the drummer decided to quit. That's show biz.

***Las Vegas Visitor,* September 1977:** *Golddiggers, a talented group of lovely entertainers whose frequent appearances on network television specials have earned them an enthusiastic following. The Golddigger portion of the show is non-stop entertainment, singing, dancing and comedy with a vast variety of material and solo numbers to display the girls' individual talents. They will hold the Celebrity Room MGM Hotel spotlight....*

Darlene (Alberici) Cianci, Golddigger 1977: The family traveled to Las Vegas to see my sisters open for Dean Martin. It was then that Maria and Linda encouraged me to audition. I was into theater arts and doing serious dramas from Chekhov and Shakespeare in summer stock; I didn't think I was right for the part but I went along. Maria and Linda snuck me backstage at the MGM and I tried on a couple of the outfits that the girls wore in the show. They took Polaroid pictures of me in glamour poses as I tried to suck in my gut and look natural. My sisters sent the pictures to Greg Garrison's office in California; when they saw the photos I got an audition.

After the Las Vegas engagement the entire family continued our trek to Los Angeles for the tryout. I thought nothing of it, "Oh sure, these girls never leave the group." It was a long shot to think I could be in The Golddiggers because they had been together a long time. I already knew some of the act, having seen it so many times, so I sang, 'Maybe This Time' from the show at the audition. Lee Hale seemed pleasantly surprised that I could 'deliver' such a strong song. They auditioned me further by having me dance. That was easy because of all the dance lessons my parents provided me with and also because I knew the style they liked. After the whole process, they said the proverbial, "I'll keep you in mind." I didn't know

Photo: The Barracuda Sisters.

whether I would hear from them or not but within a month they phoned me in Pennsylvania to say, "You made the group."

Without delay I flew for the first time by myself to California. They had a limousine waiting for me at the airport to take me directly to costume fittings with all of these wildly theatrical Hollywood-type hairdressers, costume people, and makeup artists. They were all poking me while I was trying on the outfits and talking about me like I wasn't in the room. I heard them comparing my 'look' to a woman I never even heard of. I felt like I was in a scene from a movie where the young actress gets the 'star treatment.'

I had about a week of rehearsals to cram in as much of the show as I could. My sisters volunteered to teach me behind the scenes and then I was out on tour.

Maria: The Alberici sisters were now half of the Golddiggers but still it's hard to be the new kid on the block. All in all, it was a good experience for Darlene and she enjoyed the bus trip with Tim Fowlar and the musicians. They were very gracious and took her into their circle.

Darlene (Alberici) Cianci: I could tell it was a lot for the other girls to now have three sisters in the group. They were already used to each other so when I arrived I found it difficult to fit in. I was trying to figure out who would be my friend and who would not. I bonded with the musicians right away.

When I was about sixteen, I started singing with my mother during her big band and club gigs so I had a great rapport with musicians. They were street-wise and laughed about everything but their jokes would fly right over my head. I didn't get most of their earthy humor because they'd use this strange lingo with double entendres. It was so intriguing to me. They would spin a statement and start to roar with

"The courage came with practice." – Donald O'Connor

laughter and then another guy would add onto that and onward it would fly. The laughter was contagious.

Most mornings I'd rush onto the bus after a jog and the other girls kind of tisk-tisked because I was wearing shorts, looking like someone who just ran in off the streets. My two sisters had a lot to teach me about image. It wasn't really my style to be glamorous all the time.

Tim Fowlar, musical conductor, Roy Radin Vaudeville Revue 1973-1978: On the first tour we were told, "Do not bother the girls or you're going home." On the second trip we knew them so well and liked them so much that we were all friends by then.

The stars would all sit up toward the front of the bus and the musicians took up the back of the bus because there were so many of us. We had a little platform that we put across the seats in the aisle to make a table or we'd set it up on a cooler because we always had beer in the cooler. So they'd sit back there and drink beer and play poker. Frank Fontaine was on the tour, he was one of the big poker players on the bus. Frankie would be in his seat for a while and when he heard the poker game breaking out he'd come back and join us.

He was a real heavy drinker and he was also a very heavy eater, he was a big, huge guy by that point.

Jack Salley, trumpet player, Roy Radin Vaudeville Revue, 1973—1979: Frank Fontaine was really funny, just hilarious on and off stage and a great guy, but the booze and the cigarettes—he had to be four hundred and fifty pounds by this time.

One afternoon the bus was parked with only a couple of people still on. I had to go back in to get something and Frank was

Photo: Darlene and Donald O'Connor.

just sitting in the front of bus, air conditioning on, just staring into space. As I passed him I said, "Hi Frank" which he responded to with a slurred "Hi." He really didn't look all that good but then again he never did as he was always panting and short of breath.

As I was coming back out I looked at him and watched his eyes go back and at that point it hit me, "Uh oh, here it comes." All hell broke loose at that point, I think Carl the bus driver got to him first then everyone else. Nobody could get him off the bus because he was so huge; then with rescue working on him we were pinned in the back until they moved him. It took four guys to carry him down the stairs and out of the bus door.

Tim Fowlar, musical conductor, Roy Radin Vaudeville Revue 1973-1978:
After his heart operation, Frank thought having a pacemaker was just like having a new heart. So he partied just as hard, didn't sleep, stayed up all night drinking and eating anything he wanted and just living horribly for his condition.

A year later he was up in Spokane, Washington doing a Heart Fund telethon. He walked out on stage, did his act, went off, they gave him his check, he signed it over to the heart benefit, walked back out on stage, gave it to the host, and as he got off the stage he had a massive heart attack and died.

Dick Haymes replaced Frank Fontaine as the tour continued. Dick Haymes was a big band singer and starred in movie musicals like *State Fair*. He was mainly with the Dorsey band, a very big singer along the lines of a Sinatra or a Bing Crosby. He had some huge hits.

At one point in the show we did a whole vaudeville routine, like the old burlesque acts. One of them was The Makeup Artist where every time the star, the good looking guy, goes to do something the director yells, "Makeup!" and Billy Barty runs out with a huge powder puff and smacks him over the face with it so there's powder everywhere. It was hysterical.

Dick Haymes was the male lead who got the powderpuff in the face—or he'd duck and the director would get nailed or somebody else would get it. It was a lot like the old Three Stooges shorts.

Darlene (Alberici) Cianci: Dick Haymes was the style of singer I was, he was a big band singer, 'It Might As Well Be Spring' was his big number. His vocals were so beautiful, he caressed the tones, everybody loved him just like they all loved Donald O'Connor.

Maria: The highlight of this tour for me was being asked to play the leading lady in the Makeup Artist skit with the male stars including Donald O'Connor and Dick Haymes. I really enjoyed doing slap-stick comedy with these seasoned pros. I wore a slinky gown and developed a character, adopting a New York accent, while I playfully chewed bubble gum. Apparently, Tim Fowlar and his band decided one night that I was going to get a pie in the face at the end of the Makeup Artist skit. I saw Dick Haymes touch the pie and hesitate and that's when I saw the band cracking up out of the corner of my eye. Before he could pick up the pie, I grabbed it and smacked him right in the face with it. It was either him or me and I had makeup on!

This comedy spot gave me the opportunity to get a little more chummy with the rest of the cast and have some serious talks too. I was touched by the honesty of Dick Haymes as he pensively spoke about his marriage to Rita Hayworth and how stardom affected his reality.

Dick Haymes, *The Life of Dick Haymes: No More Little White Lies,* **1975:** *One of the big problems was that I became a superstar when I was too young to handle it. Under those circumstances a lot of negativism raises its ugly head—like ego, like feeling it's going to go on forever, like spending too much money. I sensed that I was living a false existence, and out of that came over-indulgence.*

Peter Marshall, Host *Hollywood Squares, JazzConnectionMag.com:* *Dick made a lot of mistakes. Women and booze got in the way. You got to remember, Sinatra was down, too, at one time. But he made this marvelous comeback. He was handled beautifully. Dick just blew a great career. At one time he had a better career than Sinatra. He sold more records than anybody.*

For two years in a row, Dick was the highest paid American, including the head of AT&T...
Money to him was nothing. He wasn't organized that way. If you needed money and asked Dick, he'd give you, say, $100. If he needed money and you gave him $100, he would forget that he owed you!

Tim Fowlar, musical conductor, Roy Radin Vaudeville Revue 1973-1978: Dick Haymes was a pretty heavy drinker but a real sweetheart of a guy and a true gentleman. When the Hollywood musicals and the big bands disappeared so did Dick's career. I talked to him before he passed away in 1980, he had throat cancer. He was a big pipe smoker but I don't know if that contributed to it or not.

Joyce Garro, Golddigger 1976-1978: I would stand backstage listening to Dick Haymes sing every chance I got on that tour. Billy Barty was very sweet to me. I became friends with Charlie Boy from The Drifters and we stayed in touch.

Robyn Whatley, Golddigger 1976-1987: On tour you never knew what to expect, you never even knew where you were. We performed in some of the original vaudeville theaters and you could feel the history in those places.
Tim Fowlar was so great, our young, but already "fatherly" conductor was a joy. We were so confident with him at the helm. There was always an aura of calmness and knowledge he projected, he really knew his craft. Not a surprise that he went on and was the conductor and friend for such legends as Donald O'Connor and Robert Goulet. Tim actually married Robert's daughter and has a wonderful daughter from this union.

Tim Fowlar, musical conductor, Roy Radin Vaudeville Revue 1973-1978: When you talk about the old adage "the show must go on" this was the ultimate example of that. Our job was to make sure that show hit, every show, every single night. If that meant everybody

Photo: Tim Fowlar & Robyn Whatley.

getting out a half an hour before it's time for the bus to leave and shoveling snow and getting behind the bus to push our way out of a snow bank, we did it. One time we ran so late we had to set up the rhythm section first so we could start the show and set up the rest of the band while the first act was already on. No showers, no nothing, we put on our tuxes and went on.

Jack Salley, trumpet player, Roy Radin Vaudeville Revue, 1973-1979: Showers?!? Our tuxes could do the show without us. We were just plain out there. The most we could pack was our tux, as many tux shirts as we could afford, usually at most three, a pair of jeans, and as much underwear as we could possibly fit into the suitcase. Add your most valued possession, your Ax (horn), and you were set for months.

Tim Fowlar, musical conductor, Roy Radin Vaudeville Revue 1973-1978: This time around Donald's wife Gloria came out on tour with us for a while. She wanted to see what was going on and she loved every minute of it. Everybody behaved while Gloria was awake. She was like the Den Mother on the tour, she had a ball.

Maria: Gloria O'Connor was very glamorous. Donald's wife was able to help him stay sober on our second tour, you had to respect a marriage like that. He seemed so lost on the first tour. She probably had a lot to do with him getting his drinking under control through this whole ordeal.

Patti (Pivarnik) Gribow, Golddigger 1973-1985: Donald O'Connor had a boyish, sincere charm that made him one of the nicest and most genuine people on the tour. His dancing and singing talents were quite astounding, he made musical theater look effortless.

Photo: The Drifters & The Golddiggers.

Linda: We learned so much from Donald seeing him one way and then seeing him mostly sober on this tour. It was a good life lesson for us that he was able to pull himself completely away from his addiction shortly afterward.

Tim Fowlar, musical conductor, Roy Radin Vaudeville Revue 1973-1978: Donald was brilliant. His opener was 'Without a Song' and he had his own lyrics written for it so it all pertained to him. He did a lot of things from the movies he starred in—*Singing in the Rain*, numbers from *Call Me Madam*. He worked with Anthony Newley a couple of times so he did 'Who Can I Turn To' and 'What Kind of Fool Am I' and he always closed his show with 'And I Love You So' sung to the audience.

Joyce Garro, Golddigger 1976-1978: Donald was a very kind, kind man. He was full of personality, we spent time hanging out. He was actually kind of quiet although he had this Quasimodo imitation he would do on the bus, every so often he'd muss up his hair and make this funny face.

Maria: Stanley Myron Handelman was along also; coincidentally he had been a regular on *The Golddiggers* TV show for two summer seasons when they substituted for *The Dean Martin Show* on NBC. Of course, that was before we joined so we talked about some of the previous girls. His humor was offbeat and extremely intelligent; he would open for Frank Sinatra at times so Frank must have liked him as well.

Tim Fowlar, musical conductor, Roy Radin Vaudeville Revue 1973-1978: Stanley Myron Handelman was a funny guy, his only problem was he was much too hip for the audiences we played. One of my favorite bits of his—he'd say, "I'm going to do a number with the band" and start clicking his fingers so the whole band would be snapping their fingers in tempo to him and he'd do like a coffee house poem. My favorite was, "My dog was dying by inches and dying by inches is hard so I took him out on the back porch and let him die by the yard." The musicians would be in tears but the people in the audience would just kinda go, "Huh?" His timing was impeccable, he was brilliant but he needed a hip audience to work to.

Neil Daniels, former NBC VP and founder Dean Martin Fan Center: Stanley Myron Handelman was one funny guy, it was amazing how he saw into real everyday things and made comedy bits out of it. He had this Jewish sense of humor, I think he appealed more to men than to women, some people do that. Stanley Myron Handelman basically walked away from the big time. When he was doing the Golddiggers summer show Greg Garrison was going to put him out with Vegas acts and what not but Garrison wanted a big percentage of his money. And Stanley didn't quite see it that way, he told me, "It dawned on me just then, I didn't want anybody to own me." And I think that's why his whole career just kind of fizzled.

Tim Fowlar, musical conductor, Roy Radin Vaudeville Revue 1973-1978: We were out with Charlie Thomas' Drifters, there were several groups at that time touring as The Drifters.
Sheila MacRrae was just a sweetheart, she was a great singer and treated the band wonderfully. She didn't hang with us much, she finished a show and would go back to her room or maybe every once in a while come down to the bar and hang with everybody.
Everybody adored Jackie Vernon, he was too funny. He had two weird things going for him that nobody knew about. One was he had a luggage fetish. He'd find a sale in the local newspapers and he'd go out and buy luggage. So every couple of weeks Carl the bus driver would have to go somewhere and ship it home for him; otherwise it would take up too much room on the bus.
The other thing was he was a kleptomaniac. I think we were in Johnstown, New York and it was kind of chilly at that time, we were doing a fall tour so everyone had jackets on. Jackie and Eddie Mekka were walking around a store and Jackie kept bumping into Eddie.
Eddie finally looked at him, "What the hell are

Top photo: Billy Barty & Stanley Myron Handelman.

you doing?" Jackie said, "Ah, nothing. I'm sorry, I keep bumping into you." They got back to the hotel and Jackie says, "Hey, come here a minute Eddie" and he starts reaching into Eddie's pockets and pulling all this stuff out that he had shoved in his jacket pockets. Eddie was like, "What the hell did you do?!?"

Jackie Vernon hated Roy Radin, he absolutely despised him. He once told me, "When Roy Radin dies it'll be the most attended funeral ever." I asked him why and he said, "Because when you give the audience what they want, they'll show up."

Linda: Billy Barty also liked to stir things up. He had a devilish nature, when you're on these kinds of tours sometimes you go stir crazy and do things just because you can, for your own entertainment. You get a 'who cares' kind of an attitude and create a little excitement every once in a while.

One night, Billy Barty was on the bus sitting next to one of the girls and he wanted to assure her that all areas of his body weren't small; the rest of him was normal, if you know what I'm saying.

Tim Fowlar, musical conductor, Roy Radin Vaudeville Revue 1973-1978: Donald called Billy "the tripod." He and Donald went to the same high school together, Donald told me that Billy was a maniac, he went out with so many women, he didn't let his size stop him at all.

There was a song called 'Think Big' that Billy opened with and that was his philosophy on life, "You have to think big if you want to be big and there's nothing you can't do."

Jack Salley, trumpet player, Roy Radin Vaudeville Revue, 1973—1979: There was usually a banquet after the shows and the food was outrageous. For the most part, these were smaller towns we played and, particularly in some of the Italian areas, you knew that "grandma" was cooking the gravy for the spaghetti and meatballs a week out. The wonderful thing about these after show parties was that they created an atmosphere of wholesome family warmth, for them and for us. As if we were being invited into these very humble but tremendously giving local people's home for their traditional Sunday Evening Family Dinner. This genuine welcome and openness with a smile was something we had the privilege of being a part of.

Jackie Vernon was the voice of Frosty the Snowman in the 1969 TV special.

Tim Fowlar, musical conductor, Roy Radin Vaudeville Revue 1973-1978: We didn't have to pay for drinks either because the booze was free at the buffets and then, when we went to the bar, Roy usually picked up the tab for everybody. He wouldn't give us a twenty-five dollar a week raise but he picked up the tab for the whole show every night at the bar. And we could drink!
As we'd get off the bus somebody'd yell, "Hey, we'll meet you at the office" and everybody knew where we were going—to the hotel bar.

Jack Salley, trumpet player, Roy Radin Vaudeville Revue, 1973—1979: We were kids, all of us. There were really no drugs out there but, boy, did we drink. None of us could afford drugs but none of us did them anyway. But the beer just flowed.
On one of the tours we had a guy, Kenny Sherburne, who was a juggling act. He would be stone drunk puking his guts out in the wings offstage just as they were announcing his entrance, and then ride around onstage on a twelve foot unicycle juggling axes only to be followed by lit fire torches.
Because the band was on stage with him, I cannot begin to tell you how fast everybody memorized his material. Nobody took their eyes off of him particularly as he was making each pass on the bike no less than three feet in front of the sax section.

Tim Fowlar, musical conductor, Roy Radin Vaudeville Revue 1973-1978: Let me tell you, there's nothing more frightening than seeing a guy over off in the wings getting ready to come out with his lit torches "Ladies and gentlemen, here he is, mister fun on wheels"—and you hear him barfing into a trash can—"Kenny Sherburne!" And he'd wipe his mouth and out he'd come.
One night Roy got mad at him and told him if he came to work drunk or with a drink on his breath he would be fired immediately. After that he started dropping everything—torches, axes—we were backed up to the trombone section trying to get away from him. It was terrifying.
After a show in Long Island our troupe headed to a big Thanksgiving dinner at Roy Radin's palatial estate in Southampton. Roy's house used to be a rum runners' stop back in the days of prohibition so it was isolated on the outer edge of the Hamptons.
After dinner we watched clips from Donald O'Connor's movies and we all went out walking along the shore just before dusk. Darlene went wandering off with a couple of the guys down the beach so Maria and Linda got panicked and we all had to go looking for her.

Linda: Instinctively, I was worried. It was getting dark. I ran frantically down the beach calling out for her. She was younger and more naive than the rest of us and after some of the stories I had heard, I was imagining all sorts of things. After a while we located her and the guys. Thankfully, there was nothing going on, they were just walking down the beach.

Tim Fowlar, musical conductor, Roy Radin Vaudeville Revue 1973-1978:
Roy Radin started out as a really, really nice guy. All he wanted to do was have fun. This tour was a giant party the whole time and when Roy was there it was even more fun because he picked up the tab for everything.

But then later in the sixth, seventh, and eighth years he became a more important producer and actually started believing his own publicity and thought he was much bigger than he was. He also got into drugs and making really shady deals.

In the late-seventies, he'd take these big stars and get them drunk or drugged up and get them to sign a contract. He'd make them all sorts of promises, get them drunk, get them stoned, and make it sound like the greatest thing in the world. He'd get them away from the people that actually cared about them, their managers and agents, and just take over.

Roy's parties could get pretty wild, when he got drunk he was a crazy son of a bitch. He'd hire narcotics and police officers from different cities on the East Coast to be bodyguards for the tour and they'd take their vacation to come work with us. They'd make a lot of money but they also had a good time.

Roy and his crew got drunk one night and they took the hotel furniture and threw it in the pool in the courtyard at the Holiday Inn in Rome, New York. They were using the furniture for target practice. The hotel called the police and, because we were doing police benefits, the cops appeased the manager so Roy paid for the damage but they threw them all in their limos and Winnebagos and sent them on to the next town.

You just had to know when to back off and get away from him because Roy would definitely get carried away.

Maria: I personally got a bizarre bad vibe from Roy Radin and his wife. Despite how wealthy they were you kinda got a feeling they weren't very classy. They seemed a little shady. Some of the guys on the tour would get together with Roy for drinks and I would hear some wild stories; so if any of us girls were invited, we declined.

On one night, a catering room was set up with music and an open bar with appetizers so the girls joined the rest of the cast for a little fun. Some of us were dancing to the music and then a slow song played through the speakers. That's when Roy asked me to dance. His wife wasn't there and I wasn't sure if he was making a move. However, this was a cast party and everyone was present so I thought it was okay.

Roy was a hefty man and I was keeping it friendly by being talkative. As we danced, he told me about the big budget movie musicals that he was going to produce. It sounded intriguing. He asked me if I would be interested in playing a starring role. Was he serious? I had to stop my heart from leaping out.

Of course I was interested. My sisters and I were planning on leaving the group to pursue our own careers. Getting work might take a while and I planned to pursue acting. Part of me was wondering, did Roy pick me out of the group to play the part of the "Movie Star" in the vaudeville skit as a test run for his upcoming movie? He told me he wanted to produce these motion pictures himself with no major film company attached to the project. I didn't like the sound of that. Where would that kind of money come from—drugs, gangsters…?

Roy asked how he could get in touch with me after the tour. He wanted my phone number but I asked Roy for his card instead. I told him I didn't have phone service because I was always on the road. I suggested that he call Greg Garrison or my father because they could always get in touch with me. He paused a while, gave me a puzzling look, took out his card and said, "Just call me."

Eddie Fisher, *Been There, Done That:* *The nicest thing I can say about Roy Radin is that he was the sleaziest person I'd ever known. He was guzzling cocaine. Along with producing the shows he was making big coke deals.*

Tim Fowlar, musical conductor, Roy Radin Vaudeville Revue 1973-1978: Skip ahead five years to 1982. It was about two in the morning, my phone rang and it was Roy's sister-in-law. She was in tears, "Roy's gone." I said, "What do you mean he's gone?" She said, "Some bitch picked him up in a limo and he's disappeared, nobody's heard from him for three days." I said, "Well, maybe he got lucky," and she told me, "No, he hasn't called his mom." Roy called his mother religiously. He could be in Figi, he could be in Hong Kong, it didn't matter, he called his mother every single day and she hadn't heard from him. The people who were staying with Roy in Los Angeles hadn't heard from him. She said, "The cops are looking into it right now but I know that bitch had him killed." She stayed in touch with me for the weeks that he was missing.
Roy's contact in L.A., Lanny Greenberger, was a drug dealer. She introduced Roy to movie producer Bob Evans, and Roy got the funding from some people on the islands to supply the money, it was a forty million dollar package, for three movies including *The Cotton Club* and a sequel to *Chinatown.*
Roy decided he wanted to cut Lanny out, just give her a finder's fee and kick her to the curb. She took offense to that, she wanted to be an equal partner in the whole thing. Lanny went to Bob Evans and Bob allegedly said, "Well, if Roy wasn't in the picture we'd still have a deal. Even if Roy was gone the money would still be there." She took that to mean, "Have him killed and everything will be taken care of." And she did. That's why Evans was investigated but they could never prove he had anything to do with it other than planting that seed.
The bizarre story about Roy is that he was born on a Friday the thirteenth, disappeared on a Friday the thirteenth, and his body was found on a Friday the thirteenth shot with thirteen bullet holes. Then the killers took an M80 and stuck it in his mouth and blew his face off to make him unrecognizable. It became notoriously known as The Cotton Club Murder.
Jackie Vernon absolutely hated Roy but he went to his funeral. After the funeral they had the wake and he was there with all these people. Afterwards he actually drove back out to the graveyard at midnight and peed on his grave. He called me from there and said, "Well, I did it. I peed on Roy's grave at midnight. I had to do it." I don't know what Roy did to him but whatever it was it must have been pretty bad.

Maria: A couple of days after Thanksgiving, The Golddiggers left the Radin tour early while everyone else continued on for another two weeks. That gave us a few days to rest up so we visited our friends, Susie and Deborah in LA.

Susie had just landed the role of head cheerleader Patty Simcox in the blockbuster musical movie *Grease* with John Travolta and Olivia Newton-John. I had never seen the stage play so I didn't know much about the musical. Susie told me, "If you weren't on the road with The Golddiggers, you could have tried out for one of the other leads, the Latino role." She was beaming with enthusiasm.

Deborah and Susie were also writing songs and recording with Lonnie Jordan, a member of the group, War. Linda and I were so happy that good things were happening for them. We had witnessed their struggle. Deborah was doing acting roles on television and during this time off, Patti had secured a theatrical agent too. Linda and I were in the midst of strong, independent women who prompted us to think beyond The Golddiggers.

Instead, Linda and I headed back to Las Vegas for a week opening for Dean starting December 1, 1977. Dean was so sweet and each of 'his girls' was delivered a bouquet of roses wishing us a Merry Christmas. We were all kindred spirits sharing so much together and I was feeling grateful.

Robyn Whatley, Golddigger 1976-1987: Maria was such a free spirit, a real nature girl. We were both more 'outdoor' types and loved exploring natural places together wherever we were performing. One glorious day she burst into a song that she had written, 'The Music of Earth' with the words, "The music of the earth, la la la, the symphony of nature, la la la la...." It was the purest and sweetest song, reflecting a sense of appreciation for the beauty of the world. It reminded me of a Nigerian saying, "from a beautiful heart comes a beautiful song."

Linda: Red Rock Canyon outside of Las Vegas was a colorful, pristine hiking spot we frequented. Maria and I looked forward to our nature excursions and had wonderful hiking adventures together.

Maria: It's a long way up to the highest plateau at Red Rock Canyon but something drove me to continue climbing. When I got to the top a melody filled my heart and I sing it daily like a Psalm. 'I sing a song of praise to you, Lord. I sing a song of praise to You. I'd like to thank you Lord for everything You do. I sing a song of praise to You.' I never thought I'd receive a spiritual message so close to Sin City!

Robyn Whatley, Golddigger 1976-1987: As time went by, it turned out we were playing every six weeks with Dean in Las Vegas. There would be women who would come every six weeks and sit in the front row and we got to know them. They would come backstage and ask us everything about Dean and try to get closer to Dean. There were quite a few of them.
We would go out and play around Vegas because everybody knew us there, that was a time when the town wasn't a corporation; it was actually people. We were always running around the Strip getting comped to other performers' shows.
Of course, there were some disagreements and there were fiery, passionate personalities but we mostly hung out together and shared the experience together.

Joyce Garro, Golddigger 1976-1978: I would stand backstage and watch Dean's show almost every night in Vegas. There were so many incredible talents working in Las Vegas. I probably saw Wayne Newton's show ten or fifteen times, he would always invite us backstage. I was still with the Golddiggers when he approached me to be one of his backup singers. I told him, "At least I get a solo every once in a while with The Golddiggers."

We were always going out dancing, that's the best exercise to keep our figures trim. So we went dancing a lot at The Jockey Club; it was a private club, the owner gave us all lifetime memberships.

Maria: Our times in The Golddiggers gave us a lifetime of experiences. All of us girls were very different but very alike in many ways. We had a deep sense of caring for each other and professionalism. Besides our talent, we all contributed a special something to the group. Patti relished the role of captain for many years and when Patti left the group to pursue theatrical work, Joyce took on the captain role for a bit. Robyn organized most of our social outings after the show; while Peggy was helpful managing the costumes—with a whine. Linda and I taped the shows to make sure everyone's voices were blending together; each voice, a part of the whole. Harmonizing and praying together became our special bond. Linda and I always knew how blessed we were to be a part of the 'Big Time' and the magic that surrounded Dean Martin. He worked

with our favorite entertainers like Shirley Jones but he treated us like we were his favorites too. We celebrated special occasions and shared private jokes and messages together. Dean was so dear to us.
Linda and I were looking forward to going home for Christmas. The road and the Roy Radin tour in particular had taken a toll on our spirit leaving us feeling drained.
We had taped Dean's second *Christmas in California* special before the tour and it aired on December 18th, 1977, during our Christmas vacation.
Lee Hale had put Linda and I right in front of the microphone during the pre-record of the theme song, so everyone in our family recognized our voices right away.
Taping the Christmas specials always put me in a holiday frame of mind. Somehow, Greg seemed more hospitable and relaxed with us and all the guest stars when we shot the special at his Hidden Valley ranch. The setting was so picturesque, with green hills, sometimes shaded by huge oak trees. Of course, there were always a few prized horses galloping freely across the field, enclosed by a white picket fence. It made me homesick.

Robyn Whatley, Golddigger 1976-1987:
The horses we used in the special were Greg Garrison's, they were Andalusians; he had the world wide grand champion Andalusian at the time. I'm a horse woman so I can appreciate somebody who can really ride and Dean was a wonderful rider. I think Dean was probably the happiest when he was riding a horse.
He looked gorgeous in a tuxedo, he looked fantastic in Vegas, but when he was in cowboy gear, with the boots and the jeans and a nice flannel type open shirt, that was when he was most comfortable. Working in the tack room with the saddles and all of that, that's when he was really at ease.

The Andalusian Society exists today because of Greg Garrison.

Linda: Dean made a very handsome cowboy and was right at home strolling through the rooms of the ranch, singing Christmas songs. This special gave the illusion of a bunch of friends enjoying togetherness for Christmas on Dean's ranch. The reality was, it was the Garrison's ranch and it was all staged.

Because of the added expense and unpredictability of working outdoors, thousands of dollars could be wasted if one of us missed our mark or made a mistake and a retake was needed.

Besides Dean and The Golddiggers, appearances on the show were made by country singer Crystal Gayle, Linda Lavin of TV's *Alice*, French chanteuse Mireille Mathieu and our old friend Jonathan Winters. As a group, some of us went on hay rides and country strolls, singing together along the way, like one big happy family.

It was nice getting to see Greg with his family at home on their ranch. Greg's daughter, Patricia, was a sweet and home spun young lady who had a love and deep knowledge of horses. Ray

Ellen, Greg's wife, was a sophisticated, serious looking woman and had no interest in the taping going on at the ranch. After our short introduction she mostly kept out of sight. When Greg married her she had quite a bit of money and was in no way enamored by what he did or his success. I saw Greg's son, Michael, around every so often. He seemed very interested in his dad's television directing skills and his relationship with Dean Martin.

Robyn Whatley, Golddigger 1976-1987: You could tell Greg Garrison just adored Dean, you could see the mutual respect. They worked on a handshake for twenty-three years or so and that's unheard of. But that was Dean with Mort Viner his manager and that was Dean with Kenny Lane his piano player that wrote the hit song 'Everybody Loves Somebody Sometime.' They just did it out of loyalty and friendship.

Dean Martin roasted Frank Sinatra, Ronald Reagan and George Burns in 1977.

Darlene (Alberici) Cianci: The first time I saw Dean Martin backstage, I felt a magnetism that made me want to stop, step back and collect myself. He had many people fawning over him, so I watched and admired how he handled it all. When my sisters pulled me closer to introduce Dean, he welcomed me with a strong handshake. He had a muscular hand that was very powerful. I smiled and was speechless as he charmingly said, "Oh, another sister? Your mother and father sure made beautiful girls."

Over the years, I witnessed the changes in The Golddiggers and the development of each one of their stage personalities and talents. When a different girl joined the group it brought a new flavor to their show. When my sisters started in The Golddiggers with 'Patti from Cincinnati' and the rest of the girls from all over the country, their show was like a glamorous Busby Berkeley presentation, a unified well-oiled machine. Everything was so exciting that I didn't want to turn my head for a second. After a few years, Wendy and Peggy joined the group and all hell broke loose because these girls were not the typical image of a 'Golddigger'. Now, the group started to look like a review of leading ladies vying to give the most extraordinary moment on stage. Later, when Robyn and Joyce joined the group, the unit had become more sophisticated and fine-tuned. Each girl developed their sense of style when they entertained and it seemed that people were enchanted to hear what each one had to say besides applauding their talent. The audiences had grown up along with The Golddiggers and appreciated these confident women who were no longer giggling girls. When I was a part of the group, I had to learn to pace my day and reserve my energy so I could give my best to the show. The girls performed like Olympic athletes, focused and disciplined. They were like well groomed thoroughbreds. I enjoyed racing alongside them for a while but my heart yearned to play other characters in the theater as well.

Linda: Dean's journey to becoming an entertainment legend was based more on relationships than ambition and that's unusual for this town. Dean once said that if it was up to him he might have been a gambler, a card dealer or croupier. When Dean was a young man that was what he was doing but God gave him so much more to work with, more than he ever could have imagined. And Dean was very grateful, he never imagined himself being a big star.

I recalled how I happened to find myself in this position; it started out as an uncertain adventure with my sister. Even though we had experienced things with this group we never could have conceived of, I still had the sense that God could offer a new challenge for us.

By this point, we were sure we were going to leave the group to pursue a career as a sister act. The time seemed right for a change and we'd been developing some material over time. Robyn kept reminding us that this was a "dream gig" and she was right but our family was very supportive of our move away from the Golddiggers. My dad repeated what we had said from the very beginning, that we were only supposed to do it for a couple of years and move on. He wanted us to stay in Pennsylvania and follow leads in New York. I think he wanted to be more involved in our career but mostly he wanted to have all his children around him.

Maria: With strong family ties Linda and I were able to be worldly-wise without losing ourselves. our dad always reminded his children to keep a positive attitude, "Look at the doughnut, not the hole."

Where was I going to find another boss like Dean? Before our last shows, I made a point of visiting Dean for more than the usual few minutes. I asked him if he thought he would do another tour with Frank Sinatra. In his loose Dino way he shook his head, pointed his finger and said, "He's too pushy...." I finished his sentence with, "And you're an easy going guy." I knew Dean's remark was truth said in jest. I was going to miss this pre-show ritual of give and take.

I could feel the buzz and energy of the audience on the other side of the curtain which always got my heart pumping faster. Backstage we had our own buzz. While a few of the musicians tuned up, Ken Lane joked around with them.

I was going to miss the girls and all the fun we had hanging out together. We had become like sisters over the last five years as we watched each other's backs.

Linda: Vegas was fun, easy, comfortable—too comfortable. I was getting this 'now or never' feeling about branching out in show business. There was so much more I wanted to do. But I was torn between enjoying this moment of success or pushing ahead to what was next, career wise. We were developing friendships, getting chummy with the guys in the orchestra and with Roger, Dean's personal valet and assistant. Roger said that Dean liked to have a hotel room where he could sneak backstage without using any common areas or elevators. According to him, Dean had lots of quirks and was driving him crazy. Roger once confided to one of the girls that Dean wore lifts in his shoes. I don't know why Dean would have to; he was the perfect height as far as I was concerned.

Peggy started and continued a lovely tradition. Every year at Christmas she would give Dean a sentimental letter with a photo of the group. What do you get the guy who has everything? He appeared to treasure those moments and, little by little, during our Vegas stays, he warmly unveiled his vulnerability and softer side to us.

On the last night of our engagement Dean held me a little longer than usual during our pre-show greeting, our eyes met as he gently and slowly stroked my back in a way he had never touched me before. I felt a little weak in the knees. Oh boy, I sensed we could take our relationship in a whole other direction. So there was that also to think about.

Maria: My sister Darlene decided to take her money and use it to pound the pavements, auditioning in New York for musicals and touring companies which landed her some starring roles. Linda and I returned to California with another vision. We wanted to continue writing songs, record them and do our own show. While we were with The Golddiggers, we had made some solid connections with the managers of the clubs where we performed. Greg Garrison had given Linda and me his blessing, telling us, "use the Golddiggers name if you need to" and we did! We knew he had faith in our talent both as individuals and as a sister act. We were going to gear our show to be the caliber of entertainment like The Golddiggers but with a more updated image.

Photos: Dean backstage with Peggy at Christmastime.

We loved the current style of music and decided to change our name to make it more disco sounding. We thought the "Alberici Sisters" sounded too much like a trapeze act so we called ourselves "Silk." We already had gigs lined up and a new rights of passage ahead of us.

Linda: So too, Joyce was leaving the group to continue her career as solo singer. I was feeling sentimental about us all moving in different directions and my heart was overwhelmed with gratitude for being given the opportunity to get to know such wonderful ladies. Each had touched my life in so many positive ways.

It wasn't easy to say goodbye to 'Crazy' Peggy and Robyn, 'the goddess,' the two ladies who chose to remain with the group. I didn't even want to think of how Peggy, Robyn and Lee Hale would train four new girls but they did. The Golddiggers continued on in grand form with another Mexico tour and also as Dean's opening act in Vegas. The group was booked for television and more *Christmas in California* specials. Maria and I were happy for them but we were eager to create our own identity as we embarked on a new chapter in our lives.

We did indeed strike out on our own. There were major career and life choices to be made and sometimes danger would come knocking on our door. As a duo, we became an opening act for stars like Jay Leno as we continued to play the main rooms in Atlantic City and Las Vegas. Audiences in Singapore and other exotic locales beckoned us to perform as well as the familiar clubs we frequented in The Golddiggers. Our sister, Darlene, soon joined us—but this time we were billed as The Alberici Sisters when we returned to Monaco to perform for the Royal Family.

What we didn't know was the world of entertainment was changing faster than we knew. Within a year almost all of the large venues where we were performing around the country began to rapidly disappear including the Fairmont showrooms, the Nanuet Theatre-Go-Round—even the Latin Casino was converted into a discothèque before mysteriously burning to the ground a few years later.

Now and then, fate would sweep us back into The Golddiggers when some of the girls pursued new ventures but with a wink and a smile we were back doing our sister act again. Before long, we rejoined The Golddiggers. Working with Dean was a safe haven for us and we continued performing with him until he retired in 1991.

Those were the happiest of times. We also felt Dean's profound loss as he dealt with the tragic death of his son and we were there when Dean shared the details of his falling out with Frank Sinatra.

Looking back, it was a blessing to have each other to share this journey. There were many more adventures to challenge us and surprises beyond our wildest dreams but those are stories for another day.

Former Golddiggers today! From left to right: Linda Eichberg, Robyn Whatley, Patti Gribow, Marie Halton, Linda Snook, Maria Lauren and Joyce Garro. (Marie Halton and Linda Snook were part of the last Golddigger group of the 80s and 90s.)

Today, the Alberici Sisters are active in Fitness & Entertainment!

Certified in the exercise principles of Pilates, Yoga, Tai Chi, Muscle Conditioning and Aerobics. As entertainers, Maria and Linda still sing and dance to rave reviews and enjoy personally coaching fitness and singing.

:ABOUT THE AUTHORS:

Maria Lauren (Maria Elena Alberici - Riccio)

The winner of two national fitness awards, Maria produced and hosted a TV series promoting a positive lifestyle called *You Got the Power*. She has applied this message and trademark to CD's, sportswear and directing after-school programs recognized by our nation's capital and the city of Los Angeles. A Lifestyle Educator for over two decades, Maria continues to share her expertise at corporate medical and wellness centers. As a performing artist, Maria made co-starring appearances on several hit TV series and carried the leading role in numerous musical comedy stage shows such as *Company*. "Charismatic, Maria Lauren displays persuasive acting ability." – *L.A. Weekly*. Rave reviews have followed her production of *Showstoppers* which featured some of the former Golddiggers. "Showstoppers live up to acts name." – Wickenburg Sun Newspaper. Maria and her daughter Marianna were guests on *Larry King Live*. Marianna Riccio is a singer-songwriter, actress and dancer who has sang for a variety of venues including star-studded events such as Jamie Foxx's Award party. Maria balances the rigors of show business and being a fitness practitioner with spending time with her friends and family, her husband Carmine and daughter Marianna in West Hills, CA..

Linda Eichberg (Linda Alberici Eichberg)

Linda and her sister Maria, have shared success as singer-songwriters with two charting recordings. Both went on to individually use their acting talents in several prime time television shows. Linda was a featured actress on *Knight Rider, St. Elsewhere, Mike Hammer* and *The KTTV Bedtime Movie Show*. Presently, Linda is working as a certified fitness instructor teaching personal fitness and group exercise classes. Giving time to her church and community is important to Linda. Her work for Lily of the Valley Endeavor raises funds and awareness for the plight of orphans and children affected by HIV/AIDS. She has traveled to South Africa for this cause. Linda sings in a Christian worship band and continues singing and dancing in a variety of venues around the world. Getting together to perform or hang out with her brothers and sisters or Golddigger buddies is still an enjoyable part of her life. Linda lives in Westlake Village, Ca. with her husband Steven, an Attorney/Mediator, and daughter Lindsay, who is a senior at UC Berkeley.

Billy Ingram produced this book

Billy launched TVparty.com in 1997 and it quickly became one of the Internet's hottest spots for entertainment attracting millions of users a month; *TVparty!* was the first to broadcast clips of TV shows online. In 2002 he released the best-selling book *TVparty: Television's Untold Tales* to rave reviews from around the world. He wrote and starred in two TV series for the VH1 and Bravo networks and produced the Eisner Award nominated book *Dear John: The Alex Toth Book*. He was a designer on some of the most successful Academy Award campaigns, film trailers, and movie posters of all time, for stars like Harrison Ford, Barbra Streisand, Tom Cruise, Steven Spielberg and many others. An internationally acclaimed actor, Internet pioneer, artist, and writer, Billy Ingram starred in the 2011 indie motion picture *Swimming in a Lake of Fire*.

The last Golddigger group to appear with Dean in Vegas pictured from the top: Linda Snook-Bott, Peggy Gohl, Marie Halton, and Maria Lauren. (Linda had left to prepare for the birth of her daughter but was a part of the group for most of Dean's final performances at Bally's.)

WHERE ARE THEY NOW?

Darlene Alberici – Cianci
After Darlene's exciting times in The Golddiggers she traveled throughout the world with her sisters, The Alberici Sisters, where they were honored to do a Command Performance for the Royal Family of Monaco. In the tri-state area, Darlene lends her vocal expertise to commercials and radio jingles and finds success leading and organizing ensembles from cabaret to big band. One memorable show was televised for presidential hopeful George W. Bush at the Franklin Institute, where the Philadelphia Boys Choir accompanied her powerful vocal range in "God Bless America." While performing as a featured vocalist, she met the musician and leading man of her dreams who is the perfect complement to her most coveted role of being a mom to her son, David. Darlene harmonizes her artistic passions into busy days as a teacher of Yoga and Tai-Chi, helping others to find their expression in health and vitality.

Theresa Bishop
Theresa Bishop Miller has performed all over the world, on stage and television, as a singer-dancer with The Young Americans, Dean Martin's Golddiggers, Disney's Kids of the Kingdom, Disney Company, and The Los Angeles Rams Cheerleaders. She traveled to Spain, Hong Kong and Mainland China as a Disney Character Artist. She has designed, illustrated, and sculpted a wide variety of items, from souvenirs to collectibles. She can occasionally be seen performing in a musical or at church.

Theresa is married to Glen Miller, who is a drummer and photographer. They have three beautiful daughters. Jesika is a singer, actress and artist; Kristen is a manager, wife, and mother of Kambria; and Natalie is a singer, dancer, actress and songwriter.

Susan Buckner

Besides starring in the movie *Grease* as Patty Simcox, Susan Buckner starred in Deadly Blessings with Sharon Stone and Lisa Hartman and in the ABC series *When the Whistle Blows* and *The Nancy Drew/Hardy Boys* series. Susan guest starred in *The Love Boat, Starsky and Hutch, Police Woman, Switch* and *Friends*. She also co-wrote and produced two albums with Lonnie Jordan of the famed R&B group, War. Susan was a featured dancer on the *Sonny and Cher Show, Mac Davis Show, The Brady Bunch Hour* among others. She started her professional career at age sixteen as a dancer/comedian in Seattle in local stage and theater and then became Miss Seattle in the Miss America Pageant before being hired for television with the Dean Martin Golddiggers. She is the mother of two children, Samantha and Adam.

Joyce Garro

Joyce Garro, a native of Chicago, is a singer, musician and entertainer. Joyce has twice sung our National Anthem at Wrigley Field. She has recorded numerous CDs and commercials. She continues to sing in LA and Chicago for corporate events, Italian festivals, nightclubs, churches, and senior centers, and often donates her talent to charity, including VA Hospitals and USO shows. Joyce sings jazz, popular music, gospel, and standards from the Great American Songbook. Often she will accompany herself at the piano, singing not only in English but also in Italian, Hebrew, Spanish, Armenian, Greek, and Japanese. Joyce is also a long time member of Society of Singers since her dear friend, the late Ella Fitzgerald encouraged her to join this amazing charity. Joyce lives in LA and has two children, Anthony and Kimberly. She has a special place in her heart for her Golddigger sisters!

Peggy Gohl

Peggy Gohl studied at the Civic Light Opera and was a featured soloist at Radio City Music Hall backed by a 65-piece orchestra. Peggy starred as Ado Annie in *Oklahoma!* with John Davidson and was the opening act for magician David Copperfield. Peggy performed with a wide variety of celebrities, Tennessee Ernie Ford, Kenny Rogers, George Burns and Patrick Swayze, to name a few. But Peg's most favorite performances were the seventeen years she spent as one of the Dean Martin Golddiggers. Dean himself graced her with the moniker, "Crazy." Peg lives in South Florida with her husband and still finds the time to sing and charm audiences across the U.S. She was honored to be the featured entertainer for Leeza Gibbons at Circle of Care Leeza's Place, a support group for Alzheimer's caregivers and their families.

Patti Gribow

Patti Pivaar Gribow (formerly Pivarnik) cherishes the lifelong relationships created during her 13 years with the Golddiggers. This past decade, Gribow has produced and hosted 500 plus professional business and entertainment talk shows: *The Patti Gribow Show, Patti Gribow's RoundTable* and *Leading Experts*. Currently she is President of IMPRINT Media Productions, a digital media production company. Recently Patti was named International Spokesperson for FoodHUB organic meats, as seen on QVC. In addition she is a guest artist on the inaugural album, *The World is Getting Colder* recorded by the group "Old Sand Mill" released by SHP Records and Universal Music. Patti has received numerous awards for her advocacy for women in Palm Desert, California where she resides with her husband, Dale. Their daughter, Gina, is attending UC Hastings Law School.

Marie Halton

Marie began her career as a child actress, singer, dancer, performing in local theater and eventually, professional theater and television. Her love of musical theater resulted in roles in various productions including Robert Stigwood's production of the rock opera *Tommy, JB, Oklahoma, Funny Girl, Sugar* and *Lorelei* with the great Carol Channing. Returning from Broadway, Marie was invited to join the group The Establishment, which toured and performed with Perry Como. Marie had worked on *The Dean Martin Show* in the 1970s as a skit player and had come to appreciate the amazing talent that was Dean—so, the transition to Golddiggers was a natural. The sisterhood that formed with the other Golddiggers, both past and present, and the wonderful talent and man that was Dean, led to a thirteen-year commitment. Marie went back to school and received degrees in Art and Interior Design. Marie is happily married to Howard Peck, she has three terrific stepsons and three beautiful grandsons. She is grateful for the opportunities, the friends, and of course, for the music.

Robin Hoctor-Horneff

Robin Hoctor-Horneff won a scholarship at the American Ballet Theatre when she was just 16 years old. While still in high school, she modeled for the Eileen Ford Modeling Agency. After graduation, Robin earned a part in the Broadway show *Sugar* starring Robert Morse. At age twenty, Robin met Gene Kelly and started a professional working relationship as his assistant choreographer and friend from 1974 until his death. One of Robin's most memorable experiences was being the assistant choreographer for the MGM film *That's Entertainment* starring Fred Astaire and Gene Kelly. Robin opened her Performing Arts Center in the fall of 1979. Since then she has not only trained hundreds of students but has also been involved with the National Alliance for Excellence, an organization that gives college scholarships. Robin and her husband Van have four children, William, Vanessa, John and Samantha.

Wendy Kimball

Wendy Kimball's eclectic career started with a tour of *Annie Get Your Gun* starring Barbara Eden. Her first Broadway show was *Music Man* starring Dick Van Dyke and Christian Slater, and other Broadway credits include *Annie* and *Rags*. Wendy has toured the country with *The Rocky Horror Show* and worked for Disney Productions playing Minnie Mouse to thousands of children. She was the voice of Birthday Bear on the *Care Bears* albums and the dancing partner to John Travolta in a Wyler's lemonade commercial. In recent years Wendy joined The Benny Goodman Band as its featured singer. In her spare time, Wendy is deeply committed to improving the lives of animals and is an advocate for animal rights. Her years with The Golddiggers conjure up some of her fondest memories, producing lifetime friendships.

Colleen Kincaid Jackson

Raised in Fresno, California, Colleen, a former Miss Fresno County, followed her lifelong dream to sing and dance and auditioned for the Golddiggers in 1973. After 2 memorable years, Colleen ventured out on her own, working in clubs and touring with the comedienne, Marty Allen. But show business paled in appeal to a new found faith and in 1978 she married Randy Jackson (Sacramento) and joined him in his work with Young Life, a Christian outreach to teens.

For employment, Colleen moved behind the camera and worked in a variety of genres from commercial broadcast to web delivery. Adding Instructional Design from SDSU to her skill set, she currently is production supervisor at SchoolMedia, Inc., producing award winning educational videos and learning games.

Thirty-three years later Colleen and Randy are still active in Young Life as are their 2 daughters, Lydia (Jackson) Arguelles and Elizabeth Jackson.

Lee Nolting

Through a combined passion for teaching and community involvement, Lee Nolting has emerged as one of St. Louis' most valued and beloved art educators. Lee is a founding faculty member for COCA (Center of Creative Arts). Over her 24 years with COCA, Lee has played an instrumental role in establishing a pre-professional dance scholarship TIP (Talent Identified Program), student performance companies and award-winning outreach programs, one being the Coming Up Taller Award from the White House. Lee was recognized in 2003 by the National Foundation for Advancement in the Arts for her encouragement and support of students who have been recognized for exceptional artistic achievements. She has been and remains a believer that dance can be used to guide children toward achievement and hope.

Deborah Pratt

Deborah M. Pratt is a television director/writer/producer and author of the Science-Fantasy trilogy *The Vision Quest*. Deborah was co-executive producer and head writer of the award winning sci-fi hit *Quantum Leap* and executive producer for *The Net* on the USA Network. She directed 'Cora Unashamed' for *Masterpiece Theater*. She is also author of *Inner Knowings and Visionary: Being One*. She is writer, director and producer for the upcoming WEB Series *Warrior One* and in development with her passion feature film epic, *Chevalier & Antoinette*. Deborah is a single mother of two great children Troian and Nick. Troian Bellisario has gained recognition for her dramatic acting on the ABC family television series, *Pretty Little Liars* by the Teen Choice Awards. Deborah lives in Southern California and donates her time to El Nido Charities. Her mission in life is for the advancement of humanity. Her motto is: Life in Honor, Love and Light.

Linda Snook-Bott

Linda Snook joined The Golddiggers in 1978 at the age of 19, after placing in the Miss California Pageant. She considers being one of the Dean Martin Golddiggers to be the "greatest" gig of a lifetime spending eight years with the group. Between Golddigger dates, Linda Snook headlined in Las Vegas as "Miss City Lights" at the Flamingo Hilton and toured several countries with her show. Linda is still involved with the music industry today and has recorded four albums. She spent five years in Nashville as a songwriter, performer and promoter of women in music. She continues to entertain to sold out concerts in venues throughout California. She now resides in Redding, California and owns a popular radio station with her husband and has both a daily talk show and a weekly entertainment show. Early this summer Linda will begin a daily TV show that reaches the entire Northern California area with her husband, Carl. Linda Snook remembers performing with the Alberici Sisters, who were both incredibly talented, specializing in tight harmonies.

Robyn Whatley-Kahn

Robyn has had an incredibly fortunate life. She was born in Louisiana and has ended up on the Greek "island of longevity" Ikaria. She's lived a dream come true as a former Dean Martin Golddigger, singing with the entertainment legends of the century... and with her best buddies. She's been blessed with a son, Shanen, a daughter, Tamara, two grandchildren and a devoted husband, David. She's lived in Hawaii and the Caribbean, traveled by air and car over 500,000 miles, directed and starred in her own one-woman shows *Touch of Showbiz*, to raise monies for Hospice Care. Also, Robyn has written an acclaimed lullaby album, *Skye's Lullabies*, for her son and grand daughter and for the past 30 years has been an alternative health instructor. Big congrats to "the sisters."

Patricia Booth-Julius

Patricia received her Actors Equity Card when she joined the St. Louis Municipal Opera during her teen years. There, she performed in over 32 musical comedies and light operas with Ethel Merman, Douglas Fairbanks Jr., Eddie Albert, Florence Henderson and John Raitt. Later, Patricia auditioned for Greg Garrison Productions at NBC and was hired to perform with *The Gene Kelly Show* in Las Vegas. Subsequently, she was offered a position as one of The Golddiggers on the Dean Martin variety show. While the TV series was on hiatus, Patricia was hired for the "FoliesBergere" at The Tropicana Hotel in Vegas as the lead singer. "I did not know until dress rehearsal night that the showgirls were topless because I was fully clothed." After two years, Patricia rejoined The Golddiggers again with all new girls. Patricia still entertains and loves a wonderful man named Jack, her husband and best friend.

Neil Daniels

Neil Daniels was West-Coast liaison for NBC starting at the age of 14 for shows including *The Tonight Show, The Flip Wilson Show, Rowan & Martin's Laugh-in, The Bob Hope Specials*, Elvis' comeback special, and *The Dean Martin Show* to name just a few. His career has run the gamut from music historian to editor, photographer, radio performer/announcer, producer, teacher, graphic designer, writer (he has ghost written a handful of television episodes, as well as authoring the biography *Cherry's Jubilee* with famed singer/golfer Don Cherry). Daniels founded The Dean Martin Fan Center nearly two decades ago and publishes a quarterly magazine for Dean Martin fans worldwide.

Lee Hale

Lee Hale was musical director and later producer of *The Dean Martin Show* and the many subsequent Roasts and specials. He was also musical director of *The Golddiggers* summer shows and produced *The Golddiggers* 1971 TV series. He is the creative consultant and editor for the 29 DVD set *The Best of The Dean Martin Show*. A six-time Emmy nominee and one of the most sought out producers in television today, Lee Hale is the author of the critically acclaimed *Backstage at the Dean Martin Show* and has a new book coming in 2011. Throughout the years, Lee Hale has supported the arts and continues to donate his producing and musical talents to organizations such as the Singer's Society and the Dancer's Society.

PHOTO CREDITS

No photos may be reproduced without written permission from the copyright owners. We did our best to track down the owners of all photos in this book. If you feel we used a photo in error please contact tvparty@bellsouth.net and we'll correct the situation.

Photos on pages 7-22, 24, 27-29, 34-46, 48, 50, 52, 55-57, 60-67, 71-75, 76, 78, 80-92, 94-96, 98, 99, 100, 104, 105, 108, 109, 110, 111, 113-115, 117-120, 124-126, 128, 129, 131, 133, 136, 139-144, 146-148, 150, 152-154, 157, 159, 160, 165, 170, 173, 175, 176, 179, 180, 185-190, 192, 195, 196, 198, 199, 202, 204, 206-208, 210, 212, 213, 215, 217, 218, 220, 224-231, 250, 236, 237, 239, 241, 243-245, 247, 250, 253, 254, 258, 260-266, 268, 269, 271, 274, 275, 277, 281, 282, 284, 285, 287-293, 295-301, 305, 313, 315, 317-322, 326-328, 332, 337, from the archives of Maria Lauren & Linda Eichberg.

Photos on pages 23, 25, 32, 58, 59, 69, 74-77, 81, 82, 84, 85, 86, 89, 93, 94, 97, 103, 106, 107, 109, 112, 121, 123, 124, 128, 129, 130, 133-135, 147, 148, 149, 155, 156, 158, 159, 161-164, 166, 174, 176, 178, 184, 185, 191, 193, 200, 211, 213, 217, 222, 223, 233, 235, 328, 247, 249, 252-259, 262, 264, 267, 270, 272, 274, 276, 293, 303-305, 309, 310, 329, from the TVparty! archives,

Photos on pages 57, 140, 148, 175, 176, 180, 188, 189, 313, courtesy of Robert Scott Hooper Photography.

Photos on pages 65, 71, 81, 85, 94, 95, 98, 100, 109, 143, 173, 190, 199, 208, 215, 245, 258, 262, 271, 277, 293, 320, 326, courtesy of Susan Rothschild Photography.

Photos taken at the Nanuet Theatre-Go-Round on pages 165 and 167 courtesy of Mark Glick.

Photo on pages 95 & 333, courtesy of Lee Hale.

Photos on pages 101, 137, 335, courtesy of Lee Nolting.

Photos on pages 151, 169, 171, 181-186, 160, 203, 233, 333, courtesy of Wendy Kimball.

Photos on pages 151, 200, 201, 220, 230, 259, 286, 294, 311, 323, 330 courtesy of Peggy Gohl.

Photos on pages 191, 193, 197, 204, 330 courtesy of Theresa Bishop Miller.

Photos on pages 205, 219, 240, 248, 281, 308, 317, 330 courtesy of Joyce Garro.

Photos on page 177, 222, 280, 332 courtest of Patti Grobow

Photos on page 335 courtest of Patty Booth-Julius.

Photos on pages 66, 82, 85, 181, 200, 202, 205, 207, 210 226, 228, 231, 232, 234, 251, 283, 290, 291, 294, 307, 316, 318, 324, 334 courtesy of Robyn Whatley-Kahn Photography.

Photos on pages 91, 209, 212, 222, 306, 309, 312, courtesy of Tim Fowlar.

Photos on pages 87, 199, 302, 303, 307, 324, 330 courtesy of Darlene Alberici Cianci.

Photo on pages 102 & 335 courtesy of Neil Daniels.

Photo on pages 96, 97, 132, 224, courtesy of Maria Jensen.

Photos on pages 79, 116, 118, 334, courtesy of Deborah Pratt.

Photos on pages 177, 221, 280, courtesy of Patti Gribow

Photos on pages 144 & 330 courtesy of Susan Buckner

Photos on pages 70 & 333 courtesy of Colleen Kincaid Jackson

Photo on page 332, courtesy of Marie Halton Peck

Photo on page 334, courtest of Linda Snook-Bott

Images from vintage Las Vegas postcards on pages 1, 4-6, 121, 123, 145, 336-340

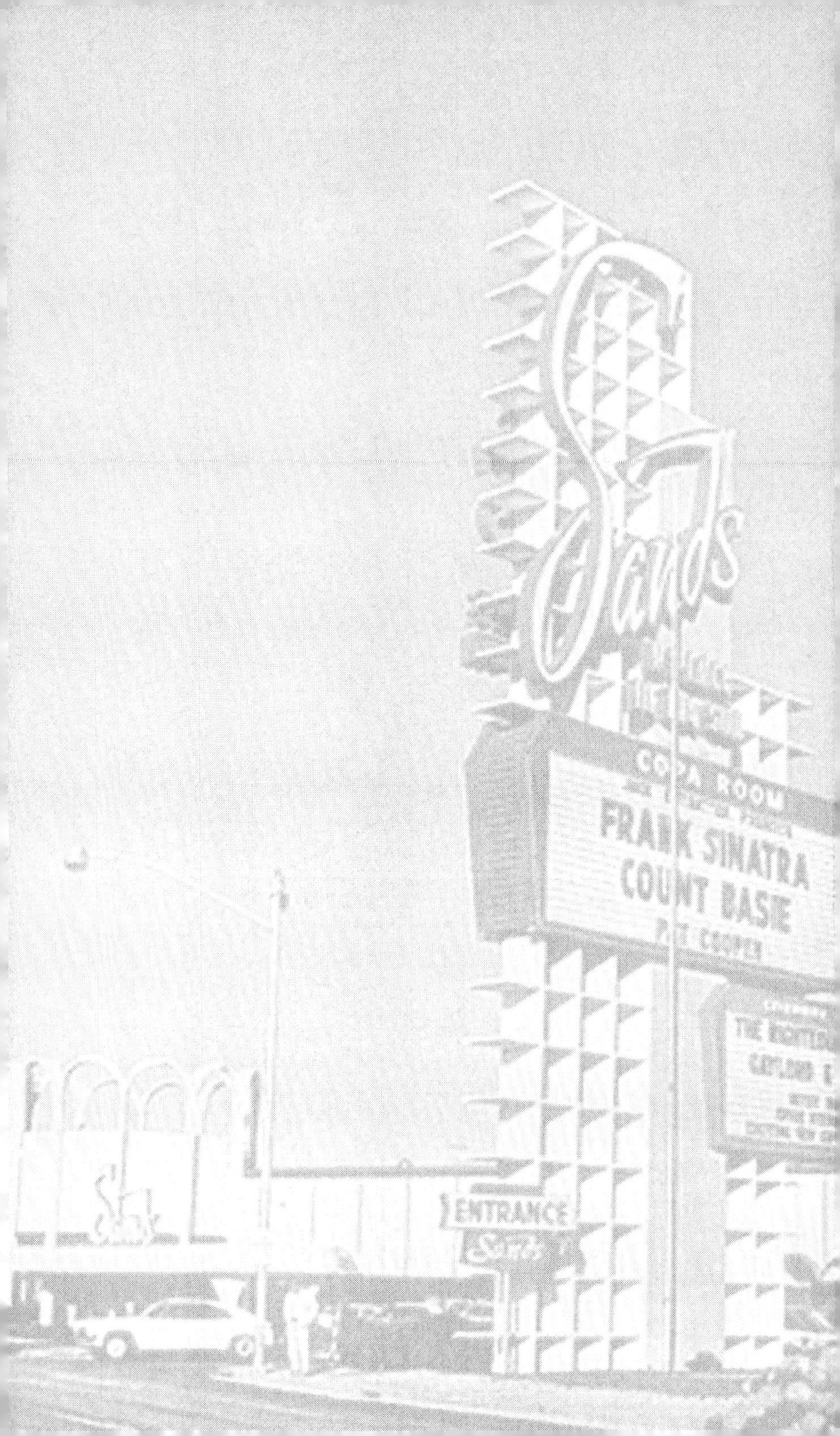
Sands
COPA ROOM
FRANK SINATRA
COUNT BASIE
ENTRANCE
Sands

Visit us online:
BeyondOurWildestDreams.com

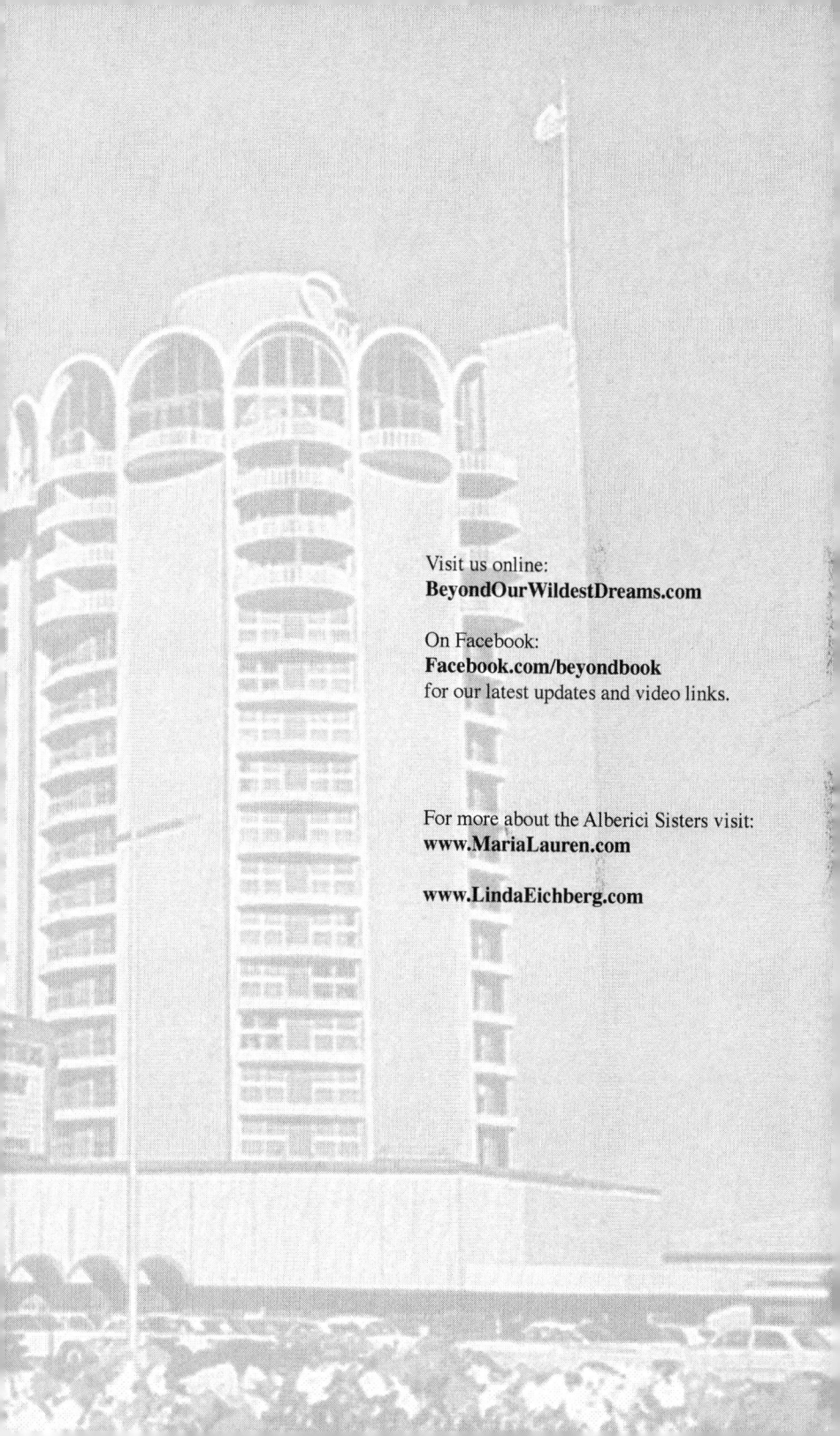

On Facebook:
Facebook.com/beyondbook
for our latest updates and video links.

For more about the Alberici Sisters visit:
www.MariaLauren.com

www.LindaEichberg.com

Dean Martin and the Alberici Sisters backstage during one of Deano's last performances in Las Vegas.

Acknowledgements...

Many thanks to Billy Ingram, your hard work was only surpassed by your passion. To all our mentors, fellow performers, 'Golddigger sisters' and all who contributed photos and stories to this book, we thank you for sharing the richness of your talents, experiences and memories with us.

Special thanks to: James Counts, Tim Fowlar, Jack Salley, Steven Eichberg, Carmine Riccio, Mark Glick, Francie Mendenhall, Demond Wilson, Channing Wade, Howard & Jennie Counts, Lillian Alberici, Ralph Pepino, Chuck Anderson, Jan Kubicki, Deborah Pratt, Patti Gribow, Robin Hoctor-Horneff, Lee Hale, Neil Daniels, Colleen Kincaid Jackson, Pat Cooper, Lee Nolting, Darlene Alberici - Cianci, Susan Buckner, Bob Mills, Don Cherry, Ichiro (Masatoshi) Mitsumoto, Ed Robertson, Wendy Kimball, Peggy Gohl, Helen Costa, Tony Horowitz, Dr. Gene Moehring, Patty Booth, Theresa Bishop Miller, Joyce Garro, Robyn Whatley, Wayne Dammert, Anthony Bruno, Shawn Levy, Jody Gerson, Russ Dunn, Misty Lee Morgan, Judith Zander, and Marty Walsh.

For classic TV on the Internet visit: www.TVparty.com

Made in the USA
Lexington, KY
12 July 2018